IRISH
Genealogical Abstracts

from the

LONDONDERRY JOURNAL

1772-1784

by

Donald M. Schlegel

CLEARFIELD

Printed for
Clearfield Company, Inc. by
Genealogical Publishing Co., Inc.
Baltimore, Maryland
1990

Reprinted for
Clearfield Company, Inc. by
Genealogical Publishing Co., Inc.
Baltimore, Maryland
2001

International Standard Book Number: 0-8063-5079-2

Made in the United States of America

Introduction

The <u>Londonderry</u> <u>Journal</u> was published in Londonderry, Ireland, by George Douglas and various partners. Beginning with issue Number 1 on Wednesday, June 3, 1772, it was published semi-weekly through Tuesday, May 1, 1781 and weekly thereafter. The paper is still published today. The abstracts published here begin with the first issue and carry through the end of 1784. A microfilm version of the paper was used in making these abstracts. A few issues and pages were missing from the series as filmed. These were numbers 313, 423, 424, and 1034 and pages 3 and 4 of both numbers 367 and 779. Any other numbers not listed in the text contain no information of direct use to genealogists. Inevitably, some words and letters were impossible to read. These have been indicated by underscores.

The genealogical nature of the items abstracted has been defined to be broadly inclusive. Perhaps the most numerous entries are those relating to marriages. Many of those included here also appear in Henry Farrar's <u>Irish</u> <u>Marriages:</u> <u>an</u> <u>Index</u> <u>to</u> <u>the</u> <u>Marriages</u> <u>in</u> Walker's Hibernian <u>Magazine,</u> 1771 <u>to</u> 1812. Many others, especially those relating to the Ulster Scots, do not appear in that work. Other evidences of marriage, such as notices of separation or non-responsibility for debts, which ususally give the wife's maiden name, are included. There are many death notices, but unfortunately these usually do not supply the names of survivors. Accounts of accidental and violent deaths and the execution of criminals are included, as are administrators' and executors' notices. A few births were reported in the newspaper, either among the aristocracy or among the common people when unusual circumstances, such as multiple births, made them newsworthy. Any other news item or notice showing family relationships has been abstracted.

Along the broader lines of interest, considering that many users of this book will be Americans searching for immigrant ancestors, all notices of migration or of potential causes of migration are noted. All notices of passenger ships are included. Examples of those who might have cause to emigrate are bankrupts, criminals, military deserters, and runaway apprentices. Conversions to the Church of Ireland are also included, since these may point to church record sources.

Many notices of persons in the newspaper contain no information of a genealogical nature, but, give useful clues to persons' locations in Ireland. As more fully described in its own introduction, these references have been gathered into the appendix.

While the abstracts cover all of Ireland, it is expected that the local notices should be especially useful to those tracing Ulster Scots who migrated to America. Ulster Scots or "Scotch-Irish" made up the largest portion of emigrants from Ireland to America in the Eighteenth Century and the port of Derry, at least before the American Revolution, outstripped even Belfast as a point of departure.

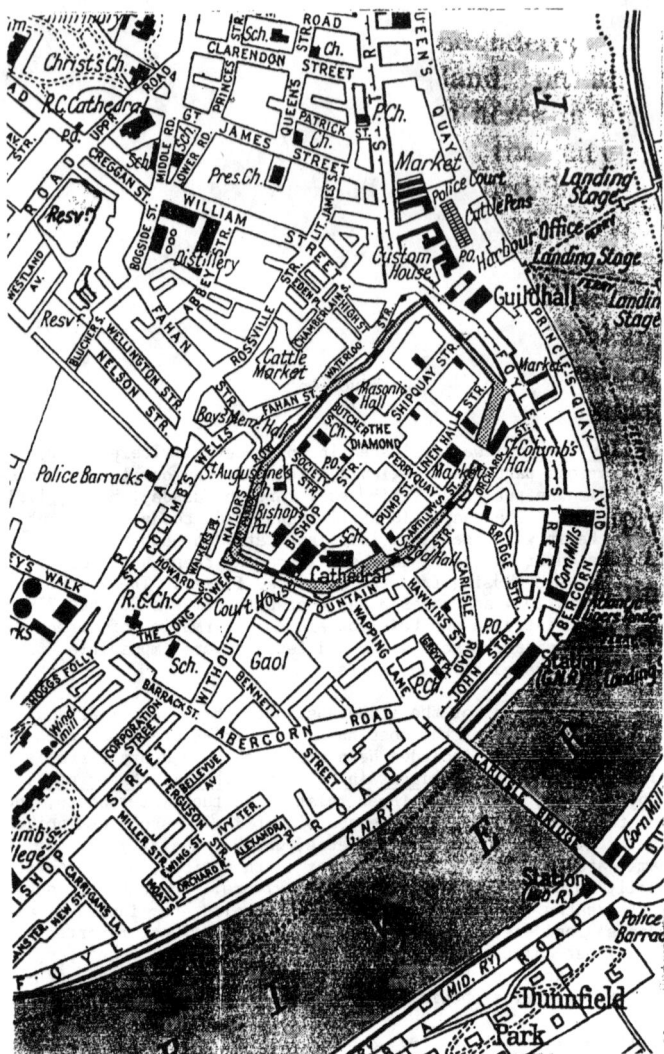

To help in locating the sites of the many Londonderry references, a portion of a map of the city is reproduced above. The old city was surrounded by its walls, which are indicated by shading on the map. Within were Bishop street, Butcher street, Shipquay street, and Ferryquay street, each leading from the Diamond to the gate of the respective name, along with Pump street and Artillery street (called Artillery lane in the Eighteenth Century). These are often mentioned in the abstracts.

The spelling of Irish place-names is always problematical. In all cases, the spelling has been kept the same as in the newspaper, even when it appeared that the paper might be in error. It ought also to be noted that names which were relatively well-known at the time of publication might now be relatively unknown or may no longer exist, such as the names of lands near the city of Londonderry which have been swallowed up by the city's growth during the intervening two centuries.

1 - Weds. June 3, 1772

Belfast, May 19.
Thomas Ohagan was hung at Downpatrick on Saturday last, but he wore a steel collar and harness and did not die. Hugh M'Ilpatrick, Thomas Stewart, Thomas Ward, and John Black were executed Saturday last at Carrickfergus.

2 - Sat., June 5, 1772

Kilkenny, May 30.
Sunday last, William Kennedy of Thurles drowned while trying to save his uncle's servant boy (who also drowned).

Belfast, June 2.
Saturday last were executed at Downpatrick: Daniel Murphy and Owen Murphy, for burglary and felony; Cormack Shiel for robbery; John Cockran and Patrick Crilly for horse stealing. Early yesterday morning Barbara Cunningham, wife of David Cunningham of Belfast, kay porter, was found dead in bed; her husband was gaoled.

Dublin.
Married: Philip Brabazon, Carrstown Co. Louth to Miss Adams of Hoathstown, Co. Meath; Samuel Barry to Miss Elizabeth Wade.
Born: a son to Lady and Sir William Pigot Piers.
Died: in London, the Countess of Londonderry; Lady Jocelyn; in Smithfield, age 82, Hon. Robert French; at Fort Singleton, Co. Monaghan, Oliver Singleton; Henry Piers, attorney; at Carrick, Rev. Mr. Purcell, Roman Catholic clergyman; Samuel Custis, bridle cutter.

3 - Weds., June 10, 1772

Dublin.
Married: at Limerick, Thomas Lawrence, Millmount, to Miss Moore, Ashgrove; at Turbetstown, Co. Westmeath, John Baggot to Miss Deale; at Carrigrohan church, William Hughes, Johnstown, to Miss Fortune Bennett, Ballingilly; Maurice Ronayne, Garran-James, to Miss Goold, Mocroom.
Died: at Gramore, age 9, Elizabeth, daughter of the Earl of Wandesford; Mrs. Bunlery; at Williamstown, Co. Kildare, John, eldest son of Adam Williams; Abraham Creighton, Lord Erne of Grum Dastle, Co. Fermanagh; William Bury.

Londonderry.
Married: Captain Thornton, Muff, to Miss Ennis, Magilligan.
Died: Sunday last, James Harvey, for many years an eminent merchant.

4 - Sat., June 13, 1772

Dublin.
Married: William Sherlock, Mt. Armstrong, Co. Kildare, to Miss Read, daughter of John Read of Summer-hill. Henry Hickey, Clonbullock, King's Co. to Miss Mary Anne Grierson, Drumcally, King's Co.
Died: Mrs. Law, housekeeper to the General Post Office, Dublin; in Pill lane, John Fidder, attorney; Rev. Thos. Vance, D.D., a minister at Usher's quay Meeting House; on Cork hill, Mr. Thomas Lagrayiere, livery lace manufacturer; in Stephen st., Miss Ganning.

5 - Weds. June 17, 1772

Dublin.
Margaret Magennis, convert to the Church of Ireland, in the church of Castle Blaney.
Married: Richard Symes, Bally Arthur, Co. Wicklow to Miss Susannah Gilbert, William St.; William Carrol, Tulla near Nenagh, to Miss Susannah, daughter of Francis Parker late of Newton, Co. Tipperary; Richard Burnet, Drumcondra, seedsman, to Miss Parry of Beaumorris.

1

Died: at Drogheda, Rev. Mr. John Brett, age 84; at Bullingate, Co. Wicklow, George Braddell; at Finglass, Mrs. Waters, widow of Richard Waters; on the same day, in Cuffe st, her sister the Widow Dudley; Isaac Jackson, Quaker, printer and bookseller.

Londonderry.
Married: Robert Stewart, of this city, merchant, to Miss Jordan of Dublin.
Died: at Carrickmines near Dublin, George Cary of Redcastle, Co. Donegal.

6 - Sat., June 20, 1772

Corke.
Garret Barry, son of William Barry of Kilbarry, was killed by Daniel Punch of Glasheen.

Londonderry.
Cleared out: the Hannah of Londonderry, ---- Mitchell, master, for Philadelphia, with 400 passengers.

7 - Weds., June 24, 1772

On Saturday the 30th ult., the ship John and James (belonging to Lt. Col. Desbrisay), James Baker, master, sailed from Newry for St. John's Island, North America, with the Rev. Oliver Hanley, the Rev. John Martin, Mr. Aicken, merchant, Mr. Wren, surgeon, (tenants to Col. Desbrisay) and 184 other persons, all of whom were in high spirits, and went off with great decency and order.
Same day, the ship Philadelphia, Captain Malcolm, sailed out of Belfast for Philadelphia, having 240 passengers on board.

Londonderry.
Cleared out: June 22, the General Wolfe, of Londonderry, for Philadelphia, Hunter, with 400 passengers; the Walworth of Londonderry, M'Causland, for Philadelphia, with provisions and passengers.
Ads: The ship Hopewell, James Campbell, 250 tons, to depart Londonderry 20 July for Newcastle and Philadelphia; Andrew M'Farlane of Eskragh near Carinteel, Co. Tyrone, who is to take his passage in said ship, can make arrangements for others. The ship Nancy, 300 tons, Norman Chevers, July 26 for Nova Scotia and possibly on to North Carolina. Warning by Rev. Alexander Colhoun, administrator and representative of the late William Colhoun, Co. Tyrone, to deal only with him concerning lease of Drumnahe, Co. Donegal, lately in possession of William Willson, deceased.

8 - Sat. June 27, 1772

Dublin.
Married: William Parsons to Lady Jane King, daughter of the Earl of Kingston; Robert Hamilton, Drumsonnis, Co. Tyrone to Miss Alice Nicolls, Lossett, Co. Cavan; Guy Bleakly, Co. Fermanagh, to Miss Jane Grier, Co. Longford; Rev. Archdeacon Hutchinson to Miss Elizabeth Tottenham; Thomas Cooke, Kilman, Co. Tipperary to Miss Bushell, Co. Tipperary; ---- Cooke to Miss Cuffe, daughter of the late Lord Desart; ---- Flin, Co. Sligo, to Miss Brown of Westport.
Died: in Co. Corke, Rev. Dennis Lehan, Romish clergyman; Mrs. Mary Bolingbroke; the relict of Francis Lodge; the wife of Patrick Ford, merchant; Miss Katharine, daughter of Lt. Col. Pierce; in Rush, John Connor alias Jack the Bachelor.

Londonderry.
Died: June 23, Mrs. Ann Craghead, age 83.
Ads: Ship Boscawan, 250 tons, George Marshall, master, to sail for Newcastle and Philadelphia on July 15.

2

9 - Weds. July 1, 1772.

Dublin.
---- M'Geagh of Cookstown, Co. Tyrone, drowned while returning from
Londonderry.
Married: Henry Jones, Knock, Co. Westmeath to Miss Dowdall, Mullingar.
Died: at Kilkenny, Robert Mulhollen, formerly captain of the 12th Dragoons;
Alderman John Cooke, June 24; Darby M'Carthy, carpenter, Nenagh, last Monday
after being bitten by a mad cat.

Londonderry.
Dixon Cuningham was elected burgess in place of James Harvey, deceased.
Ads: John Colhoun, concerning Alexander Colhoun's recent ad; he is the son of
Alexander Colhoun and has right to Drumnaho and other lands by will of
William Colhoun; executors of William's will, Charles Usher and William
Stewart, are long since dead; a bill is now pending in Chancery to recover
the rents these executors had received during John's minority; Margaret is
the wife of Alexander Colhoun.

10 - Sat. July 4, 1772.

Dublin.
Married: at Tuam, Lord Riverston to Miss Olivia French, eldest daughter of
Arthur French of Tyrone. Died: Hamilton Archdale, surveyor of Beldoyle; Pat
Duffe, linen draper; Andrew Darcy, surgeon; James Tiernan, druggist.

Londonderry.
Ads: The yard, warehouse, etc. of the late James Stewart to be auctioned by
Alderman Schoales and Richard Raby.

11 - Weds., July 8, 1772.

Dublin.
Judy Rispan, wife of James Rispan, Co. Westmeath, was delivered of three
sons, one on Friday June 26, one on Saturday, and one on Sunday.
Married: Samuel Handy jr., Collylough, Co. Westmeath, to Miss Catharine
Fleming, Drumsna, Co. Leitrim; John Shepheard, Lt. of 28th Foot, to Miss
Elinor Stafford, Crampton Court; Francis Thomey to Miss Montgomery; at
Willbrooke (seat of Rev. Dean Handcock) Michael Tailford to Miss Mary
daughter of said Dean Handcock.
Died: in Co. Roscommon, Henry Dillon, Belgard; at Sligo, Miss Charlotte
Molyneaux; at Limerick, Justin M'Carthy of Springhouse, Co. Tipperary; at
Limerick, the lady of Capt. Lancelot Hill; near Kevin's port, Mr. Morgan,
Methodist preacher.

Londonderry.
Ads: The former lands and house of the late Rev. Mr. Humble, in and near
Newtown Stewart, to be sold by John Siree, Saelfield near Rathmelton, and
Samuel Lawson, Newtown Stewart. The Prince of Wales, 300 tons, Thomas
Morrison, now at Londonderry, for Baltimore and Philadelphia Aug. 1; James
Thompson, merchant, agent.

12 - Sat., July 11, 1772.

Dublin.
Married: Capt. Despard to Miss Croaisdale of Summer-hill.
Died: at Carrickmacross, John Cassidy, apothecary; at Belfast, David Lyons,
linen draper.

Londonderry.
The Friendship, M'Cullogh, from Belfast with passengers, arrived at
Philadelphia, all well, after a passage of five weeks.

13 - Weds., July 15, 1772.

Cork, July 2.
Died Tuesday last, Robert Hill, late of County Wicklow.

Dublin.
Married: at Cargins, Co. Roscommon (the seat of Daniel Kelly), Malby Crofton, Longford, Co. Sligo, to Miss Elizabeth Kelly; Peter Kinselagh, age 63, to Miss Polly Dunn, age 13, both of Carrick near Portarlington. Died: at Ballyshannon, Co. Donegal, Thomas Dickson; at Glasnevin, Capt. Theophilus Desbrisay; Miss Anne, daughter of the late Captain Hansard.

14 - Sat., July 18, 1772.

Kilkenny.
William Mihan, Loughmore, Co. Tipperary, father of three children and the support of two old women, allegedly was murdered by Dennis and Thomas Meagher and their mother and sister, of the same place.

Dublin.
Married: John Minett to Miss Elizabeth Harding of Clonlee, King's Co.; at Tullow, Co. Carlow, Owen Courtney, age 80, to Miss Brown of Laidtown, age 25. Died: at Broomhill, Hawks Crosse.

Londonderry.
On July 2, Mrs. Ringland of the Rock, parish of Kilmore, Co. Down, age 52, bore a son, her first child in eleven years; Mr. Ringland is 64 years old.

15 - Weds., July 22, 1772

Corke.
John Connor alias Jack the Bachelor, smuggler, though reported dead by the Dublin papers, has been seen here.

Kilkenny.
Two men named Ling and Kelly (a fisherman) drowned in the Barrow at Carlow.

Dublin.
John Dunn was convicted of the murder of Patrick Quinn.

Londonderry.
Ads: Ship Jupiter of Londonderry, Alexander Ewing master, arrived in Philadelphia after 27 days, to return with wheat and flour and return to Philadelphia in September with passengers. The Nancy is now advertised for Wilmington, N.C. by Aug. 10th.

16 - Sat., July 25, 1772.

Dublin, July 21.
Wednesday fo'night died at Clackmanan Castle, Scotland, Harry Bruce, age 72, of the same, descended from John Bruce, third son of Robert, Lord Annandale (the Competitor); heir of Sir Robert Bruce who in 1359 received a charter for Clackmanan from King David; he had no issue.

Londonderry.
Died: at Letterkenny, Robert Gamble, son of Henry Gamble, late of this city. Ads: Mr. Shannon, organist, spinnet to sell. The late Mr. James Hervey's interest in High Dunmore to be sold.

17 - Weds., July 29, 1772

Dublin.
Edward Donnelan, Kevin's port, carpenter, convert to the Church of Ireland. Married: William O'Brien, Drumballa Co. Leitrim to Miss Irwin, daughter of

4

Acheson Irwin of Drumsilla, Co. Leitrim.
Died; Richard Benson, formerly ledger keeper in the Treasury; at Dunmanway,
Rev. Sir Michael Cox, bart.; at Portarlington, Capt. Francis Baillie; on the
20th, Morley Saunders of Saunders Grove; Anthony Perier, late one of the High
Sheriffs of this city.

Londonderry.
Ads: Sarah Wiley, alias Desart, has left her husband Andrew Wiley, Cororeagh,
barony of Inishowen, Co. Donegal, farmer. The ship Elizabeth is expected
from Norway, David Brown, master; to go to Newcastle and Philadelphia about
Aug. 20; Alderman Wm. Lecky, agent.

18 - Sat., Aug. 1, 1772

Galway.
Catharine Mannin was gaoled for drowning her five-year-old son Patrick Mannin
in a churn of milk.

Dublin.
The following were sentenced to death: John Dunn for the murder of Patrick
Quin; William Roe for the murder of Edward Moran; John Casey for the murder
of Thomas Penninton; John Dudgeon for robbing the house of Barth. Harrold;
Daniel Kelly for stealing seventeen sheep from Thomas Whelan. Bella
Stapleton, for robbing the house of John Carney, to be hanged, but she was
with child. Dennis Murray, to be transported for stealing clothes from the
bleach field of James Field. Valentine Devatt to be whipped for picking
pockets. James Keating to be pillored and imprisoned for riot and assault on
a watchman. John Robinson, to be burned in the hand for manslaughter. John
Maxwell, same.
Bankrupts: Alexander Alexander, Coagh, Co. Tyrone, linen draper, bleacher,
etc.; Edward Corcoran, Dublin, shop keeper; John Anderson, Dublin, silk
weaver.

Cork, July 23.
The ship Hopewell, Archibald Long, from New York, 22 days out spoke with the
brigantine William, John Thompson, from Newry to Virginia with servants, 19
days out...all well.

Philadelphia, June 11.
Saturday last arrived here the ship Jupiter, Capt. Ewing, from Londonderry,
who landed 430 passengers at Newcastle.

19 - Weds., Aug. 5, 1772.

Dublin.
Eugene M'Canna, convert to Ch. of I., Church of Benburb, Co. Tyrone.
Married: at Augher, Co.Tyrone, George Leigh to Miss Mary Wilson; Benjamin Lee
of Merrion to Miss Smith of Drogheda; Thomas Kelly, surgeon, to Widow Brown;
Thomas Armitage, bookseller, to Miss Betty Williams of Chapelizod.
Died: at Maddenstown, Mrs. Ormsby Vandeleur; at the seat of the Earl of
Milltown, the Lady of Hon. Brice Leeson; Michael Waldron, attorney; William
Luffingham, linen draper.
Bankrupt: Edmund Meagher, Nenagh, Co. Tipperary, shopkeeper.

20 - Sat., Aug. 8, 1772

Dublin, Aug. 4.
Born: two sons to Lady Viscountess Powerscourt, Sunday.
Married: at Kilmurry, Tobias Horan of Newcastle near Limerick to Miss
Meredith.

21 - Weds., Aug. 12, 1772

Dublin, Aug. 8.
Last Wednesday John Dunn was executed for the murder of Patrick Quin.
Died: last Thursday, the Countess of Westmeath.

Londonderry.
Ads: The Jupiter for New Castle and Philadelphia, Andrew Gregg and James
Thompson, agents. The Prince of Wales, 300 tons, Thomas Morrison master, to
sail on the 14th for Baltimore and Philadelphia. The ship Nancy, 300 tons,
Norman Chevers master, for Wilmington, North Carolina on the 24th. The ship
Hopewell, 250 tons, James Campbell master, for Newcastle and Philadelphia.

22 - Sat., Aug. 15, 1772

Dublin.
Owen Traynor, shoemaker, convert to Church of Ireland. ---- Reed of Sligo
committed suicide, followed by his wife. ---- Dunn, Queen's County, killed -
--- Murray.
Married: Rev. Dean Hamilton to Miss Wood, daughter of Hans Wood of Co.
Westmeath, niece to the Earl of Kingston.
Bankrupt: Craghead Kyle, Dublin, dealer and chapman.

Londonderry.
Cleared out: Boscawen, Marshall, for Philadelphia with passengers.

23 - Weds., Aug. 19, 1772.

Dublin.
Miss Jane Kelly, convert to Church of Ireland.

Londonderry.
Ads: Jane Henderson or Maxwell eloped from her husband John Henderson of
Dunrain, parish of Ardstraw, Co. Tyrone, Aug. 4th.

24 - Sat., Aug. 22, 1772.

Dublin.
Married: William Gilboarn of Peafield, Queen's County to Miss Luffingham of
Bride st.; at Waterford, Capt. Musgrave to Miss Keily, daughter of Richard
Keily of Lismore, Co. Westmeath.
Died: at Thomastown, Rev. Thomas Quinlean, of the Church of Rome; in
Meetinghouse yard, Mr. Edward Connor, merchant.

25 - Weds., Aug. 26, 1772.

Corke.
Catherine Fitzgerald, convert to Church of Ireland.

Londonderry.
Cleared: the Hopewell, Wianiag, for Philadelphia in ballast.

26 - Sat., Aug. 29, 1772.

Dublin.
Bankrupt: Henry Graves, Dublin, grocer; Leonard M'Nally, Dublin, grocer.
Married: Thomas Howison of Bride st., merchant, to Miss Mary Davy of the
Batchelor's Walk; at Ennis, Co. Clare, Denis O'Callaghan of this city to
Miss Mary Hauffort.
Died: near Roscarberry, Rev. Bart. Crotty, parish priest; at Newforrest, Co.
Galway, James de Arcy.

27 - Weds., Sept. 2, 1772

Dublin.
Bankrupt: Alexander Reynolds, Ballymoney, Co. Antrim, merchant.
Married: Thomas Shaw, linen draper, to Miss Ann White, both of Backlane; in
England, Richard Rose Drew of Exeter to Miss Hannah Spencer, daughter of
Brent Spencer, late of Bele-hill, Co. Down, dec'd; Robert Colvil to Miss
Lennox of Henry st.; at Cover Hill, Co. Down, James Tod to Miss M'Clelland.
Died: in Francis st., William Dulles, stuff-mercer; at Loughbrickland,
Francis Rourke, a captain on half pay.

Londonderry.
Cleared out, the Prince of Wales, Morrison, for Baltimore with passengers.

28 - Sat., Sept. 5, 1772.

Dublin.
Converts to the Church of Ireland: Mary Lodge at Kilkenny and Anne Fitzsimons
at Clanduff, diocese of Dromore. Wedgeworth Green's life is despaired of
after an accident. Mr. John Young's wife was delivered of three boys.
Married: in Sackville st., Thomas Pepper of Ballygarth, Co. Meath, to Miss
Moore, daughter of Richard Moore of Barn, deceased; John Neynoe of Grafton
st. to Miss Elinor Twig, Co. Wicklow.
Died: in Merrion st., Rt. Rev. Dr. Young, Bishop of Leighlin and Fernes;
William Talbot sr., of Loughane, King's County; at Ennis, Co. Clare, Thomas
Magrath, M.D.

Londonderry.
Married: at Strabane, Rev. Jocelyn Ingram to Miss Porter of the same town.

29 - Weds., Sept. 9, 1772.

Dublin.
Married: at Limerick, Lord Stavordale to Miss Grady, daughter of Standish
Grady of Capercullen; John Knox to Miss Penelope Tisdal.
Died: in Lurgan st., Patrick Savage, attorney; in County Mayo, James Gilden
sr.; in Mary's lane, Mr. Hugh Chambers, timber merchant.

Londonderry.
The ship Rose, Robert George, from Londonderry, arrived at Newcastle on July
12 with passengers.

30 - Sat., Sept. 12, 1772

Dublin.
Married: at Monaghan, Mr. James Gray of Loughdayan, Co. Down to Miss Lowry;
at Kinsale, Richard Moore, barrister, to Miss Ottiwell.
Bankrupt: Richard Quignan of Marrowbone lane, tanner.

31 - Weds., Setp. 16, 1772

Dublin.
Luke Wallis, brother of General Wallis in the Imperial service, convert to
the Church of Ireland.
Died: General Vileneve; at the Sheds of Clontarf, Edward Mocks, a boy.

Londonderry.
Ads: The sons of Bryan O'Faran, late of Londonderry, deceased, taylor, intend
to carry on his business to support his widow.

32 - Sat., Sept. 19, 1772

Dublin, Sept. 15.
Thursday the Charles, Perkins, bound from Galway to New York in America,

having sprung a leak at sea, was obliged to put into this harbour. There are upwards of 100 Highlanders with their families on board, who are at present at George's quay in great distress, waiting for the vessel to be repaired. Married: James Gray to Miss Ann Lowry of Monaghan; William Lowry of Monaghan to Miss Olivia Picken of same; Blaney Mitchel of Monaghan, attorney, to Miss Ann Forster of same; at Kinsale, Capt. Baskerville of the 50th Regiment to Miss Bishop.
Died; near Aughnacloy, the wife of James Sweeny jr.; in Dorset st., Rev. Mr. M'Clane; near Freshford, Rev. Mr. Stewart; at Tullaheady, Co. Tipperary, James O'Dwyr.
Bankrupt: Henry Graves of Dublin, grocer.

Limerick.
Johanna Cooper and Mary Mulowny, converts to the Church of Ireland, at the parish church of Kilsinane.

33 - Weds., Sept. 23, 1772.

Belfast, Sept. 11.
On Wednesday se'nnight a small boat returning to Rathlin from Ballycastle sank and Rev. Alexander Cuppage, James Gage, four other passengers, and two boatmen drowned.
At the Antrim assizes ended Tues. last: John Blair jr, found guilty of stealing four bullocks, to be executed; Hugh Douglas, to be transported.

Dublin.
John Sheehan, taylor, Limerick, convert to Church of Ireland.

34 - Sat., Sept. 26, 1772

Dublin.
Mention of George Smyth of this city, now residing among the Mowhawks in North America.
Converts to the Church of Ireland: Rev. Mr. P. Fay, at Navan; Mary Carron or Maguire, Anne Minckleroy, Catherine M'Illether, and Judith Corrigan, at Killether in the district of Kilmore.
Died: Rev. Charles Bunworth of Baltidaniel, Vicar of Killbriun and Killbrony; at Galway, Rev. Valentine Fleming of the Church of Rome; at Brookhall, Co. Antrim, in his 77th year, James Watson.

35 - Weds., Sept. 30, 1772

Galway, Sept. 21.
Bartholomew Gilligan, a servant, died last Friday of hydrophobia.

Clonmel, Sept. 21.
Last Thursday a thatched cabin near Ballindunna took fire and the wife and child of ---- Cleary died in the flames.

Dublin.
Married; Rev. Mr. Abrahan Seawright of Limerick to Miss Smyth of Belfast; at Ballyporeen, James Casey of Co. Limerick to Miss Dobbin; Tho. Pardy of Gilford, merchant, to Miss Williams of Drumbanagher.
Died: Rev. William Greenshields, Rector of Finoe etc., Diocese of Killalo; in Great Cuffe st., John Gibton; in College Green, Lt. Robert French of the marines.
Bankrupt: William Walsh of Dublin, grocer.

36 - Sat., Oct. 3, 1772

Dublin.
Married; Thomas Derham, merchant, to Miss Magennis of Drogheda.
Died: in Dawson st., in his 92nd year, Rev. Dr. Arthur St. George, Dean of Rosse, upwards of 66 years a clergyman of the Diocese of Clogher.

Londonderry.
Died: last Thursday, Thomas Moore of this city, merchant.
Tuesday last was executed at Lifford Neal Dougherty, for the murder of Mr.
Armstrong at Carn in Co. Donegal; died penitent; a Roman Catholic, age 30.
Cleared out, the Nancy, Chevers, for Wilmington with passengers.

37 - Weds., Oct. 7, 1772

Dublin, Oct. 3.
Died: Thursday, Ford Lambert, Earl of Cavan (?); at Newton, Co. Roscommon,
John Hemsworth.
Bankrupt: Charles Hearn of George's st., upholder.

38 - Sat., Oct. 10, 1772

Dublin.
Married: James Maxwell, surgeon of the Tyrone hospital, to Miss Maxwell of
Drum, near Lisburn; at Ballihaise, Co. Cavan, Capt. Stewart of the Royal
Irish Dragoons to Miss Alicia Blacker of Co. Armagh.
Died: Thomas Monck, a Burgess in Parliament for the borough of Old Leighlin;
at Bath, Edward Browne, formerly of the First Horse; at Kells, Mr. Val.
Cruise.

39 - Weds., Oct. 14, 1772

Dublin, Oct. 10
A Mr. Graham, coming to a fair at Dublin, drowned near Guilford on Friday.
Died: Wednesday, Sir Thomas Butler, bart., at his seat of Garryhunden; Arthur
Nugent of Tubbertynan, Co. Meath; James Colgan, one of the Vicars Choral of
St. Patrick's and Christ Church; at Ballynure in his 84th year, James Park.

Londonderry.
Ads: All of the goods in his wholesale and retail drapery shop are to be sold
at the house of the late Thomas Moore. Joseph Scott, Raphoe, to sell
interest in Mullangar farm, subject to annuity of 10 pounds during the life
of Mrs. Rouse, who is about sixty years old.

40 - Sat., Oct. 17, 1772

Dublin.
Constantine Murphy and Constantine Corrigan, converts to Church of Ireland,
at Killesher, Diocese of Kilmore.
Married: at Strabane, Charles Stewart of Hornhead to Miss Charleton.

41 - Weds., Oct. 21, 1772

Dublin.
Married: Rev. Dr. Henry Candler of Castlewood, Co. Kilkenny to Mrs. Aylward;
in King's County, Humphry Ellis to Miss Lucinda Armstrong.
Died: the Lady of Col. Pepper; in Abbey st., Joseph Davenport of Lifford, Co.
Donegal; at St. Wollston's, Henry Shannon.

Belfast.
Cleared out, the Pennsylvania Farmer, Robeson, for Philadelphia.

Londonderry.
Died: a few days ago at Strabane, Miss Ann Hamilton, daughter of
Claudius Hamilton, M.P.
Cleared out, the Pitt, McShane, for Baltimore in ballast.

42 - Sat., Oct. 24, 1772

Londonderry.
Died: a few days ago at Newtown Limavady, Alexander Ogilbay, bleacher.

Dublin, Oct. 20.
Married: Saturday last, William Glendowe, banker, of this city, to Miss Newcomen, daughter of the late Charles Newcomen of Co. Longford.

43 - Tues., Oct. 27, 1772

Dublin.
Michael and William Wild, at Nenagh, Co. Tipperary, converts to the Church of Ireland.
Jacob and Samuel Poole, tried for ordering soldiers to fire and thereby killing Paul Fleming and Laughlin Lawler, were found not guilty.
Died: at Belfast, the wife of Stephen Haven; near Maryborough, Mrs. Bunbury (her estate to Lt. Bunbury, late of the Third Regiment of Horse); in Linen st., Richard Montgomery, merchant.

Belfast.
Cleared out, the Hopewell, Martin, for Charlestown, beef etc.

44 - Fri., Oct. 30, 1772

Dublin, Oct. 27.
Mention of the murder of Rev. Mr. Morrell and destruction of the property of Richard Johnson of Guilford.
Married: at Ennis, William Blood jr. of Roxton to Miss Elizabeth Bindon.
Died: James Reily, one of the Vicars Choral of Christ Church and St. Patrick's; near Cashel, William Pennefather; Sunday last, the lady of Hon. John Beresford.

46 - Fri., Nov. 6, 1772

Dublin.
Died: the Lady of Lt. Col. Chesevix; in Bandon road, Thomas Bennett, age 130; at Edinburgh, Peter M'Donald, a fisherman, in the 119th year of his age; his father lived to be 110 and his grandfather to 107; in Wiltshire, Thomas Pearce, age 112, never married.

Londonderry.
Died: at Strabane Tuesday last, Mrs. Rebecca Sproul, wife of John Sproul.

47 - Tues., Nov. 10, 1772

Belfast.
Cleared out, the Britannia, Clendennen, Charlestown, beef, etc.

Londonderry.
Ads: The ship Wallworth, Conolly M'Causland, commander, arrived safe at Philadelphia after a passage of eight weeks.

48 - Fri., Nov. 13, 1772

Belfast.
Cleared, the Elizabeth, Brown, for Savannah with beef, bread, etc.

Dublin.
Married; Rev. Mr. Clark of Raphoe to Miss Elinor Nesbit of Killybegs; Peter Lewich to Miss Rebecca Irvin.

49 - Tues., Nov. 17, 1772.

Dublin.
Died; in Great Cumberland st., Ed. Ramsay, secretary to the Board of Excise; in Bolton st., John Reid, an eminent builder.

Londonderry.
Ads: Alice Gourney or Cay, wife of Joseph Gourney of Waterside, Londonderry,
has left him.

52 - Fri., Nov. 27, 1772

Sligo, Nov. 10.
Late Saturday night last was drowned Mr. William Alexander.

Dublin.
Bankrupt: Thomas Forster, Dublin, merchant.

Londonderry.
Married: in County Tyrone, Thomas Young of Sandville to Miss Ann Rife (Rise?)
of Lisslane.

53 - Tues., Dec. 1, 1772

Dublin.
Married: Lt. Watkins of the 28th Regiment to Miss Mitchel, daughter of Capt.
Mitchel of the 45th Regiment; Charles Colhon of Sixmilecross, Co. Tyrone, to
Miss Scarlet Anderson of same.
Died: at his house at Stephen's green, Edward Brabazon, 7th Earl of Meath;
Rev. Daniel Jackson, age 84 (Church of Ireland); at Galway, Captain M'Kay of
the Highland Regiment.

Londonderry.
Tuesday the 24th died James Maxwel sr. of Omagh.

54 - Fri., Dec. 4, 1772

Dublin.
Died: in Yorkshire, Viscount Galway, brother of General Monckton; at
Clontarf, William Rochfort, brother to the Earl of Belvedere.

Londonderry.
The Boscawen, Captain Marshal, arrived in Philadelphia with passengers after
an agreeable passage of six weeks. The Hopewell of Londonderry, John
Winning, arrived at Philadelphia after five weeks, passengers all well.
Married: near Aughnacloy, Co. Tyrone, Alexander Fleming, formerly of the
linen hall, Dublin, age 65, and Mrs. Mary Mitchel, age 76.

55 - Tues., Dec. 8, 1772

Londonderry.
Ads: Mention of the estate of the late Alderman Hogg.

56 - Fri., Dec. 11, 1772

Londonderry.
The Prince of Wales, Thomas Morrison, master, from this port arrived safe at
Baltimore with passengers after six weeks.

57 - Tues., Dec. 15, 1772

Dublin.
Owen Devlin, at Shankill, Lurgan, convert to the Church of Ireland.

Londonderry.
Capt. John M'Gauran and his brig Delight were lost on the coast near
Liverpool, with the crew and twenty-six passengers from Drogheda.
Died in childbed last week, age 16, at Strabane, Mrs. Hamilton, lady of John
Hamilton of Dunemana, daughter of the late Lord Boyne.

58 - Fri., Dec. 18, 1772

Londonderry.
Ads: Pat Maguigan ran away from the service of Gust. Hamilton.

59 - Tues., Dec. 22, 1772

Dublin.
Bankrupt: Michael Griffin, merchant, Dublin.

62 - Fri., Jan. 1, 1773

Cork.
Mrs. Mary Dawly, convert to the Church of Ireland.

Londonderry.
Isabel Coll and William M'Award, parish of Aughanuntian, converts to the
Church of Ireland.
Died: a few days since in the parish of Ardstraw, Co. Tyrone, Robert
M'Creary, age 106; he had been a soldier under King William; his youngest
child was two years old.

63 - Tues., Jan. 5, 1773

Dublin.
Died: at Aix in Provence, David Hay, bookseller of this city; the wife of
William Sall, late of Back-lane.

66 - Fri., Jan. 15, 1773

Dublin.
---- Smyth, baker, beat his wife and has not been heard of since.
Bankrupt: Richard Arnold of Dublin, distiller and dealer.

Londonderry.
Ads: Darby Carr has run away from the service of George Ash of Ashbrook.
Monro Denning, from London, watchmaker, has settled in Strabane.

67 - Tues., Jan. 19, 1773

Dublin.
James Burden, Cork, convert to Church of Ireland.

Londonderry.
The ship Jupiter, Alexander Ewing, arrived at Philadelphia about seven weeks
ago and landed passengers in good spirits.
Ads: Martha Donnelly separated from James Buchanan jr. of Londonderry.

68 - Fri., Jan. 22, 1773

Dublin, Jan. 19.
James Cassidy and Ann Cassidy alias Monaghan, converts to Church of Ireland,
at Killesher, diocese of Kilmore.
Died: a few days ago, Thomas Faulkner of Raan, Co. Donegal, late Captain of
the 11th Foot.

69 - Tues., Jan. 26, 1773

Carlow, Jan. 20.
A few nights ago Rev. Mr. Patrick Lawler, Roman Catholic clergyman, missed
his way and drowned in a bog.

71 - Tues., Feb. 2, 1773

Londonderry.
Died: last Saturday, George Gordon of this city, apothecary.
Ads: Martha Lockart alias Wilson alias Cook has left her husband, James
Lockart of Newtown Limavady, baker. The late Andrew Delap's share of the
Woods of Ray to be sold; his partner was James Watt of Rathmelton.

72 - Fri., Feb. 5, 1773

Corke.
Captain Savage of the Industry drowned in a wreck in Dingle Bay.

73 - Tues., Feb. 9, 1773

Londonderry.
Died: on Thursday the fourth, in Capel st. in Dublin, Arthur Dougherty,
Register of the Bishop's Court.
Ads: Sarah Work alias Stephenson has left her husband Frederick Work of
Rushhall. Ann Sinclare alias Brown has left her husband John Sinclare,
Newtown Limavaddy.

74 - Fri., Feb. 12, 1773

Londonderry.
Married: yesterday, Alexander Wilson of this city, merchant, to Miss
Elizabeth M'Conegal; yesterday, William Smith of Newtown Limavady to Miss
Mary Lecky, daughter of Alderman Thomas Lecky of this city.
Ads: The ship Minerva, Capt. Francis Ferris, 350 tons, lies at Warren-point
to take passengers for Newcastle and Philadelphia; a very fine ship, "full 5
Feet 4 Inches high between the decks." (Newry)

75 - Tues., Feb. 16, 1773

Londonderry.
Cleared out: the Sally, Thomson, for Baltimore in ballast.

Ads: Ship Jenny, Capt. Arch. M'Illwaine, 250 tons, at the ship quay, for
Newcastle and Philadelphia on March 20. Property of the late Capt. Thomas
Faulkner to be sold at the house of Raan, near Letterkenny.

77 - Tues., Feb. 23, 1773

Londonderry.
Ads: Tradesmen for Baltimore in America wanted; apply to Charles Hamilton,
Armstrong's Inn, Enniskillen and later at Glascow's Inn, Omagh, Knox's Inn,
Strabane, and Pat Bradly's Inn, Londonderry.

78 - Fri., Feb. 26, 1773

Londonderry.
Married: last week, William Dysan to Miss Jane Mitchel, both of this city.
Ads: Brant Homan, woollen draper, Francis st., Dublin, has taken into his
company his late partner's brother, Richard Homan.

79 - Tues., Mar. 2, 1773

Galway, Feb. 18.
Captain Morgan of the sloop of war Hunter died Sunday before Tuesday last.

Dublin.
Patrick Smith, parish of Killesher, Diocese of Kilmore and Samuel Taylor,
Tulla, Co. Clare, converts to the Church of Ireland.

Londonderry.
---- Thompson, a poor farmer of near Cookstown, Co. Tyrone, was shot and
killed returning home with his bride.

80 - Fri., Mar. 5, 1773

Londonderry.
Ads: The business of the late George Gordon is to be continued by his son,
Gardner Gordon. Ship Hannah, 40 tons, Capt. James Mitchell, to sail Apr. 10
for Newcastle and Philadelphia.

81 - Tues., Mar. 9, 1773

Dublin.
Notice of the trial of William Creighton, who was found guilty of robbing the
mail and was to be hung.

Londonderry.
Ads: Ship Walworth, Capt. Conolly M'Causland, 300 tons, to sail Apr. 6 for
Newcastle and Philadelphia. Ship Jupiter, 300 tons, Alexander Ewing, for
same on 20 April. Ship Betty, 250 tons, Richard Hunter, for Baltimore on
March 19. The executors of Thomas Moore, deceased, to let (at the house of
Mr. Lepper at Three Trees) the lands that John Quigley of Clenally formerly
possessed in Glentaugher, held under William M'Ilwaine of Lisfanan.

82 - Fri., Mar. 12, 1773

Londonderry.
Ads: The Alexander, James Hunter, 400 tons, to sail April 15 for Newcastle
and Philadelphia; not six months old, at least six feet high between decks,
and at all points calculated for the accomodation of passengers,
redemptioners, or servants; Robert Alexander, owner.

83 - Tues., Mar. 16, 1773

Londonderry.
Robert Gibson of Portaferry was washed overboard from the Acorn on Dec. 26,
on way from Carolina (to Liverpool?).
Died: in Grafton st., Dublin, George Harvey, of Maulin hall, County Donegal.
Ads: Notice of executors of the late Thomas Moore, late of Butcher st.,
woollen draper.

84 - Fri., Mar. 19, 1773

Londonderry.
Died: a few days ago, John Harrison, at his house near Culmore; this morning,
Mrs. Jonathan Nicolls, wife of one of the city sheriffs.

85 - Tues., Mar. 23, 1773

Dublin, Mar. 20.
Thursday night the Richard of Corke, from the West Indies, ran on a bank and
sank; all were lost except one sailor, including the master, Dennis Twohigg.

86 - Fri., Mar. 26, 1773

Dublin.
Died: Sunday, Lt. Agnew of Prussia st.

Londonderry.
Cleared out, the Friendship, M'Culloch, for Philadelphia with beef etc.
Died: a few days ago at Strabane, Mrs. Ingram, wife of Rev. Ingram, daughter
of Mr. Porter, post-master of Strabane.

Dublin, Mar. 30.
Last Wednesday died in London Rt. Hon. Philip Dormer Stanhope (born 1695).
Saturday last were executed George Crinnion, postman, convicted of opening
letters, and Francis Gore, for street robbery.

Londonderry.
Cleared out: the Elliott, Pym, for Newcastle in ballast.
Ads: The brig Louisa, Isaac Kirkpatrick, 200 tons, for Charleston, S.C., to
sail May 1; Robert Alexander, owner. The ship Walworth, Conolly M'Causland,
300 tons, for Charlestown, S.C. and Cape Fear, N.C. on May 10.

89 - Tues., Apr. 6, 1773

Sligo.
At the last assizes, John M'Gown was found guild of horse stealing; to be
executed April 10.

Dublin.
Bankrupt: Andrew Chaigneau of Cork-hill, Dublin; Richard Davys, Theobald
Jennings, and James Tuke, grocers, Dublin; and William Beirne of Elphin, Co.
Roscommon, merchant.

Londonderry.
Yesterday were tried here certain persons having on the 19th of June
assaulted three brothers named M'Donald, of Inniskillen, one of whom was shot
dead and another desperately wounded; they were found not guilty. [See number
137.]
Ads: Alexander Morrison has advertised to sell 50 acres of Graysteelmore, but
he only has the rent of 14 acres; it belongs to his brother-in-law, one
Mackey, now in America. James Crawford is recruiting redemptioners and
servants for America.

90 - Fri., Apr. 9, 1773

Dublin, Apr. 6.
Died: Capt. Robinson of the Royal Highlanders, in Galway; Monday last, James
Byrne, last surviving son of Charles Byrne of Byrne's grove, Co. Kilkenny;
some time ago in France, ---- Fitzgerald, a general in the French service; at
Ahanakishe near Mallow, James Nagle, at an advanced age; at Kilkenny, Hans
Bailie, an alderman of Dublin.
Married: Hon. Gustavus Hamilton (eldest son of Richard Lord Viscount Boyne)
to Miss Somerville, only daughter of the late Sir Quayle Somerville; at
Bulruth, Co. Sligo, John Healy, age 79, to Margaret ----, age 64.

Londonderry.
Article on emigration. Ships and tonnage that sailed with passengers to
North America, taken from ads published in the Belfast Newsletter:

	1771		1772		
	ships	tuns	ships	tuns	Total
Londonderry	13	3650	9	2650	
Belfast	7	1751	10	2650	
Newry	9	2800	5	1600	
Portrush	1	250	1	250	
Larne	2	450	5	1300	
	32	8900	30	8450	62	17,350

The number of passengers was estimated to be the same as the number of tuns.
Most paid their passage, at 3 pounds 10 shillings each. Most were employed
in the linen manufacture or farming. Emigration was increasing. ..."till
now, it was chiefly the very meanest of the people that went off, mostly in

the station of indentured servants and such as had become obnoxious to their mother Country." In the last five or six years, one quarter of the trading class and one quarter of the manufacturing people had left.

91 - Tues. Apr. 13, 1773

Dublin, Apr. 10.
Died: Wednesday, James Dunn, age 73, at his house on Ormond quay.

Londonderry.
The ship Jenny, Capt. M'Elwaine, to sail the 17th.

92 - Fri., Apr. 16, 1773

Dublin.
There are now fourteen ships at Belfast taking in passengers for America, also ships at Cork, Limerick, and Galway.

Londonderry.
A few days ago a new brig Louisa, the property of Alderman Alexander, was launched on the river.
Ads: Ship Rose, Robert George, 300 tons, for Newcastle and Philadelphia on June 1.

93 - Tues., Apr. 20, 1773

Dublin.
The Dublin, Power, from this port to Maryland with convicts, was entirely lost the middle of January on the Horse Shore in Chesapeake Bay; the people were saved.
Died: at Athlone, Loftus Glass; at Carrick mines, Rev. Henry Wright; Stephen Sibthorpe of Newtown, Co. Louth; in Dame St., David Ribton, one of the Sheriff-Peers of the County.
Bankrupt: Francis Hunter of Antrim, Co. Antrim, shop keeper.

Londonderry.
Died yesterday, the widow of Arthur Dougherty, lately deceased.

94 - Fri., Apr. 23, 1773

Dublin.
Nicholas Lawless, parish church of St. Werburgh's, convert to Church of Ireland.

Londonderry.
Ads: The ship Jupiter is at Culmore, for Philadelphia May 10. Brig Hellen, 200 tons, Capt. James Ramage, for Charlestown, South Carolina and Cape Fear, N.C., on May 20.

95 - Tues., Apr. 27, 1773

Dublin.
Born: at Leinster house, a son to Dutchess of Leinster; in Henry st., a son to the Lady of Sir Lucius O'Brien.

Londonderry.
Died: Apr. 18, Rev. Mr. Hind, near Magheracross, Co. Fermanagh, while riding from Mr. Lendrum's.

96 - Fri., Apr. 30, 1773

Dublin, Apr. 27.
Died: at Milltown, Eyre Evans; Thursday in Sackville st., Mrs. Malone; at Saunderscourt, Co. Wexford, Arthur Gore, Earl of Arran; in Carlow, Major

Astle, age 100; in Ross lane, James Taylor, counsellor at law; Rev. Michael Storey of Wicklow.

97 - Tues., May 4, 1773

Dublin.
Died: at his house in Peter st., Edward Donovan, counsellor at law; at Esker, Co. Dublin, Mrs. Elizabeth Lyster, relict of John Lyster; Charles M'Donnell, member of parliament for the borough of Ennis.

Londonderry.
The Elizabeth, Robert Johnson, has arrived from Belfast at Savannah, Georgia with 300 passengers.
Mention of Rev. Mr. Orr, deceased, of Magherafelt (Church of Ireland).
Cleared out; the Jenny, M'Ilwaine, for Philadelphia in ballast.

98 - Fri., May 7, 1773

Dublin.
Bankrupt; Marsden Warren, Dublin, merchant; Ignatius Andrews, Dublin, grocer; William Ahern, Co. Cork, tanner.
Cleared out: [from Belfast?] Agnes, Ewing, for Philadelphia with beef, cloth, etc.

Londonderry.
Ads: Alexander Cochran jr., Clashgowny, has to let two tenements in Strabane lately held by Joseph Brown, deceased, at the house of William Porter.

99 - Tues., May 11, 1773

Newry, May 3.
Last week Mrs. Charles Grant of Ballygorrian had a baby; the mother is 64 and the father is 95.

Dublin, May 8.
Died: Col. Thomas Burton, killed in an accident; Saturday last, Hugh Moran, at the Royal Hospital, a soldier aged 113; a few days before, James Keating, an old soldier there, age 103.
Bankrupt: John Maguire, Enniskillen, dealer and chapman; John Lynch, Dublin, merchant; John Glenholme, Magherafelt, Co. Londonderry; Nicholas Hart, New-row, Dublin, dealer; Thomas Yeats & James Donaldson, Bride st., dealers and chapmen; John Mannin, Bridge st., linen draper.

Londonderry.
Ads: Daniel M'Laughlin is taking up sail making in addition to his business of rope making, to be helped by James Parkinson, who served his apprenticeship in Liverpool.

100 - Fri., May 14, 1773

Londonderry.
Mr. Aul of Newtown Lemavady was swindled; his son was in America.

101 - Tues., May 18, 1773

Dublin, May 15.
Died: at Belfast, Rev. Gilbert Kennedy, dissenting minister there for near thirty years; at Belfast, William Wallace sr., age 80; Mr. Todd, merchant of Fleet st.; Thomas Lynch of Lavally, Co. Galway.
Londonderry.
Died: last Friday, age 88, Rev. Mr. John Holmes, fifty-five years a minister of the Gospel, 31 years in the parish of Glendermot. [See also number 102.]

102 - Fri., May 21, 1773

Londonderry.
Died: Saturday last Rev. John Holmes, Dissenting Minister of Glendermot, age 88.

103 - Tues., May 25, 1773

Dublin, May 22.
Married: last Saturday, Lord Townshend to Miss Anne, daughter of William Montgomery.
Died: Pierce Evans of the 28th Regiment; in Francis st., John Emerson; in Earl st., Mr. Joseph Greenhow, a Quaker; Cliffe Tottenham; Rev. Mr. Blashford, librarian; Alderman Robert King; at Waterford, Rev. Mr. Shea, (Roman Catholic); in Watling st., Mr. Anthony Magawly, an excommunicate Romish priest.

Londonderry.
Cleared out: the Alexander, Hunter, for Philadelphia with passengers; the Hannah, Mitchel, for same with passengers; the Wallworth, M'Causland, for Carolina with passengers.
Ads: For Newcastle and Philadelphia, the brig Louisa, 200 tons, June 7; owner Robert Alexander; capt. Isaac Kirkpatrick. For Charlestown, S.C., the ship George, 250 tons, Capt. William Pinkerton, July 1. For Baltimore, the ship Prince of Wales, 350 tons, Thomas Morrison, July 10.

104 - Fri., May 28, 1773

Belfast, May 25.
Saturday, old Mary Doggart was murdered in Mill-held; yesterday her daughter Jenny Doggart was committed to gaol on suspicion; her son Edward Doggart has absconded.

Dublin.
Lamby Higgins of Mountmelick drowned on Tuesday the 18th.

Londonderry.
Ads: Hugh Shannon, apprentice, age about 18, ran away from the service of Joseph Carr of Aughasessy. The ship Philadelphia, John Winning, 250 tons, for Newcastle and Philadelphia June 20. The ship Rose, Robert George, 300 tons, for Newcastle and Philadelphia June 10.

105 - Tues., June 1, 1773

Londonderry.
Cleared out: the Jupiter, Ewing, for Phladelphia with passengers.

106 - Fri., June 4, 1773

Londonderry.
Letter from John Wesley: Emigration is caused by tenants being turned out of farms by landlords when leases are up; it is draining money from poor Ireland; all emigrants are Protestants and Romanists are already a majority even in Ulster. He thinks they should rather beg in Ireland than starve in America, based on what he saw in Georgia in former times.

Ads: For the Prince of Wales, going to Baltimore: "The town of Baltimore is commodiously situated for a ready Communication with all the back parts of Pennsylvania, Maryland, and Virginia, to which most new Settlers resort. It is a hundred miles nearer than Philadelphia to Fort Pitt on the River Ohio -- a new Province of vast Extent, of the most fertile fine Lands in North America, and in the most agreeable moderate Climate, is now settling very fast along the Banks of that famous River, where Tracts of the richest Lands in the World and of greater Extent than most Kingdoms in Europe, are yet

unsettled, and will for many Ages to come afford the most happy Asylum for
all that choose to exchange a Land of Poverty, for Freedom, Wealth, and
Happiness."

107 - Tues., June 8, 1773

Dublin, June 5.
Last week the Venus, Captain Oliffe, sailed from this port for Virginia and
Maryland, with a valuable cargo, and a considerable number of servants and
redemptioners (not criminals, due to the present general distress among the
middle and lower classes).
Ulick Roche of Gortatibee, convert to the Church of Ireland, parish church of
Lower Shandon.

Londonderry.
Ads: Samuel Smiley, carpenter, apprentice of James Hamilton and Thomas
Miles, ran away.

108 - Fri., June 11, 1773

Londonderry.
Ads: The Boscawen, Geo. Marshall, 250 tons, for Newcastle and Philadelphia,
July 20. The Ann, Patrick Miller, 300 tons, for Charlestown, S.C., July 20.

109 - Tues., June 15, 1773

Londonderry.
Married, last Friday, Robert Cochran of Glashgowan near St. Johnston, linen
merchant, to Miss Catherine Maxwell of Omagh.
Ads: Mention of the late George Vaughan of "Burncranagh"; Gustavus Brooke,
agent and receiver; Thomas Abraham, new agent, of Londonderry; Edward
Ledwich, treasurer of trustees. The Elizabeth, Robert Johnson, 300 tons, for
Charlestown, S.C. Sept. 1.

111 - Tues., June 22, 1773

Dublin.
Bankrupt: Samuel Byan [Bryan in No. 125] of Coleraine, distiller; George Knox
of Strabane, merchant.

Londonderry.
Ads: An auction for the payment of debts of the late James Cochran.

113 - Tues., June 29, 1773

Dublin.
Philip Harvey, parish of Clommagh, diocese of Leighlin, convert to the Church
of Ireland.

Londonderry.
Cleared out: the Louisa, Kirkpatrick, for Philadelphia with passengers; the
Hellen, Ramage, for Charles-Town with passengers.

115 - Tues., July 6, 1773

Londonderry.
The Boscawen was reported off Anapolis May 20, seven weeks out, all well.

116 - Fri., July 9, 1773

Belfast, July 6.
On Wednesday Edward Hagen, gauger of Port Glenone, was fatally shot as he was
about to arrest a man for keeping a concealed still.

Dublin, July 6.
A duel Friday between Mr. Shannon and ---- Ryan (of Queen st., see No. 117) at Glassnevin; Mr. Ryan died.
Married: Luke Gardiner to Miss Montgomery, daughter of Will. Montgomery; Thomas Newcoman of Callaghstown, Co. Louth, to Miss Daly, daughter of Joseph Daly of Castle Daly, Co. Westmeath.
Bankrupt: William James of Londonderry, shopkeeper.

117 - Tues., July 13, 1773

Dublin.
Captain Samuel Williams was found not guilty of killing Lt. James Wolsely in a duel.

Londonderry.
Died: yesterday, Mrs. Ledlie, wife of Thomas Ledlie of this city.
Ads: The Prince of Wales is at Culmore; for Baltimore July 22.

118 - Fri., July 16, 1773

Londonderry.
Ads: Catherine Babington, executrix of Humphry Babington, deceased, vs. Andrew Knox, William Wray, et alia; legal notice.

119 - Tues., July 20, 1773

Londonderry.
Died: Thursday last, Mrs. Towel, relict of the late Mr. Towel, daughter of the famous Mr. Murray of the siege of Derry.
Ads: Stock etc. of the late Rev. Edward Spence, Ballyrattan, to be sold.

121 - Tues., July 27, 1773

Dublin.
Bankrupt: William Sloan, Roan, Co. Armagh, merchant; John Tomb, Cole Island, Co. Tyrone, shop-keeper.

122 - Fri., July 30, 1773

Dublin.
Thomas Arthur, a native of Ireland, has opened a manufactory of carpets, etc., in Paris.
Rev. Roger Boyce, convert to the Church of Ireland, in parish church of St. Nicholas Without.
Bankrupt: Samuel Mayfield, Dublin, linen draper.

123 - Tues., Aug. 3, 1773

Dublin, July 31.
The wife of ---- Wilkinson a few days ago was delivered of triplet boys.

Londonderry.
Saturday last died Alexander Stewart, late master of the brig Ann.
The ship Elizabeth, at the Quay, wants fifty to sixty people for Cape Fair, North Carolina.

124 - Fri., Aug. 6, 1773

Dublin, Aug. 3.
Executed Saturday were Henry Fitzsimons for robbing Matthew Sullivan, John Magee, and Richard Gray on the King's highway; and Hugh Dogherty, for robbing Gavin Thompson on the King's highway.

125 - Tues., Aug. 10, 1773

Londonderry.
Ads: Thomas Short, administrator of the estate of the late John Ardess of
Lower Crossbellanree, near Newtown Stewart, Co. Tyrone. Property of the
bankrupt Samuel Bryan of Coleraine to be sold. Martha Lamrock has left her
husband John Lamrock of Letterhandry, parish of Comber, Co. Londonderry.

126 - Fri., Aug. 13, 1773

Dublin, Aug. 10.
Married: a few days ago, Capt. Nixon of the 25th Foot to Miss Frances Nixon
of Mullaghduff near Newtown Butler; Dr. William Gardiner of the 62nd
Regiment to Miss Peacock, daughter of George Peacock of Barnrick, Co. Clare.
Died: a few days ago in Co. Waterford, Richard Earl of Barrymore; in Co.
Meath, Lord Dunboyne; near Newcastle, Arthur Brudenell.

Londonderry.
Ads: William James, bankrupt; John Campbell of Fannett, assignee; Robert
Murray, Londonderry, attorney.

127 - Tues., Aug. 17, 1773

Limerick.
Converts to the Church of Ireland: William Dwyer and John Morony, carpenter,
Cahirconlish.

Londonderry.
The Jenny, Capt. Archibald M'Ilwaine, has arrived at Newcastle after five
weeks and three days, all well and a birth on board.
The Betty, Capt. Richard Hunter, arrived at Baltimore on July 4 with
passengers, from Waterford in six weeks.
Cleared out: the Ann, Miller, for Charles Town with passengers.

128 - Fri., Aug. 20, 1773

Londonderry.
Ads: Joseph, Isabella, and Mary Dening of Dromore are charged with the murder
of John Gallagher, late of Letterkenny. Richard Caldwell wants apprentices
for the America.

130 - Fri., Aug. 27, 1773

Dublin.
Died: in Channel row, Viscountess Mountgarret, age 66; at Castlecoole, Co.
Fermanagh, Margelson Armat [difficult to read, perhaps Annal ?].

Londonderry.
Ads: Debtors of the late Andrew Woods of Atreame in the parish of Donagheady,
Co. Tyrone are to pay Thomas Bond of Bond's Glen, parish of Cumber, Co.
Londonderry or Robert Galbraith, Castlemellon, parish of Donagheady,
administrators.

131 - Tues., Aug. 31, 1773

Waterford, Aug. 25.
A Kennedy was killed by an Ellard, between Nenagh and Clogjordan.

Dublin, Aug. 28.
---- Wheeler and his family went down with the Mermaid.
Married: George Berford, Co. Roscommon, to daughter of Peter Sproule,
Longfield, Co. Roscommon; at Corke, James Regan of Londonderry to Miss Ward
of Bandon; at Sligo, Thomas Williamson to Catherine Babington; Benjamin Yeats
of William st. to Miss Butler, daughter of Mr. Butler of Dublin Castle.

Died: in Glamorganshire, Philip ap Morris; at Ballygalane near Lismore,
Thomas Power, M.D.; at Galway, John French Fitz-Andrew; in Grafton st.,
Captain John Atkins; in Dame st., William Smith, bookseller.

Londonderry.
Ads: Brig Charming Polly, George Murren, for Baltimore Sept. 16.

132 - Fri., Sept. 3, 1773

Dublin.
Mary Moran, Clonmell, convert to Church of Ireland.

Londonderry.
Died: Tuesday last, Mrs. James Knox, the result of an accidental blow.
Ads: Isabella Strabridge, otherwise Caldwell, of Tull__ab, parish of Donagh,
Inishowen, has left her husband John Strabridge.

133 - Tues., Sept. 7, 1773

Dublin, Sept. 4.
Married: Drury Shepey, Dublin, to Miss Elizabeth Newburgh, daughter of
Brockhill Newburgh; Mr. Kelly to Miss Perrier of Kevin st.; William Coleman
of Baltray, age 86, to Miss Rosanna Murphy of Gormanstown, age 76 [unclear
print; could be 16 or 46].

Londonderry.
Cleared out: the Philadelphia, Winning, for Philadelphia, with passengers.

134 - Fri., Sept. 10, 1773

Londonderry.
The Jupiter, Capt. Ewing, arrived at New Castle on July 29 after seven weeks,
all well.

135 - Tues., Sept. 14, 1773

Dublin.
Bankrupt: William Callahan, Dublin, druggist; Charles Kiernan, Dublin,
grocer; Daniel Sullivan, Dublin, wine dealer; John Gregg, Belfast, merchant.

Londonderry.
Ads: Bryan Laun, of near Strabane, is accused of murdering Philip Carlon of
Islandmore, Co. Derry, and has fled; reward offered by John Carlan.

136 - Fri., Sept. 17, 1773

Sligo, Sept. 5.
Samuel Black or Sergeant Slack was found guilty of murdering his wife.

137 - Tues., Sept. 21, 1773

Cork, Sept. 9.
Mary Sullivan and Mary Smith, found guilty of the murder of John Brien,
butcher, are to hang.
Edmund McDaniel, Patrick Sullivan, Timothy Foord, and James Sullivan were
tried for riot at the rope walk of John Young at Leitrim, June 21. McDaniel
and P. Sullivan were sentenced to death; the others were acquitted.

Newry, Sept. 12.
Catherine M'Glown, found guilty of the murder of her son, age five, was given
the death penalty.
Charles M'Gowan, alias Smith, and Hugh M'Ilvenna, two of the Black Faces,
were to hang for robbing Pat M'Conewell at Derrykeen.
Terence Corrigan and ---- Kelly to be transported.

Dublin, Sept. 18.
The Venus, Oliffe, from Dublin May 1 for Baltimore, arrived after nine weeks.

Londonderry.
At the assizes, Tues. Sept. 14: John Watkins of Derrybrusk, Co. Fermanagh, was acquitted in the murder of Thomas M'Donnell [possibly related to the incident mentioned in number 89]; James M'Donald to be transported for stealing yarn; Samuel Gregg and John Baptisto to be transported.
Married: Sept. 16 in the Cathedral church, Peter Benson of Eloghbeg, Co. Donegal, to W--- Bachop of Londonderry.
Died: Mrs. Peter M'Donagh of this city.

138 - Fri., Sept. 24, 1773

Sligo, Sept. 14.
Samuel Slack alias Sergeant Slack was executed.

139 - Tues., Sept. 28, 1773

Londonderry.
Cleared out: the Boscawen, Caldwell, for Philadelphia with passengers.

141 - Tues., Oct. 5, 1773

Dublin.
Hannah Roche, Murin, Co. Kerry, now of Corke, convert to the Church of Ireland.

Londonderry.
Died: Miss Rebecca Mitchel, daughter of William Mitchel of this city.

142 - Fri., Oct. 8, 1773

Dublin, Oct. 5.
Married: at Swords, William Bunbury of Co. Carlow to Miss Kane, daughter of Redmond Kane; at Drogheda, Hugh Carmichael, attorney, to Miss Rogers of Balgeen; Samuel Lawrence to Miss Anna Maria Wallace, Kevin's Port.
Died: Robert Jaffray, merchant, Eustace st., age 70 years; John Harwood, Co. Roscommon; Lady William Brabazon; Mrs. Rev. Lightburne of Trim, Co. Meath, age 78 years; Lt. Col. Hawke, 6th Regiment, son of Admiral Hawke; John Coughlan, M.D., Ballyporeen.
Bankrupt: Robert and William Sloan, Roan, Co. Armagh, linen drapers.

Londonderry.
Died: Tuesday at Birdstown, Peter Benson, attorney.

143 - Tues., Oct. 12, 1773

Dublin, Oct. 9.
Bankrupt: George Fox, Dublin, tobacconist.
Died: at Cloonterk, Co. Mayo, John Jones, age 102 years; Rev. Mr. Ryan, rector of Leixlip; Dr. Span, Grafton st.; at Woodhill, Co. Donegal, Oct. 2, John Irwin of Dumfilis (?), Co. Leitrim.

144 - Fri., Oct. 15, 1773

Dublin, Oct. 12.
Thomas Mullally was executed for robbing James Dolan.
Mary Bandon, convert to the Church of Ireland at St. Canice Cathedral.

Londonderry.
Died: Wednesday, Miss Elizabeth Crookshank, maiden sister of Alderman Crookshank, late of this city.
Ads: Mary Lee alias Jones has left her husband Robert Lee; of Ballaghaneaden.

145 - Tues., Oct. 19, 1773

Wexford, Oct. 11.
---- Jones fell from his horse and died.

Dublin, Oct. 16.
Mr. Harper, linen draper, fell from his horse and died; he was doorkeeper of
the House.

Londonderry.
Cleared out: the Elizabeth, Johnson, for Charlestown with passengers.

147 - Tues., Oct. 26, 1773

Dublin, Oct. 23.
James Gordon and Thomas Mulhall were executed for robbing Mr. Bulkeley near
Rathcool.
Married: the Earl of Ross to Miss Clements, daughter of Rt. Hon. Nathaniel
Clements; Col. Simon Hart to Widow Campbell; Lt. John Hardy of the First
Horse to Miss Susannah Bernard; ---- Sherlock to Miss Jennet; ---- Darley to
Miss Margaret Jordan; at Newry, John White to Widow Mathews.

Londonderry.
Married: Joseph Thompson to Miss Guy.
Died: William Mackey, Cosquin.
Ads: Ann M'Closky alias Turkington, wife of Henry M'Closky, threatens to
contract debts; at Ovill, parish of Dungiven.

148 - Fri., Oct. 29, 1773

Limerick.
At Clounlehaird, near Glin, lives ---- Kelly, age 120 years.
Near Shaneagolden lives Mrs. Mary Fowle, age 109, with over one hundred
descendants living.

150 - Fri., Nov. 5, 1773

Dublin.
William Meares, Michael Reily, Philip Deane, and Michael Conroy were
executed.

151 - Tues., Nov. 9, 1773

Belfast, Nov. 5.
Rev. John Neeson, parish priest of Ballymena, Skerry, etc., convert to the
Church of Ireland.

152 - Fri., Nov. 12, 1773

Philadelphia, Sept. 22.
The following ships arrived lately with passengers:
    - brig Louisa, Kirkpatrick, Derry, 180
    - Rose, George, Derry, 350
    - Britannia, Peter, Holland, 250
    - Rea Galley, Hunter, Lewis Islands, 300
    - snow Sarah, Corry, Dublin, 120
    - snow Sally, Jones, with English and Dutch, 80
    - Catherine, Sutton, London, 50
    - snow Peggy, Hastie, Glasgow, 40

Londonderry.
The brig Louisa brought a letter addressed: To Ireland to the County
Cavan Coot hill to the cair of Thomas Maghan traden to Barney Smith In

24

the Parish of Aughmulan in the County Monaghan lives on Francis Johnsons
Land.

153 - Tues., Nov. 16, 1773

Dublin.
Died: Lt. Gen. Daniel Webbe of the 14th Dragoons; Blennerhasset Grove; Oliver
A___, M.D.; Edward H___, governor of Kinsale; Luke Dillon, Clonbrock, Co.
Roscommon; Rev. Mr. Dobbs; John Hobbs; Percy Fenton, Coomb, merchant.
Bankrupt: John Grace, Smithfield, Dublin; Cornelius Clarke, Dublin, linen
draper; Richard Beaghan, Dublin; Thomas Hacket, Dublin, breeches maker.

155 - Tues., Nov. 23, 1773

Dublin.
Died: James FitzGerald, Duke of Leinster etc.
Bankrupt: William Andrews, Rich Hill, Co. Armagh, innkeeper; Robert
Fitzsimons, Limerick, mercer; Michael Connor, Dublin, merchant.

156 - Fri., Nov. 26, 1773

Dublin.
John Magee alias Capt. Firebrand was executed.

Londonderry.
Ads: Rev. Dr. Torrens, exr. of the late Mrs. Lucy Cary, selling land.

159 - Tues., Dec. 7, 1773

Londonderry.
The Prince of Wales, Tho. Morrison, from Londonderry Aug. 8, arrived at
Baltimore Oct. 7, passengers well.

List of ships advertised in the Belfast News-Letter to sail with passengers
for America, in 1773.

From Londonderry:	March	2, Jenny	250	Philadelphia
		9, Hannah	400	"
		12, Jupiter	300	"
		16, Wallworth	300	"
	April	15, Alexander	400	"
		27, Hellen	200	Charlestown
	May	1, Louisa	200	"
	June	1, Rose	300	Philadelphia
		8, Pr. of Wales	350	Baltimore
		18, Ann	300	Charlestown
	July	6, Philadelphia	250	Philadelphia
	August	3, Boscawen	250	"
		10, George	250	"
		13, Elizabeth	300	Charlestown
From Larne:	April	16, James & Mary	250	Charlestown
	May	18, Lord Dunluce	400	"
	Sept.	10, Betty	250	"
	Nov.	23, L.Dun.2d voy	400	Baltimore
From Belfast:	Jan.	15, Friendship	300	Philadelphia
	Feb.	5, Agnes	200	Charlestown
		9, Peggy	200	Philadelphia
	April	20, Yaward	350	St. John's Island
	June	11, Two Brothers	200	Baltimore
	July	6, NewBetyGreg	200	Philadelphia
		9, Frshp.2d vo.	300	"
		20, Lord Bangor	200	Wilmington

```
                27, Charm.Molly    250 Baltimore
       August   6, Lib.& Property  250 Charlestown
                20, Betty          300 Philadelphia
                31, Catherine      300   "
                31, Waddell        450 Charlestown

From Newry:    Feb. 12, Minerva    350 Philadelphia
                    19, Charlotte   250   "
                    23, Betsy       300   "
                    23, Nedham      400   "
               Mar.  5, Robert      350   "
                    12, Newry Assist. 300 "
                    23, Elliot      300 Charlestown
               Sept. 10, Betsy 2d voy. 300 Philadelphia
```

	1771		1772		1773		Total	
From	sh.	tons	sh.	tons	sh.	tons	ships	tons
Derry	13	3650	9	2650	14	4050	36	10350
Belfast	7	1750	10	2650	13	3400	30	7100
Newry	9	2800	5	1600	8	2550	22	6950
Larne	2	450	5	1300	4	1300	11	3050
P.Rush	1	250	1	250			2	500
	32	8900	30	8450	39	11300	101	28650

[Note: the common calculation was that one ton of shipping would carry one nominal (adult) passenger.]

160 - Fri., Dec. 10, 1773

Clonmel.
Margaret Meehan, Shanraghan, and William Kennedy, Rathronan, converts to the Church of Ireland.

Kilkenny.
Daniel Donovan, Waterford, convert to the Church of Ireland.

Dublin.
John Power, educated for the Romish clergy, convert to the Church of Ireland at Enlafad, Co. Sligo.

161 - Tues., Dec. 14, 1773

Londonderry.
Mrs. John Minnan, wife of the blacksmith of Raphoe, delivered a remarkable son last week; she is 60 years old, he is seventy and a retired soldier; they were married thirty years.
Ads: Frederick Coyle, apprentice, ran away from John Siree.

162 - Fri., Dec. 17, 1773

Dublin.
Married: Rev. Mr. Rentoul, dissenting minister of Lurgan, to Louisa, daughter of Solomon White.
Died: Rev. Luke Doude of Church st. chapel; at Waterford, Rev. Mr. Moore; at Sligo, Mrs. Thomas Burrows; William Braddel; Powell Eyre; John Roe; in Monaghan, James Sweeny.

164 - Fri., Dec. 24, 1773

Dublin.
Married: Lord Sydney to the daughter of St. Laurence, Earl of Howth; Lt. Hewet, son of the Lord Chancellor, to daughter of Thomas Strettle of Corke; John C. Maudesley of Killea, King's Co., to Miss Alton; at the Royal

Hospital, Benjamin Potts, age 86, to Miss Mary Hodgings, age 64.
Died: at Kilmainham, Sir Simon Bradstreet; John Brown of Castlebrown, Co.
Kildare; Samuel Harper.
John Bonynge, Yorkfield, Co. Westmeath, was shot dead by his son Paul.

Newry.
Died: Robert Scot.

Londonderry.
Ads: Meave M'Closkey, alias Kelly, wife of Michael M'Closkey of Templemoyle,
parish of Banagher, has left him.

165 - Tues., Dec. 28, 1773

Dublin.
Married: at Portadown, Co. Armagh, Ralph Wilson, linen draper, age 80, to
Miss Millar of Killycamain, age 16.

166 - Fri., Dec. 31, 1773

Londonderry.
Died: at Clashgowan, near St. Johnston, Mrs. Margaret, wife of Alexander
Cochran jr.

170 - Fri., Jan. 14, 1774

Dublin.
John Sullivan, Rathcoony parish, convert to the Church of Ireland.

Londonderry.
Died: Richard Thorp, woollen draper.

171 - Tue., Jan. 18, 1774

Dublin.
Mr. Moore, goldsmith, was murdered in the house of ---- Fitzmaurice.
Dennis M'Carthy, Holycross church, and Cath. Waldron, Limerick, converts to
the Church of Ireland.

Londonderry.
Married: at Strabane, John Barclay, son of Robert Barclay, to Miss Sproul.
Died: Sam Scot, Strabane.
Ads: Darby alias Jeffrey M'Feeley ran away from Henry Cary. Michael
M'Closkey is reconciled with his wife Meave.

172 - Fri., Jan. 21, 1774

Dublin.
John Scully, servant of Rev. Mr. Smith of Enniskillen, was shot dead by ----
Crawford.
Died: Thomas Richey, bookbinder.

173 - Tues., Jan. 25, 1774

Cork, Dec. 10.
Daniel Healy of Donaghmore was killed.

Londonderry.
Died: Mr. Ambrose Colhoun, Letterkenny.
Ads: The leased farm of the late James M'Ilwaine jr., deceased, to be sold.

174 - Fri., Jan. 28, 1774

Londonderry.
Died: Andrew Knox, of Prehen, near Londonderry; Thomas Abraham, surveyor of this port; Samuel Perry, Mullaghmore, Co. Tyrone.
Ads: The Alexander, James Hunter, arived yesterday with flax seed and eighty passengers; is to leave for Newcastle and Philadelphia Apr. 20; she is two years old, 400 tons; Robert Alexander, owner; Henry Newton, Coleraine, and Alexander Clerk, Maghera, passenger agents.

176 - Fri., Feb. 4, 1774

Baltimore, Maryland, Oct. 16, 1773.
Arrived yesterday: the Prince of Wales, Morrison, from Londonderry with two hundred passengers.

Londonderry.
Died: John King, Newtown Lemavady; Mrs. Hughes of this city, late of Dublin; William Beaty, Dungiven, age 130 years.

177 - Tues., Feb. 8, 1774

Londonderry.
Ads: The ship Mary, Robert George, for Newcastle and Philadelphia Apr. 10; owners William Hope, William Glen, Thomas Chambers, and Abraham M'Causland, merchants, Londonderry.

178 - Fri., Feb. 11, 1774

Belfast.
Rev. Bernard O'Doran, priest of Laid and Ardclinis, convert to the Church of Ireland.

Kilkenny.
Margaret Boyd, convert to the Church of Ireland.

Londonderry.
Married: near Ballyshannon, James Smith, Legnadavagh, to Miss Jones.
Died: at Alla, parish of Cumber, Rev. George Gwynn; Mr. Humphry Ewing, aged 72 years.
Ads: Debts due to John King, late of Newtown Lemavady, are to be paid to Mrs. Ann King.

179 - Tues., Feb. 15, 1774

Dublin.
Died: Surgeon Whiteway's son.

Londonderry.
Ads: Mary Scott, administratrix of Samuel Scott of Strabane, to sell property; debts payable to Robert Nelson of Strabane.

180 - Fri., Feb. 18, 1774

Londonderry.
Contributions are solicited by Mrs. Kennedy and Mrs. Thompson for Anne Moore of Ballymoney, wife of James M'Cann of Lisburn; he is now a sailor on the Hynd sloop of war; she and their son are destitute.
Died: Wednesday last, Archibald M'Curdy, former sailing master.

182 - Fri., Feb. 25, 1774

Londonderry.
Ads: The Jupiter, Alexander Ewing, will return to New York soon with

passengers. Cormick O'Sheal and Edward Dougherty of the parish of
Kilmacranon, are indicted for their pact to murder Shane M'Attigert of
Kilmacranon; to be tried at next assizes. The _Hannah_, James Mitchell, 400
tons, two years old, to sail Apr. 10 for Newcastle and Philadelphia; apply to
James Stirling, Willworth, or William Neely near Ballygawly, Co. Tyrone. The
snow _Baltimore_, Robert White, 250 tons, for Baltimore on March 20; apply
Samuel Brown, Londonderry, or William White, Larne.

183 - Tues., Mar. 1, 1774

Dublin.
Died: a child of Mr. Moore, Dame st.

Londonderry.
Ads: Samuel Galbraith, executor of Samuel Perry, Mullaghmore, Co. Tyrone,
household furniture to be auctioned; Wybrants Olpherts and James Hamilton,
attorneys. Major Henry Caldwell is seeking settlers for estates in Quebec
Province; apply to him at Sir James Caldwell's Bart. at Castle Caldwell, or
Dr. Michael Law, Strabane, or Patrick Hamilton, garrison, or Henry West,
Downpatrick, or Mr. Mauleverer or Samuel Montgomery or William Caldwell at
Londonderry; their ship of 400 tons to leave in the first week of May. Ann
M'Aneverton alias O'Donnell, wife of Joseph O'Donnell, has left him.

184 - Fri., Mar. 4, 1774

Dublin.
Bankrupt: William and John Phibbs, Sligo, merchants.

Londonderry.
Ads: _Jupiter_, Alexander Ewing, 350 tons, to depart Apr. 15 for Newcastle and
Philadelphia. Robert Steel of the Third Horse, King's County, warns tenants
in Lifford parish not to pay their rent to Flora Steel alias Hamilton.
Holdings of Alexander M'Causland, deceased, are to be auctioned at Omagh, by
William Hamilton, Omagh, attorney.

185 - Tues., Mar. 8, 1774

Dublin.
Died: John Knox, M.P.; John Wolverton, attorney.

186 - Fri., Mar. 11, 1774

Letter from John Harvey, Malin Hall: recently "in one of the public papers"
there was published a list of 167 tenants of the Earl of Donegal who had left
Enishowen for America because of high rents, etc. He denies that they left;
he is the Earl's agent in Enishowen. Mentions Rev. Robert Huey in the list,
Donegal's only direct tenant; he sold his lease to Moses Scott of Derry. Two
others are John Doherty and John Vance; Doherty's lease was sold to George
Charleton.

Londonderry.
Ads: Richard Mason and George Kerr deserted from the 53rd Regiment at
Belfast.

187 - Tues., Mar. 15, 1774

Corke.
Died: Rev. Mr. Emanuel Moore.

Londonderry.
Ads: Hugh Hill, David Ross, and Will. Lecky, executors of William Hogg, vs.
Henry M'Neill and Elizabeth M'Neill; and Samuel Broderick vs. same, Co.
Londonderry; notice.

188 - Fri. Mar. 18, 1774

Dublin.
Mrs. Elmer Hunt, Diocese of Cashell, convert to the Church of Ireland.
Charles Fanning, who had been convicted of highway robbery, was executed.

190 - Fri., Mar. 25, 1774

Londonderry.
Died: Mrs. Catherine Lecky, widow of Alderman Lecky and sister of the late
bishop of Limerick, age 75 years.
Ads: The new ship Hill, George Marshall, 300 tons, for Newcastle,
Philadelphia, and New York, May 10; two months old; Robert Houstoun,
Londonderry, merchant and Will. Gregg, Coleraine, agents.

191 - Tues. Apr. 5, 1774

Londonderry.
At the recent assizes: William Dinsmore, convicted of stealing cows, to be
executed; Frederick M'Cun, convicted of theft, and Catherine Dogharty, of
stealing money, are to be transported.
Ads: Col. Maguire, deceased, horse breeder, mentioned. The Baltimore, for
Baltimore, is delayed until April 6; will go via Larne. The Hope, Robert
M'Clenaghan, a new vessel of 350 tons, is now at Newry; will sail for
Newcastle and Philadelphia; apply to Andrew Thompson, merchant, or to John
Hagan at Thomas Hyndman's, who came in said ship and proposes to return in
her. Ephraim Campbell, son of Ephraim Campbell, innkeeper of Derry, is
missing with the horse of Owen Rooney of Dundalk.

192 - Fri., Apr. 8, 1774

Cork.
Died: Felix Dryer, master of the Sarah, his wife and crew, and Mr. Cowan, a
revenue officer, all drowned; Mrs. Harding.

Dublin.
Died: at Athy, Rev. Kene Kerceval, D.D.; at Balicasidy, Co. Fermanagh,
Alexander Steel.

Londonderry.
---- Kerr and ---- Gallagher, converts to the Church of Ireland.

193 - Tues., Apr. 12, 1774

Dublin.
Bankrupt: James Leadly, Newry, shopkeeper.

Londonderry.
Edward and William Dillon, at the Church of Carrigans, converts to the Church
of Ireland.
Ads: Isabella Hamilton otherwise Shaw is calumniating Alexander Hamilton.
The Minerva, Robert Macky, 200 tons, built last summer in Philadelphia,
leaves for Newcastle and Philadelphia on May 10; owners Andrew Gregg and
James Thompson of Londonderry; she is eight feet high in cabin, seven feet in
steerage, six feet between decks.

195 - Tues., Apr. 19, 1774

Ross.
John Lynch, also known as Thomas Fox, was executed for murder.

Carlow.
John Kenny, butcher, was gaoled for causing the death of Patrick Sullivan.

Belfast.
Mary Develin and Patrick Colgan, Stewartstown, Co. Tyrone, converts to the
Church of Ireland.

Dublin.
Cornelius O'Driscoll, Ballyisland, Co. Corke, convert to the Church of
Ireland.

196 - Fri., Apr. 22, 1774

Letter from Matthew Wetherby, carpenter, from Malone near Belfast (who went
to New York last year) to John Wilson of Malone. He was eight weeks on the
voyage, nearly in the winter; mentioned in Ireland: James Hudson and family,
Christopher Hudson, Edward Liddy, and Bridget Gillesy.

Belfast, Apr. 19.
Friday last sailed the Prosperity, M'Culloch, for Newcastle and Philadelphia,
470 nominal passengers, about 520 souls or more.

197 - Tues., Apr. 26, 1774

Dublin.
Died: near Kilkenny, Rt. Hon. Somerset Hamilton Butler, Earl of Carrick;
Edmund Malone, justice of the Court of Common Pleas; Rev. James Dowdall, of
the Church of Rome, on Constitution Hill.
Bankrupt: William Caldwell and Richard Caldwell, Londonderry, merchants.

Londonderry.
Ads: The Jupiter, Alexander Ewing, at Culmore, for Philadelphia May 12.

198 - Fri., Apr. 29, 1774

Jane Reavy, over 100 years old, lives at Eagle Hill, near Hacket's town, Co.
Carlow.

199 - Tues., May 3, 1774

Dublin.
Trial of Andrew T. S. Moore vs. other heirs and heiresses of Archibald Moore,
dec'd.

Londonderry.
Robert Newell, bailiff of the barony of Ennishowen, died in an accident.
Patrick Dinsmore received a reprieve and will be transported instead of being
executed.
Married: Alexander Brown, tanner, to Miss Sharky, both of this city.
Ads: Deposition of Elizabeth Moore of Newtown Lemavady, widow of Ezekiel
Moore, concerning activities of Rev. Wm. Moore, his wife Elizabeth born
Hazlet, and Manus M'Nirlan in 1767-1771. Rev. Moore was in America for ten
months as of May, 1767.
Another deposition on the same subject, by Doctor William Moore, Sessnogh,
Co. Londonderry. In Nov. 1767 Elizabeth Moore arrived in Halifax on the
Hopewell, M'Gowan; her brother was then in Pennsylvania; Dr. William Moore
was in Halifax then but returned to Ireland and she went to London. [See
also Numbers 201 and 208.]

200 - Fri., May 6, 1774

Died: at Kilkenny, Eland Mossom, Member of Parliament.
Bankrupt: John Vance, Dublin, merchant.

Londonderry.
John Duglass, James Duglass, and John M'Ginnis, converts to the Church of
Ireland, at Dungiven.

201 - Tues., May 10, 1774

Cork.
Cornelius, Dennis, and Daniel M'Carthy were executed for robbing James Brown
near Macroom; they denied any guilt in the matter.

Londonderry.
Hannah Dermond of Ballybofey, convert to the Church of Ireland.
Ads: Letter concerning William and Elizabeth Moore; their son died of
smallpox. [See Number 199.]

202 - Fri., May 13, 1774

Dublin.
Letter of Samuel McCulloch at Heckenseek, Sept. 24, 1773 to his father Samuel
McCulloch at Carrickfergus. On the ship 19 June Tommy Jackson died and on
the 20th two girls died, seven weeks on board, near the coast. The mate,
several men and women, and about twelve children died of a fever on board.
His own children died. Mentions brother Billy [and Mary, his wife ?], who is
with him; children Sammy and Jammy; sister Eve already there; brother James a
merchant there, at York. Still in Ireland are John Baird, Sarah Euant,
William Harper, John Tennart, two Miss Campbells. [Apparently is in
Hackensack, New York; mentions the Dutch inhabitants.]

203 - Tues., May 17, 1774

Belfast, May 13.
On Tuesday sailed the Peace and Plenty, M'Kenzie, for Newcastle,
Philadelphia, and New York, with upwards of 400 passengers.

Dublin.
William Forster, Ballydogan, Co. Down, a Steel Boy, has been gaoled. Numbers
of Steel Boys are flying to Belfast to take shipping to America.
Died: Capt. Tindall of the snow Collier; Patrick Ewing, former High Sheriff
of Dublin; Hill Matthewes, at Ringsend, attorney; Francis O'Brien, merchant,
at Chester.
Bankrupt: James Fisher, Londonderry, distiller and innkeeper.

Londonderry.
Margaret M'Callem, of near Raphoe, had quadruplets; they did not survive.
Ads: The Alexander, Hunter, to sail for Philadelphia a few days after May 25.

207 - Tues., May 31, 1774

Dublin.
The Sea Horse, Capt. Bowson, from Cork to Philadelphia, was cast away in a
gale near Cape Delaware; the cargo was lost and a great part of the crew
perished.

Londonderry.
Ads: The Rose, Joseph Curry, 300 tons, for Newcastle and Baltimore, 15 July;
apply to Samuel Curry or William Hope. The Betty, George Campbell, 250 tons,
for Charles-town, S.C., 20 July; owners Patterson and Fletcher; Nathaniel
Hunter, merchant, agent.

208 - Fri., June 3, 1774

Belfast.
Patrick McCann and Patrick Mayns, parish of Disertlin, Diocese of Armagh,
converts to the Church of Ireland.

209 - Tues., June 7, 1774

Londonderry.
Cleared out - Hannah, Mitchel, for Philadelphia with passengers.
- Jupiter, Ewing, for same with passengers.
- Mary, George, for same with passengers.
- Amity's Admonition, Knowles, for Quebec with Major
  Caldwell and family.
Ads: Alexander Allison is not responsible for his wife, Eleanor Allison. The
Minerva, Robert Macky, for Philadelphia June 20. George Eakins vs. John
Caddle; to sell interest in a tenement in Newtown Stewart, formerly in
possession of James Caddle, deceased, between former house of William Stewart
and former house of Hu. Blair; property held by deed from Barbara Caddle.
The George, Will. Pinkerton, 250 tons, for Newcastle and Philadelphia Aug. 1;
owners James Miller and Samuel Curry, merchants.

210 - Fri., June 10, 1774

Dublin.
Married: Rt. Hon. John Beresford to the daughter of William Montgomery and
sister of Lady Viscountess Townshend and Mrs. Gardiner.

Londonderry.
Died: May 22, Mrs. Elizabeth, wife of Rev. Hugh Young, Dissenting Minister of
Dirg, near Strabane.
Ads: Deserted from the 37th Regiment of Foot (Lt. Stephen Cook) at
Londonderry, John Calcraft, age about 20 years, and Abraham Kenmon, age about
28 years. William Caldwell, Londonderry, bankrupt; his ship Philadelphia to
be sold.

211 - Tues., June 14, 1774

Bankrupt: George Cottinham, Drumcondra, Co. Dublin, bleacher.

Londonderry.
Died: Sunday last, Mrs. Elizabeth, wife of William Glen, merchant of this
city.
Cleared out: Alexander, Hunter, for Philadelphia with passengers.

213 - Tues., June 21, 1774

Londonderry.
Ads: The Ann, Patrick Miller, 300 tons, for Charlestown, S.C. on July 10;
Robert Alexander owner; Henry Newton, merchant, Coleraine, and Alexander
Clark, Maghera, agents.

214 - Fri., June 24, 1774

Dublin.
Died: at Wolverhampton, Rt. Hon. Francis Andrews, provost of Trinity College.

Londonderry.
Died: on the 21st, Rev. John Hood [or Hoop, see Number 217], Dissenting
Minister of this city.
Ads: John Peery, not responsible for his wife Martha Peery alias Lithgo.

215 - Tues. June 28, 1774

Londonderry.
Ads: William Hamilton, attorney, Omagh, to sell the holdings of Alexander
M'Causland of Correnary, deceased.

33

217 - Tues., July 5, 1774

Londonderry.
Tribute to the late Rev. Mr. John Hoop [or Hood, see Number 214].

219 - Tues., July 12, 1774

Dublin.
Married: Mr. Mitchell, merchant of Bordeaux, to Miss Lynch of the Batchelor's
walk; at Limerick, Capt. Taylor of the 28th Foot to Miss Boyle; B. Eife to
Miss Eife, daughter of Luke Eife, Co. Meath; Capt. Drought, of the Prince of
Wales' Light Dragoons, to Miss Homan, daughter of Richard Homan, Co.
Westmeath.
Died: Richard Scott, son of John Scott of Newhay, Co. Wexford.

Londonderry.
An account of the number of ships which have sailed with passengers to
America from the ports of London-Derry, Belfast, Newry, Larne, and Port Rush,
taken from an account sent from Belfast to Sir Edward Newenham and by that
Gentleman inserted at large in the Freeman's Journal.

From	From 25 July 1769 to 25 Mar. 1771, 1 year and a half.		From 25 Mar. 1771 to 25 Mar. 1773, two years.		From 25 Mar. 1773 to 25 July 1774, 1 year and a half.	
	ships	tons	ships	tons	ships	tons
L:Derry	7	1950	22	6300	21	6350
Belfast	7	1820	17	4450	19	5350
Newry	4	1200	14	4400	20	6450
Larne	2	400	7	1750	7	2450
Po. Rush	2	500	2	500	1	250
	22	5170	62	17400	68	20450

N.B. The number of emigrants is supposed fully to equal the number of tons of
shipping; the emigrants then will be forty three thousand and twenty.

A gentleman has favoured us with the following account of the emigrantions
from this Kingdom from the 3rd of August 1773 to the 29th of November
following, which was taken in Philadelphia and the other towns upon the
emigrants being landed there.

At New York	1911
At Philadelphia	2086
At Charles Town	966
At New Jersey	326
At Halifax	516
At Newport, Rhode Island	717
Total of emigrants from Ireland in four months	6522
From England, Scotland, and Germany landed in the same period	1400
From the Isle of Man	56
Total emigrants to America in four months	7978

220 - Fri., July 15, 1774

Londonderry
Ads: David Richy will not be responsible for his wife, Sarah Richy or
Con.

221 - Tues., July 19, 1774

Dublin.
Three ships in the south are now taking passengers for America and one of 300
tons bound for Baltimore is now at Dublin harbor. Henry Griffin, Cahinary
Church, near Limerick, convert to the Church of Ireland.

Londonderry.
Ads: The Rose, Joseph Curry, for Newcastle and Baltimore August 1; apply to
Samuel Curry or William Hope, merchants.

222 - Fri., July 22, 1774

Dublin.
Mary Magarry, convert to the Church of Ireland in the parish church of Saul.
Married: John Parnell, son of Sir John Parnell, Member of Parliament, to Miss
Brooke, daughter of Sir Arthur Brooke; John Adlercron of Rathinhill, Co.
Meath, son of the late Lt. Gen. Adlercron, to Miss Bermingham; Rev. William
Darby to Miss Olivia, daughter of Chidly Morgan.
Bankrupt: George Ellis, late of Snugborsug, Co. Cavan, dealer and chapman;
Patrick Long, Pimlico, Co. Dublin, dyer; Robert McKeon, late of Newry, Co.
Down, grocer, now of Dublin.

223 - Tues., July 26, 1774

Dublin.
Michael Hyland, Edward Bermingham, Michael Coningham, and Margaret Doolan,
converts to the Church of Ireland in the Diocese of Meath.

225 - Tues., Aug. 2, 1774

Dublin.
John Karr, near Templepatrick, parish of Dunigore, convert to the Church of
Ireland.
Married: Earl of Carrick to Miss Taylor, daughter of Edward Taylor, late of
Askeating, Limerick; John Sutton to Miss Jackson.
Died: in London, Percy Windham O'Brien, Earl of Thomond; Capt. Graydon, age
80 years, former Member of Parliament.

Londonderry.
Died: July 23 at Coleraine, Mrs. Oalt; Sunday, Mr. Mark Bellew; Sheelah
M'Alester, Drummeal, Co. Derry, aged 118 years.

227 - Tues., Aug. 9, 1774

Corke.
---- Stokesbury, near Carrigalive, a murder/suicide.

228 - Fri., Aug. 12, 1774

Dublin.
Bankrupt: Thomas Major, Londonderry, shopkeeper.

229 - Tues., Aug. 16, 1774

Dublin.
Married: Edmund Malone, Ballynahown, Co. Westmeath, to Miss Mary O'Conner; at
Belfast, Rev. James Cromby, Dissenting Minister, to Miss Simpson; Rev. John
Coleman, Templepatrick, to Mrs. White, relict of Dr. White; George Bell to
Widow Atkinson.

Londonderry.
Died: George Evary, apothecary of this city, at an advanced age.

230 - Fri., Aug. 19, 1774

Londonderry.
Ads: Samuel Bryan, bankrupt, sale in Dublin by assignee Samuel Dick; includes
lease held under the late John M'Alester of land near Coleraine; rent rolls
to be seen also with James Hamilton, the Clerk to the Commissioner, at
Ballymoney, Co. Antrim.

231 - Tues., Aug. 23, 1774

Dublin.
Mention of Michael Clark, deceased burgess for the borough of Ballyshannon.

232 - Fri., Aug. 26, 1774

Corke.
---- Dorney, a farmer near Carrigaline, killed three of his children.

Dublin.
Married: Earl of Bellamont to Lady Emily Fitzgerald; at Lisburn, Thomas
Graham of Co. Down to Miss Graham; at Clogher, Allan Bellingham, merchant of
Dublin, to the daughter of John Elliot Cairns, of Kill___day, Co. Tyrone; at
Castle Bellingham, Capt. William Cairns of the 39th Regiment to the daughter
of Allan Bellingham of Castle Bellingham, Co. Louth.

Londonderry.
At the Lifford assizes, Patrick Gordon and Henry O'Neil were found guilty of
the murder of James Ferguson; to be hanged. Mrs. O'Neil was also found
guilty but was with child and not to be hanged until the baby was born.
Died: in this city, Rev. Thomas Daniel, age 86.
Cleared out: the Minerva, Macky, for Philadelphia with passengers.

233 - Tues., Aug. 30, 1774

Londonderry.
Ads: Edward Davenport, apprentice, ran away from George Douglas, printer, of
this city. Edward Tonar, apprentice, ran away from James Fulton, tobacco
spinner. The Philadelphia, John Winning, for Newcastle and Philadelphia
Sept. 10, James Thompson, agent.

234 - Fri., Sept. 2, 1774

Dublin.
Christopher Eustace, Dublin, linen draper, bankrupt.

Londonderry.
At the Omagh assizes: Dudley Donnelly is to be transported for stealing cows;
Thomas Kelly and Hugh M'Golrick are to be pillored two market days for
attempting to pass bad money; Francis Dougherty is to be burned in the hand
for theft.

235 - Tues., Sept. 6, 1774

Londonderry.
Ads: the George, for Philadelphia Sept. 15, James Miller and Sam. Curry,
merchants, agents.

236 - Fri., Sept. 9, 1774

Dublin.
Married: at Corke, Richard Meade to Miss DeCourcy, daughter of Lord Kinsale;
Lt. Gudgeon of the 55th Regiment to Miss Garstin of Arran quay; Rev. Edmund
Leslie of Rockfield, Co. Antrim to Miss Portis of Belfast; at Parsonstown,
Co. Meath, Tim. Fitzpatrick to Dorothea, daughter of James Wilson.

Londonderry.
Ads: The household furniture of the late Mr. Mark Bellew to be auctioned at
Mrs. Bellew's, Shipquay st.

238 - Fri., Sept. 16, 1774

At the Antrim assizes, at Belfast: Mary Adair, of Lady Hull near Antrim, to
be burned for poisoning her husband. James Horner, to be executed for
robbery of Mr. Stafford Gorman of Glenavy. John Spence to be transported for
stealing from Hugh Kirk of Larne.

239 - Tues., Sept. 20, 1774

Belfast.
John Morgan, Goward, convert to the Church of Ireland.

Dublin.
Sarah Thornbury was found guilty of robbing the shop of Mrs. Mary Kane and
was to be executed after the birth of her child. Patrick M'Daniel (alias
Paddy Melt), William Galley, and John Burke were found guilty of robbing
Arthur Neil and were to be executed October 11.

240 - Fri., Sept. 23, 1774

Dublin.
One day last week a young man named ---- Clements was killed and his father
was wounded by a recruiting party in Armagh.

Londonderry.
Married: William Ross of Beaufort Lodge to Miss Mary, daughter of the late
John Knox of this city.
Cleared: the Philadelphia, Winning, for Philadelphia with passengers; the
Betty, Campbell, for Philadelphia in ballast.

241 - Tues., Sept. 27, 1774

New York.
Arrived here and at Philadelphia between July -- and Aug. 15: Peace and
Plenty, M'Kenzie, from Belfast, 400 passengers; ------, Mitchell, from Derry
with 400; Charlotte, Gaffny, from Waterford with 110; ----own, Keith, from
Newry with 350; and ----dham, Chevers, from Newry with 300.

Londonderry.
Ads: The Elizabeth, Robert Johnson, for Baltimore in ten days, Mr. Lecky,
agent.

242 - Fri., Sept. 30, 1774

Belfast.
Mary Adair was executed Saturday last at Carrickfergus for poisoning her
husband William last May.

243 - Tues., Oct. 4, 1774

Belfast.
The passengers who sailed from Newry to Philadelphia this summer were
remarkably sickly; in one vessel upwards of 140 souls died and in the other a
considerable number.

Dublin.
Jane M'Donnel, convert to the Church of Ireland, church of of Sainrone (?),
Rev. Mr. Armstrong.

Londonderry.
Arrived at Philadelphia, the Hannah, James Mitchell, from Londonderry with passengers in eight weeks, all well.
Died Thursday last, Mrs. Ferguson, wife of Andrew Ferguson.

244 - Fri., Oct. 7, 1774

Dublin.
Married: Christopher Deey to the widow of the late Richard Robbins; at Corke, Mr. Keeff to the daughter of Mr. Heaphy; Dr. John Purcel of Fleet st. to Miss Fitzgerald.
Died: Lady Caroline White, wife of W. White of Upton, Co. Wexford; at Spa in Germany, John Dalton, collector of Athlone; at Lisburn, John Hastings; at Mercury near Sligo, Lawrence Casleboe.

Londonderry.
Ads: Sarah Weylie alias Reed has left her husband Nathaniel Weylie.

245 - Tues., Oct. 11, 1774

Dublin.
Catharine Tough, convert to the Church of Ireland at the parish church of St. Andrew.

246 - Fri., Oct. 14, 1774

Dublin.
Died: Rev. Mr. Vincent, rector of the parish of Donamore, Co. Tyrone.

Londonderry.
Died: Sunday last, Mrs. Patterson, wife of James Patterson; Monday last, Edward Cary of Castle Cary, Co. Donegal.

247 - Tues., Oct. 18, 1774

Dublin.
Bankrupt: Nathaniel Walker, Dublin, linen draper.

248 - Fri., Oct. 21, 1774

Dublin.
Mary Wright, Newry, convert to the Church of Ireland.
Died: Friday, Mrs. Scott, wife of Hon. Mr. Baron Scott.

249 - Tues., Oct. 25, 1774

Dublin.
--- Wabby was sentenced to death for cutting two of a man's fingers off.
Married: Mr. Mitchel, comedian, to Miss Shewcraft, singer; Rev. Henry Palmer to Miss Smyth; Rev. Thomas Smyth, rector of Enniskillen, to Miss Ford, daughter of James Ford of Dawson st.; at Cavan, Rev. Charles Mears to Miss Nixon.
Died: Wednesday, Rev. Dr. Domville, former Dean of Armagh.

250 - Fri., Oct. 28, 1774

Londonderry.
Died: at Strabane, Mrs. Ingram, wife of Rev. James Ingram.
Ads: Mark Davis, shoemaker, newly from London.

251 - Tues., Nov. 1, 1774

Dublin.
Died: a son of Will. Clifford, at Bellevue.

Londonderry.
The Alexander, James Hunter, arrived in Philadelphia after nine weeks, passengers all well.
Cleared out: the Elizabeth, Johnson, for Baltimore in ballast; the Endeavor, Caldwell, for New York in ballast.

252 - Fri., Nov. 4, 1774

Waterford.
James Power of this city, cooper, convert to the Church of Ireland.

Dublin.
The following were sentenced to death: Neal Lamb and Charles Gronin or Wabby, for chalking; James Brennan for the robbery of Rev. Mr. Moody; and Thomas M'Gauran for burglary. Elizabeth Dugan and Elizabeth Peppar are to be pilloried and imprisoned.

Londonderry.
Married: on the 27th, James Alexander, member of Parliament, to Miss Ann, second daughter of James Crawford of Crawford-burn, Co. Down.
Died: on the 3rd, Thomas Balley, long a master of a vessel.

253 - Tues., Nov. 8, 1774

Newry.
On Oct. 12, James Bingham, a farmer near Waringstown, was found hung.

Dublin.
Mention of Michael Clarke, deceased member of Parliament.
Married: Alexander Adams of Larne to Miss Jane Alexander of Doagh, Co. Antrim.

Londonderry.
Married: Thomas Simpson of Ballyards, Co. Armagh, to Miss Jane Stirling of Wallworth.

254 - Fri., Nov. 11, 1774

Dublin.
Converts to the Church of Ireland: Francis Carden of Castle ----, Co. Meath; Daniel Whelan and wife Lucy, of --arrowhouse, Queen's County; James Rainy, Mary Caffery, John Quin, John Dowling, Sarah Ingham, Michael Walsh, Han-- Carrol, and others.

Londonderry.
Ads: Daniel Morgan, butcher, ran away from Roger O'Donnell, Derry, with his father, Patrick Morgan.

255 - Tues., Nov. 15, 1774

Dublin, Nov. 12.
Wednesday last, Neale Lamb and Charles Groom were executed for maiming, wounding, and chalking.
Married: Lt. Col. Mason to Miss Mosse, daughter of the late Dr. Bartholomew Bodde; at Dundrum, Ed. Eaton, excise officer, to Miss Mitchel; at Waterford, Richard Bowe, taylor, age 18, to Widow M'Daniel, age sixty.

Londonderry.
This morning died Jane, wife of John Thompson, sailing master, of this city.

256 - Fri., Nov. 18, 1774

Dublin.
James Brennan was executed near Kilmainham for robbery of Mr. Moody.

Died: Rt. Hon. Robert Rochfort, Earl of Belvedere. Hugh Holmes of Richardstown, Co. Louth, bleacher, bankrupt.

Londonderry.
Married: yesterday, John Barclay of Ballybofey, linen draper, to Elizabeth, eldest daughter of Samuel Curry, merchant, of this city.

257 - Tues., Nov. 22, 1774

Clonmel.
John Lewis, farmer near Birr, drowned.

Dublin.
Married: at Clonmel, Richard Moore of Lord Drogheda's Light ---- to Widow Lowe; Michael Sweeny of Mill st. to Miss Sweeny, daughter of Rev. S. Sweeny of William st.
John Molloy, Castle st., merchant, bankrupt.
Died: at Nenagh, Mr. and Mrs. Pierce Butler; Mrs. Downs; at Cork, Walter Edward.

Londonderry.
Married: on the 19th, Rev. Stewart Blacker of Carrick, Co. Armagh, to the daughter of Hugh Hill, member of Parliament.
Died: Friday, at Strabane, Mrs. George Knox.
Ads: Brent Homan and Richard George Homan, woolen drapers, partnership dissolved; late brother was William Homan. Martha Holmes alias Barclay has left her husband William Barclay.

259 - Tues., Nov. 29, 1774

Belfast.
Rev. Mr. Diamond, clergyman of the Church of Rome, convert to the Church of Ireland at the parish church of Kilrea.

Dublin.
A court case, Lord Castlestewart vs. the daughters and heirs at law of the late Acheson Moore of Aughnacloy, Co. Tyrone (the daughters got his lands in Tyrone, Monaghan, and Dublin).
Died: Rt. Rev. Dr. Dennison Cumberland, Bishop of Kilmore; Richard Wilson; James Crowe.

Londonderry.
The **Hill**, George Marshall, arrived at Philadelphia in eight weeks, all well.

261 - Tues., Dec. 6, 1774

Dublin.
Died: Sir Robert Blackwood, baronet, of Ballyleedy, age 81; at Newry, George Stevenson, printer and bookseller; at Belfast, Joshua Hutton; in Dame st., Francis Lord, gunsmith; in London, William Alexander.

Londonderry.
Died: Friday at Strabane, Rev. James Ingram.
Ads: The furniture and medicines in the shop of the late George Evory are to be sold; Alexander Kennedy and Mrs. Evory, executors.

262 - Fri., Dec. 9, 1774

Kilkenny, Nov. 30.
Died last Thursday, Thomas Doyle, gardener to Benjamin Burton Doyle of Saho, Co. Clare.

263 - Tues., Dec. 13, 1774

Kilkenny.
Nov. 25 died at Athy, Co. Kildare, James Purcell, age 79, head of the Porter
Drinkers, piper, etc.

265 - Tues., Dec. 20, 1774

Dublin.
Married: Luke O'Neil, Co. Antrim, to Miss Lucinda Tobin, Co. Wexford;
Cornelius O'Callaghan, Co. Tipperary, to Miss Ponsonby, daughter of John
Ponsonby; Capt. Grumley of Rush to Miss Coulter of Rush house.

Londonderry.
Ads: Daniel M'Neill, Armoy, concerning lands advertised by Elizabeth M'Neil
as executrix of Daniel M'Neil and by Henry M'Neil.

266 - Fri., Dec. 23, 1774

Londonderry.
The Minerva, Robert Macky, which left Derry on Aug. 23, arrived at
Philadelphia after five weeks and three days and landed its passengers in
good health.
Ads: John Spencer jr. of Co. Donegal inherited property from his sister,
Dolly King, late of Dublin.

267 - Tues., Dec. 27, 1774

Londonderry.
Ads: Another ad regarding the M'Neills; mentions marriage agreement between
Elizabeth Gage and Daniel M'Neil dated 19 Mar., 1747; furture renewals of
land leases vested in William Scott, now Baron of the Exchequer, and John
Gage, now deceased.

268 - Fri., Dec. 30, 1774

Dublin.
Alexander Reynolds, Ballymoney, Co. Antrim, shopkeeper, bankrupt.

269 - Tues., Jan. 3, 1775

Waterford.
In a fight between James Warren, weaver, and Charles Clarke, sailor, Warren
was slain.

Dublin.
James M'Mahon, former Roman Catholic priest who converted to the Church of
Ireland, was gaoled for stabbing and killing ---- Lowry.

Londonderry.
Ads: The brigantine Boscawen, Noble Caldwell, for Baltimore Feb. 1; Walter
and Thomas Marshall, Stephen Bennet, and Robert Houston, agents.

270 - Fri., Jan. 6, 1774

Cork.
Rev. Jeremiah Hart, parish priest of Skull and Kilmore, convert to the Church
of Ireland.

Dublin.
Coroner's inquest held on the killing of ---- Lowrie by M'Mahon. [See No.
269.]

Londonderry.
Thomas Culbertson, Cornelius M'Laughlin, and James M'Laughlin escaped from
gaol last Monday. [See below.]
Ads: John M'Laughlin, Glen Wood Sheriff's ad concerning the above escapees:
Thomas Culbertson, butcher, is charged with the murder of his uncle, Philip
Freel; Cornelius M'Laughlin, mason, is charged with stealing linen from David
and William Ross; aged in his forties.

271 - Tues., Jan. 10, 1775

Corke.
John Cashman of Castlemartyr, butcher, killed his wife, attacked Rev. Father
Nagle, and then drowned himself. Mrs. Wilson Carberry of Bandon, suicide.
Mary Linahan, convert to the Church of Ireland.

Dublin.
Alderman Mathew Baily sailed with the East India supervisors in 1769 on the
Aurora; his fate is not known. Mr. Dempsey, grocer, was robbed.
Died: Edward Mathews, Johnston, Co. Dublin, servant; in London, Henry Mossop,
Irish-born actor.

273 - Tues., Jan. 17, 1775

Dublin.
Captain Brereton's house was robbed; he had been away because of his uncle's
death.
Died: in France, Charles O'Brien, Earl of Thomond, etc., Colonel of a
regiment of infantry; at Sligo, Rev. Tho. Taffe, Provost of Sligo; near
Dundalk, Mr. Foster.

Londonderry.
Ads: John Hamilton, deceased, of Castlefin, Co. Donegal, left minor co-
heiresses; creditors are to apply to Rev. Robert M'Ghee, near Strabane. The
Mary, Robert George, 350 tons, for Baltimore March 1; William Glen, William
Hope, Tho. Chambers, and Ab. M'Causland, agents.

274 - Fri., Jan. 20, 1775

Londonderry.
Ads: Samuel Perry, Moyloughmore, Co. Tyrone, deceased; debts payable to
Samuel Galbraith, Greenmount, near Omagh.

275 - Tues., Jan. 24, 1775

Dublin.
Patrick Berrit, Crossmalina, parish of Killaloe, convert to the Ch. of Ire.
Married: Lt. George Gough of the 4th Horse to Miss Bunbury, daughter of the
late Thomas Bunbury, Co. Carlow; Mr. Minchin, linen draper, to Miss Sirr,
daughter of Major Sirr; William L. Stanford to Miss Mary Poe of Dorset st.;
at Waterford, Robert Paul, attorney, to the daughter of Darius Drake; John T.
Ashenhurst to the daughter of Mathias Read of Richmond; Paul Mazych of
Charlestown, S. C. to Elizabeth Julia, only daughter of Rev. Dr. Hamon;
Major Kelly of Essex st. to Miss Mary Brown of Lazer's hill.
Died: at Cavan, Mark Magrath; at Friendville, near Leighlin bridge, Samuel
Bradstreet; at Booterstown, Rev. Mathias Kelly, PP; James Hamill, silk
manufacturer; Peter Lawless, linen draper; William Deane, fan maker; at
Mounteban, on his way to France, Rev. Manly Gore, rector of Sligo and
Poorstown; at Ardee, William Lee; at Killcro, Richard Moore; at Clonmell,
John Carleton of Darling hill; Thomas Hunt; H. Millar, organ builder.

276 - Fri., Jan. 27, 1775

Londonderry.
Mr. Murray, master of the outward-bound brig Molly, apparently drowned.

277 - Tues., Jan. 31, 1775

Dublin.
The following were committed to Newgate prison: John Costigan, murderer of
John M'Kiernan; Lawrence Coleman, for cutting and maiming Alexander Graham of
the 40th Foot; George Campbell and Charles Byrne, slaters, for robbing
William and Robert Alexander's warehouse; John Dougherty; Mary Bourne for
theft; Thady Tisdall, sedan chairman, for assaulting Mary Coghlan.
Married: Lt. Joseph Shewbridge of the corps of Engineers to Miss Frances
Vallancey; Robert Mayne, attorney, to Mary Kellet, eldest daughter of James
Kellet, Co. Meath; Peter Hoey, book seller, to Miss Woods of Drogheda.
Died: at Coleraine, Mrs. Jane, relict of John Macky of Agivy, Co.
Londonderry, age 71; at Corke, Counsellor Murphy of Co. Kerry; at Limerick,
Rev. Mr. Laughlin, (Roman Catholic); at Thomastown, Co. Louth, Francis
M'Dermott.

278 - Fri., Feb. 3, 1775

Londonderry.
Died: at Raphoe, Miss Eliza, youngest daughter of the late Mr. Francis
Knightly of Raphoe.
Ads: Archibald Stewart, gardener, ran off from the service of Mary Sampson,
Port Hall. Elizabeth Leech or Alexander has left her husband Walter Leech.

279 - Tues., Feb. 7, 1775

Dublin.
James Palmer, Dublin, iron monger, bankrupt.
Died: Lt. Col. Charles Pearce, age 78, son of the late Lt. Gen. Thomas
Pearce.

Londonderry.
Ads: The Old Annuity Company of Londonderry to meet at Pat. Bradley's; to
elect members to replace Mr. Knox and Mr. Ormsby, deceased. Elizabeth Leech
says her husband has left her, not vice versa. [See Number 278.]

280 - Fri., Feb. 10, 1775

Peter Galan and Robert Thompson, partners, merchants of Belfast, bankrupt.

281 - Tues., Feb. 14, 1775

Dublin.
Catherine Nugent or Hatch, wife of Henry Hatch of Kells, Co. Meath, convert
to the Church of Ireland.
Died: Rev. Dr. John Obins; at More, Co. Meath, Sir Henry Lynch Bloss; on Aug.
20 in passage from Jamaica, Thomas, son of Mr. Burke of Pimlico; in
Irishtown, Mrs. William Philips, sister of Lord Viscount Jocelyn.

282 - Fri., Feb. 17, 1775

Dublin.
James Armstrong, Usher's quay, merchant, bankrupt.

283 - Tues., Feb. 21, 1775

Dublin.
William Burnside, Londonderry, merchant, bankrupt.

284 - Fri., Feb. 24, 1775

Dublin.
Dwyer Carrol of the 49th Regiment surrendered to the sheriff; he was accused
of killing ---- Franqueford last December.

Died: the Lady of Sir Robert Staples, bart., Dunmore, Queen's Co.; Mr.
Blundell, watch maker.

Londonderry.
Died: Wednesday last, Miss Frances Scott, age 59 years.
Ads: Servants for America are being received by James Crawford, to go on the
America. The America, James M'Cay, for Newcastle and Philadephia 15 days
hence; Richard Caldwell and James Caldwell, agents; the master was staying at
Mrs. Miller's. The Hill, George Marshall, for Newcastle and Philadelphia by
May 1; she was one year old and this was her second voyage; agents were
Robert Houston, Londonderry, merchant, William Gregg, Coleraine, merchant,
and the Captain at his house on Shipquay street.

285 - Tues., Feb. 28, 1775

Dublin.
Married: at Drumcarin, Co. Cavan, Rev. George Cary Hamilton to Miss Newburgh,
eldest daughter of William Newburgh; John French to Miss Daly.
Born: on the 21st, a son to Lady and John Stuart Hamilton (Member of
Parliament for Strabane).
Died: on the 4th, at Nice in the Piedmont, Dr. John Ryder, Archbishop of Tuam
and Bishop of Ardagh; Thomas Lehunte, attorney and member of Parliament.

Londonderry.
Married: Rev. Mr. Taylor of Convoy, Co. Donegal to Miss Jane Miller of
Trench, Co. Londonderry.

286 - Fri., Mar. 3, 1775

Londonderry.
Married: Feb. 27, Dougall Campbell of Lagan, Islay, Argyllshire, to Miss
Dunlap of Chatham hall, Co. Antrim.
Ads: Rose Downs, wife of Roger Coll of Lettermuck, has left him. Darby Quin,
Ann Quin, James Maloghry, and Bridget Maloghry, all of the parish of
Termonomangan, Co. Tyrone, were accused of the murder of John Clark, late of
Killeter. John Cairns, late of Waterside, distiller, will pay no debts of
his wife Sarah Cairns alias M'Closkey.

287 - Tues., Mar. 7, 1775

Dublin.
Mrs. Lettice Robinson, parish of Donaboine, diocese of Clogher, convert to
the Church of Ireland. Dwyer Carrol, ensign in the 49th regiment, was
acquitted in the murder of Lt. Henry Franquefort of the 49th. William
Overend, Portadown, Co. Armagh, merchant, bankrupt.

Londonderry.
Charles M'Donnell, at St. Columb's Cathedral, Derry, convert to the Church of
Ireland.
Ads: The Minerva, Alexander Ewing, 500 tons, for Newcastle and Philadelphia
by Apr. 20; owners James Thompson and Andrew Gregg, merchants; she is one
year old. The Hannah, James Ramage, 400 tons, for same by April 10; agents
James Stirling of Wallworth, Capt. James Mitchell of Londonderry, or William
Nealy, Co. Tyrone.

288 - Fri., Mar. 10, 1775

Londonderry.
Died: Tuesday last, George Stewart, brother of Charles Stewart of Hornhead,
Co. Donegal.

289 - Tues., Mar. 14, 1775

Dublin.
John Doyle, watchman for James Dowde, sentenced to be executed. John Birch,
guilty of robbery, to be executed. James Hand and John Murphy were executed.
Married: John Burden, Lisburn, to Miss Blow, Belfast; Morris Grayson Brown,
Glenmore, to Miss Ormsby; Fred. French, attorney, to Miss Stewart; William
Miles, age 82, to Elizabeth Morgan, age 17.

Londonderry.
Married: Richard Babington, merchant of this city, to Letitia Wray, daughter
of William Wray of Ards, Co. Donegal.
Cleared: the Boscawen, Caldwell, for Philadelphia in ballast.

290 - Fri., Mar. 17, 1775

Dublin.
Died: at Trinity College, Rev. George Lewis Shewbridge; Mr. Arnold of the
Vicars Choral; Mr. Vaughan, Roman Catholic clergyman of John's lane chapel;
George New, hatter.
Skeffington Smith Jameson, merchant, late of Larne, Co. Antrim, bankrupt.

Londonderry.
Died: at Cookstown, Co. Londonderry, Mrs. Cairns, wife of Rev. Samuel Cairns.
Ads: The ship George, Will Pinkerton, 250 tons, for Newcastle and
Philadelphia by 15 April; James Miller and Sam. Curry, merchants, agents.

291 - Tues., Mar. 21, 1775

Belfast.
Roger Henery, Antrim, convert to the Church of Ireland.

Dublin.
Miss Mary Farrelly, at parish of Knockbride, Co. Cavan, convert to the Church
of Ireland; after which she married John Caffray; both of Ballyharrow.
John Birch, attended by Father Austin, was executed.

292 - Fri., Mar. 24, 1775

Dublin.
Michael Connor and John Tomey were executed for robbing Mr. Nesbit.
Married: John Hu[s]band to Miss Catherine, daughter of the late Alderman
Reynolds; Henry Wildenham of Glin to the relict of James Crow; Robert
Percival, Knight's brook, Co. Meath to Miss Armstrong of Henry st.; Lt.
Corker to Widow Wilmore of Abby st.
Died: in France, Hon. Charles Nugent, brother of the Earl of Westmeath; at
Waterford, Rev. Mr. Browne; at Mantua, Co. Roscommon, Barth. Plunket; the
wife of Alderman Emerson; Henry Broomer, one of the town clerks of Dublin.

Londonderry.
Ads: The furniture of the late Matthew Clarke to be auctioned.

293 - Tues., Mar. 28, 1775

Dublin.
Lucius Molony, convert to the Ch. of Ireland, at the cathedral of Limerick.

Londonderry.
Ads: The Rose, Joseph Curry, 300 tons, for Baltimore by Apr. 15.

294 - Fri., Mar. 31, 1775

Dublin.
---- M'Glyne, weaver, was killed at Kilcock by Patrick Priest, miller,

45

Maynooth. Triplet sons were born to the wife of William Frost, late of
the 44th Regiment.
Married: William Hodder of Hodderfield, Co. Cork, to Miss Lysaght, daughter
of Lord Lisle; at Newry, Jonathan Blackwell to Miss Jane Cochran.
Died: Brinsley Burrowes, age 20, at the College; at Articliff near Coleraine,
Hugh Caldwell.

295 - Tues., Apr. 4, 1775

Dublin.
James Beahan, tenant of Mr. Annesley, Ballyfax, Co. Kildare, died of
hydrophobia.

Londonderry.
Married: Rev. William Chichester of Dresden, Co. Donegal, to Miss Hart,
daughter of Rev. Ed. Hart of Linsfort.
Died: Tristram Balfour of this city.
Ads: Will. Hargon's wife Margaret has left him. James Evory, William
Kennedy, and Mary Evory, executors of George Evory, deceased, vs. Thomas
Warburton, executor of Phillis Warburton, deceased; (among other lands) land
held under the will of the late Gabriel Whistler to be sold.

296 - Fri., Apr. 7, 1775

Dublin.
Rev. Neal Quin, Rev. William Parsull, parish priest of Dunleckny, James
Dowling jr. of Leighlin bridge, apothecary, and Mrs. Elizabeth Buds of
Carlow, converts to the Church of Ireland.

Londonderry.
Married: on the 6th, James Ramage, a sailing master of this port, to Miss
Hannah, eldest daughter of James Mitchell, of this city.
Cleared: the America, M'Cay, for Philadelphia in ballast.

297 - Tues., Apr. 11, 1775

Belfast.
John Horner sr. and Dennis Horner, found guilty of robbing the bleach green
of Nicholas Oakman near Glenary, to be executed. John Horner jr. to be
transported. Patrick Malone, to be executed for highway robbery.

Dublin.
Mention of the will of Mrs. Mary Knight, widow of Rev. Dr. Knight, rector of
Omagh.

Londonderry.
Ads: Rev. Galbraith Richardson vs. William Moore, Jane his wife, George Ley,
Mary his wife, John Christie, and Ann Ley; legal notice.

298 - Fri., Apr. 14, 1775

Dublin.
Died: at Clontarf, William Jessop, Doory, Co. Longford; on the 27th, at
Atticlive near Coleraine, Hugh Caldwell, leaving a widow and six children.

Londonderry.
At the Omagh assizes: Dudley Donnelly, for horse theft, to be executed May
25; James Hughes, for sheep stealing, to be transported; Davis Ducart, for
killing Charles Coningham, found to be manslaughter in self defense. At
Lifford assizes: Patrick M'Bride, for chalking, to be executed May 23. At
Londonderry assizes: Alexander Ramsay, for rape and murder of Jane
Clandennan, trial delayed.

299 - Tues., Apr. 18, 1775

Kilkenny.
Catherine Quinlon, Clonmulch church, and Mary Fitzpatrick, converts to the
Church of Ireland.

Londonderry.
John M'Grah and Hugh M'Grah, Kilmacrenan parish, converts to the Church of
Ireland.
Married: Daniel M'Laughlin, rope and sail maker, to Miss Elizabeth, daughter
of Richard Hunter of this city.

300 - Fri., Apr. 21, 1775

Corke.
Laurence Kennedy was convicted of killing his own father.

Londonderry.
Died: Tuesday, Archibald Cuningham, son of the late Archibald Cuningham, of
this city.

301 - Tues., Apr. 25, 1775

Dublin.
Died: Rt. Hon. Lady Trembleston; William Griffith, age 84, of Ballytivnan,
Co. Sligo; Rev. Richard Lloyd, rector of Rathcormuck; Joseph Bibby, glass
seller; John Smyth, architect of the city; Stephen Haven, burgess of Belfast.

302 - Fri., Apr. 28, 1775

Belfast, Apr. 25.
On Wednesday sailed the Prosperity, M'Culloh, for Philadelphia with about 480
passengers. On Sunday sailed the John, Poaug, for Baltimore with about 30
passengers.

Dublin.
At Limerick, Lt. Reynolds of the 45th Regiment was killed in a duel. [See No.
303.]
Died: at Carrickfergus, Rev. Hill Benson, Dean of Connor; Mr. John Hoyne,
Roman Catholic clergyman of Gowran.

303 - Tues., May 2, 1775

Drogheda.
Robert Hardman and his mother were gaoled for the murder of his wife.

Dublin.
At Limerick, in a duel, Lt. Ruxton killed Ensign Reynolds, son of the late
Alderman of Dublin. Bryan and Mary Moore, Mary Goldsborough, and Elizabeth
Donohoe, converts to the Church of Ireland.
Born: on the 20th, a son to the Countess of Donegal; on the 21st, a daughter
to the Lady of Sir Edward Newenham; a daughter to the Countess of Cavan; a
son, at Dundalk, to Lady Mountflorence.
Died: Daniel Mullouny in Co. Sligo, age 126 years; he was wounded at the
battle of the Boyne and at the battle of Aughrim; survived by sons,
grandsons, etc.

Londonderry.
Married: George Charleton, Roxton, Co. Donegal, to Miss Fanny, daughter of
Rev. Edward Hart of Desertague.
Ads: John Coningham's wife Elizabeth Coningham alias M'Cormick has left him.

304 - Fri., May 5, 1775

Corke.
Thomas Lyne, only son of Captain Lyne, drowned while going to embark with his father for the West Indies.

Belfast.
Patrick Malone was executed at Carrickfergus for the robbery of James M'Clughan. John and Dennis Horner are to be executed at Carrickfergus Saturday next.

Dublin.
Died: Dr. Rutty, physician and naturalist; Leo Keating, surgeon; Hon. Arthur Dawson, his fortune going to Arthur Dawson, banker of this city.

Londonderry.
Married: Peter M'Donagh, attorney of this city, to Miss Jane, daughter of John Erskine, Muff, Co. Donegal.
Ads: The *Minerva*, Alexander Ewing, for Philadelphia by May 20.

305 - Tues., May 9, 1775

Kilkenny.
James and Patrick Farnon, Ballyvass, were accused of the April 17 murder of John Fitzpatrick of Beacon's town, Co. Kildare.

Dublin.
Married: John Mitchell, merchant, Belfast, to Miss Rebecca Barnet, Ballyagherty, Co. Down; Dowell O'Reilly to Miss Connor.

306 - Fri., May 12, 1775

Belfast, May 9.
Saturday at Carrickfergus was executed Dennis Horner, for robbery of Mr. Oakman's green near Glanavy; his brother John had died a natural death the previous night.

Dublin.
Married: at Castlefin, Co. Donegal, William Maxwell of Omagh to Miss Bell Holmes, daughter of Rev. Benjamin Holmes; William Richardson, Rich Hill, Co. Armagh, to Miss Munroe, niece of the late Countess of Ely.
Died: George Cockburn; Red. Wade; John Lord, merchant; Rev. Thomas Strain, at Middletown, Co. Armagh.

308 - Fri., May 19, 1775

Belfast.
Mrs. Margaret M'Donnell, Balymagard, convert to the Church of Ireland, Ramoan parish.

309 - Tues., May 23, 1775

Dublin.
Born: a daughter to the Lady of Rt. Hon John Beresford.
Married: Mr. Stritch, merchant, to Miss Kelly; Sir Robert Tilson Dean to Miss Fitzmaurice, granddaughter of John Fitzmaurice of Springfield, Co. Limerick.
Died: John Magill, clerk of the Deliveries in the Ordnance Office; at Harold's Cross, Mr. Arthur; at Monaghan, Robert Forster, gent.

Londonderry.
Patrick M'Bride, who was sentenced to execution at Lifford, received a reprieve.

311 - Tues., May 30, 1775

Belfast, May 26.
Wednesday sailed for Newcastle and Philadelphia the ship Charlotte, Thomas Eggar, with 250 passengers.

Dublin.
Lawrence Coleman was executed for houghing a soldier.
Died: at Corke, the Lady of Rt. Hon. Lord Blayney; Will. Neynoe; James Hoey, printer and bookseller; at Furneaux, Co. Kildare, Theobald Wolfe.

312 - Fri., June 2, 1775

Dublin.
Morgan Kennedy, parish of Burrisokane, Diocese of Killaloe, convert to the Church of Ireland.
Died: Alexander M'Clintock; at Carlanstown, Co. Westmeath, William Dardis.

314 - Fri., June 9, 1775

Dublin.
Married: Arthur Dawson to Miss Monck, daughter of Geo. Paul Monck of Stephen's Green.
Died: Sir Charles Burton, bart., oldest alderman of the city; Mrs. Cruise of Drynan, Co. Dublin; at Enniskerry, Rev. Mr. Truell, minister of Powerscourt.

Londonderry.

315 - Tues., June 13, 1775

Dublin.
Married: on the 6th, Sir Robert Tilson Deane, Dromore, bart., to Miss Fitzmaurice, sole heir of the late John Fitzmaurice of Springfield, Co. Limerick.

Londonderry.
Died: at Bristol Wells, on the 6th, Miss Elizabeth Bateson, daughter of the late Richard Bateson of this city; on the 13th, James Crigan, wig maker of this city.

316 - Fri., June 16, 1775

Londonderry.

317 - Tues., June 20, 1775

Londonderry.
Married: Thursday, David Ross of this city to Miss Catherine, daughter of Redmond Coningham, Letterkenny.

319 - Tues., June 27, 1775

Dublin.
Born: a daughter to the Earl of Bellamont, baptized Mary.
Married: in Lambeth Chapel in England, Robert Stewart, Co. Down, to Miss
Pratt, daughter of Lord Camden.
Died: William Murray; in Belfast, James M'Crone, apothecary.
John Purcell, Dublin, printer, bankrupt.

Londonderry.
Died: Thursday, Miss Margaret Scott of this city, aged 50; Saturday, James
Knox, Killcadden, Co.Donegal.

320 - Fri., June 30, 1775

Dublin.
Died: at Chatham Hall near Ballimoney, Samuel Dunlope, eldest son of George
Dunlope; Rev. Mr. Robinson, rector of St. John's; the relict of Rt. Rev. Dr.
Cumberland, Bishop of Kilmore; the relict of the late Archdeacon Smith.

Londonderry.
Cleared: the Minerva, Ewing, for Philadelphia, ballast; the Hibernia,
Morrison, for Baltimore, ballast; the George, Pinkerton, for Philadelphia,
ballast; and the Hill, Marshall, for Philadelphia, ballast.

322 - Fri., July 7, 1775

Londonderry.
Married: on the 6th, John Macky of Cosquin to Miss Mary Ann M'Nutt of Fahan.
Died: Wednesday, John Erskine, Muff, Co. Donegal.

323 - Tues., July 11, 1775

Dublin.
Married: William Glascock, attorney, to Miss Scriven, daughter of Edward
Scriven; Francis Bernard, Carlow, to Miss Rebecca Hall of this city; Elms
Healy, upholder, to Miss Mary Whitestone; near Waterford, Mr. Dwyer,
bricklayer, to Widow Sweeney (his fourth wife, her fifth husband; thirteen
children between them); Dudly Hussey, counsellor at law, to Miss Darragh,
daughter of Alderman Darragh.
Died: at Drumcondra, Hon. Joseph Hamilton, youngest son of the late Lord
Boyne; at Newtown Ards, Rev. Peter Winder; on Cork Hill, Mr. Craig, saddler.

325 - Tues., July 18, 1775

Dublin.
The St. David, Capt. Lewney, bound from Dublin for Philadelphia, foundered at
sea and all on board perished. Robert Carroll, hackney coachman, to be
executed for rape.
Married: Mr. Clayton to Miss Frances O'Neill; at Arncliffe, Yorkshire,
Robert Lindsay of Co. Tyrone to the daughter of Thomas Mauleverer; at
Drumbanagher, Co. Armagh, Gustavus Handcock of Waterstown, Co. Westmeath, to
the daughter of John Moore, Member of Parliament; James Plunket, Rocksavage,
Co. Monaghan, to Miss Piers of Lisclogher, Co. Westmeath; Charles Sirie to
Miss Stirling.
Died: at Anatrim, Queen's Co., Rev. George Saville; Mr. Darley, merchant.

Londonderry.
Ads: George Barclay, register of the Annuity Company of Rapho, new members
sought to replace Rev. John Major and James Knox, Killcadden, deceased.

327 - Tues., July 25, 1775

Died: Lady Erne; at Waterford, Alexander Gordon, of the 19th Foot; at Corke,

Alderman William Parks; at Carrickfergus, Willoughby Chaplin, alderman.

328 - Fri., July 28, 1775

Londonderry.
Died: yesterday, the wife of Arthur Eccles of this city, aged 73.

329 - Tues., Aug. 1, 1775

Dublin.
Married: at Corke, Rev. Mr. Weld to Miss Mann, niece of the Bishop of Corke
and Ross; at Ballyconroe, William Bagnell jr., Marlhill, to Miss Margaret
Smithwick; John Bland, Co. Tipperary, to Miss Chadwick; Richard White,
Greenhall, to Miss O'Donnell of Co. Clare; at Belfast, John Brown of Peter's
hill to Miss Ann Lyons.
Died: at Holyhead, the Lady of the Bishop of Kildare; Ellen Cambie, relict of
Captain Cambie; Philip Hacket; at Freshford, Mr. White, age 84, Roman
Catholic clergyman; at Omagh on the 28th, Mrs. Susannah Blain.

331 - Tues., Aug. 8, 1775

Dublin.
William Wardel to be executed for robbing the house of Lady Parsons. Charles
Mulaoney, Mary Mitchel, and Peter Flanagan to be executed for robbing Mr.
Brereton. John Robison imprisoned for breaking Mr. Forde's windows. Henry
Washington, alias James Harrison, to be transported.

Londonderry.
Ads: Robert Scott declares his right to Ballycolman, parish of Urney, Co.
Tyrone, which Sarah Scott widow of William Scott intends to sell.

332 - Fri., Aug. 11, 1775

Dublin.
Spelecy and Francis Hehir, parish of Cloney, near Limerick, converts to the
Church of Ireland.

333 - Tues., Aug. 15, 1775

Belfast.
Peter Branagan, parish of Clonduff, diocese of Dromore, convert to the Church
of Ireland.

Dublin.
Married: James Wilson, Par---town, Co. Meath, to the daughter of the late
John Knox; at Waterford, Rev. Mr. Poulter to Miss Dennis; at Galway, Mr.
Burke, Claregalway, to Miss Teresa Kirwin; at Drogheda, John Delahide to Miss
Harford; at Newry, Mr. Marsden, merchant, to Miss Catherine Corry; Mr. White,
attorney, to the widow of Annesley Hughes; at Barna, Co. Tipperary, Stumble
Phillips of Mt. Phillips to Miss Lee; at Ra___n, Queen's Co., John Kimmens to
Miss White.
Died: at Galway, Mr. D'Arcy, Roman Catholic clergyman; Mr. Dunn, grocer; Mr.
King, merchant; at Brohall, King's Co., Edmond Daly; the youngest son of Lord
Mountcashel; J. Bradford, surgeon; at Ballymahon, Co. Longford, Leonard
Jacob, former captain in the 1st Dragoon Guards; at _ollymont, Tody Dodd; at
Porto_illo, Dinnison Hume; Thomas Coffy, attorney.

334 - Fri., Aug. 18, 1775

Londonderry.
Ads: Mr. Harvey, Malin-hall, to let the farm of the late Robert Newell in
Malin. John Gibbeny, bricklayer, late from London and Dublin, lodging at
Alexander Cain's, outside Ferryquay gate; his quality attested by Mr. M'Kane,
merchant, and John Clark, Bishop's gate. William Roderey was gaoled at

Lifford, charged with the murder of Daniel Greevaughan, Edenmore, parish of
Donaghmore, Co. Donegal.

335 - Tues., Aug. 22, 1775

Dublin.
---- Mulally, a proctor, was attacked and killed by White Boys near
Loughrick, near Clonmel. Mr. Fitzgerald, parish clerk of St. John's, died
with all the other passengers when a boat sank on the Shannon near Limerick.
Died: near Thomas Court, Hannah Smith, daughter of a tape weaver (her death
was blamed on thunder); Corporal Russell, of the 46th foot, who was attacked
at Oxmantown (he had a wife and two children); Mr. Connell, sales master, of
Smithfield; a son of Mr. Dalton of Mary's abbey, six years old.
William Wardell was executed.

336 - Fri., Aug. 25, 1775

Dublin.
Mr. Ferguson, Limerick, convert to the Church of Ireland.
Married: Mr. Ferguson to Miss Garstin; Mr. Matthews, vicar of Christ Church,
to Miss Councel; Lt. Charles Dawson, of the 62nd foot, to Miss Ann Holmes.
Died: at Bath, Nuttall Green of Low Grange, Co. Dublin; at Athlone, James
Sproule, sovereign of that town; Mr. Hagan, apothecary; at Paris, Gerald
Fitzgerald, member of parliament; near Waterford, John O'Neil; in London, Mr.
Houston, native of Ireland, first metzotinto scraper in Europe; at Bellrath,
Co. Meath, Christopher Nicholson; Rev. Daniel Letablere, D.D., Dean of Tuam
etc.

338 - Fri., Sept. 1, 1775

Dublin.
Married: the Earl of Belevedere to the second daughter of the late John
Bloomfield of Redwood.
Died: Gen. Michael O'Bryan Dilkes, master of the Royal Hospital; Gen. Bligh;
at Wynnefield, Co. Kildare, John Wynne Baker; at age 92, Rev. Francis Corbet,
D.D., Dean of St. Patrick's; Rev. Daniel Dickenson, curate of St. Werburgh's.

339 - Tues., Sept. 5, 1775

Dublin.
More on the estate of Christopher Nicholson; he was brother-in-law to
Gustavus Lambert and uncle to Charles Lambert. Samuel Johnston, sr.,
Glonadreegan, bequeathed money for a monument over the grave of the late
Charles Lucas, M.D. Thomas Cuningham, George Cox, and William Smith escaped
from Newgate.
Married: Robert Townly to Miss Kirk; Captain M'Donagh, in the French King's
service, to Miss Rose Plunket, second daughter to Lord Dunsany; at
Enniskillen, John Harrick to Miss Sarah Hinds; William Conyngham, Springhill,
Co. Londonderry, to "Mrs." Hamilton, only daughter of James Hamilton late of
Brownhall, Co. Donegal; Surgeon Woodroffe to Miss Jane Whelan.
Died: aged 75 years, George Faulkner, alderman, printer of the Dublin
Journal; James Byrne; Rev. Francis Cuffe; at his seat at Castleshane, Co.
Monaghan, Edward Lucas, former member of parliament.

341 - Tues., Sept. 12, 1775

Corke.
Margaret Regan was killed by her niece's husband, John Car----.

342 - Fri., Sept. 15, 1775

Corke.
William Ahern, parish of Timoleague, convert to the Church of Ireland.

Kilkenny.
Miss Callanan of Carlow, parish Clonmusk, convert to the Church of Ireland.

343 - Tues., Sept. 19, 1775

Kilkenny.
Benjamin Stewart, Captain of the White Boys, was executed on the Aug. 24.

Dublin.
Married: Richard Crosdaile, Rye, to Miss Sandys, both of Queen's Co.; Capt.
James Cook, haven master at Dublin, to Widow Lawrence.
Died: at Charleville, William Holmes Pomeroy; Lady Sarah Taylor, eldest
daughter of the Earl of Bective; George Lyndon, LL.D., Register to the
Consistory Court of Dublin; at Milltown, Standish Sheppard; at Newtown
Lemavady on the 15th, in childbed, Elizabeth, wife of Marcus Moody, merchant.

Londonderry.
Owen M'Cartney of parish of Dungiven and John M'Kean, parish of Bovevagh,
converts to the Church of Ireland.
Died: on the 17th, Charles M'Laughlin of this city, writing master, a young
lad.

344 - Fri., Sept. 22, 1775

Corke.
The Waddel on Sept. 9 spoke with the Recovery, M'Cullogh, from Dublin with
150 passengers and servants for Philadelphia, eight weeks out, all well.

Dublin.
Mary Robinson, Bridget Paterson, Patrick Barret, James Nally, and Daniel
Murphy, church of Crosmolina, diocese of Kells, converts to the Church of
Ireland.
Married: at Glaslough, Co. Monaghan, Hugh Maffert to Miss Euphemia Murray; at
Youghal, Capt. Thomas Gregg of the Plymouth division of marines to Miss
Freeman, daughter of Jasper Freeman.

Londonderry.
At the Omagh assizes, George Osborn and James Armstrong were found guilty of
manslaughter in the death of Andrew Sproul. At the Lifford assizes, ----
M'Minamen, to be executed for a robbery at Barnesmore. At the Derry assizes,
Alexander Ramsay, found guilty of the murder of Jane Clandennan on Dec. 31,
to be executed Sept. 27.
Ads: Notice by James Sproul that George Osborn, Drysage, Co. Tyrone, and
James Armstrong, Turawinny, Co. Fermanagh, on Sept. 6 found guilty of
manslaughter of Andrew Sproul, late of Oughie, Co. Tyrone, were ordered to be
burned in the hand, which was done. Giles M'Mahon, otherwise M'Ilmurray, has
left her husband Michael M'Mahon, Bearney, parish of Cams, Co. Tyrone.

345 - Tues., Sept. 26, 1775

Dublin.
Married: on the 10th at the palace at Clogher, Sir Arthur Brooke, bart., to
Miss Ford, a near relation of the Bishop of Clogher; near Corke, Capt. Park
to Miss Brown; near Waterford, John Stone to Miss Bolton, daughter of
Cornelius Bolton, member of parliament.
Died: at Ardrum, Sir John Conway Colthurst, member of parliament; Hon. Mrs.
Burke; T. Digges Latouche, age 25.

346 - Fri., Sept. 29, 1775

Londonderry.
Alexander Ramsay was executed Wednesday last.
Ads: Joseph Orr, son of the late Widow Orr, to continue her brazier business
in Pump st.

53

347 - Tues., Oct. 3, 1775

Kilkenny.
James Tyrrell, parish of Dunmore, convert to the Church of Ireland.

Dublin.
Married: Captain Bakeup of the <u>Betty</u> of Derry to Miss Faussett of Sligo.
Died: Rev. Dr. William Lill, rector of Ardee etc. in Co. Armagh; on Sept. 12
at Spa, where he went for his health, Lord Mulgrave, brother-in-law of the
Earl of Bristol.

348 - Fri., Oct. 6, 1775

Londonderry.
Ann M'Gonegal, Derry, convert to the Church of Ireland.
Ads: Jonathan Nicolls and James Ramage, sheriffs, to sell the interest of
John M'Kim, deceased, in land in the Liberties of Derry now in possession of
John Stuart, John Clark, Neal M'Paul, John Black, Ephraim Campbell, and
Samuel M'Clure.

349 - Tues., Oct. 10, 1775

Dublin.
Michael O'Brien, Derrymore near Limerick, John Johnston, Swords, Laughlin
Fallin, Athlone, and ---- Cusack, Wicklow, converts to the Church of Ireland.

350 - Fri., Oct. 13, 1775

Dublin.
Died: at Spa, age 18, Miss Louisa Nugent, granddaughter of Lord Clare; Robert
Trimble, surveyor.

Londonderry.
James Henry, Tamlaght parish, convert to the Church of Ireland. Dennis
M'Pole, baker, died as a result of being stabbed in a quarrel with a
shoemaker.

351 - Tues., Oct. 17, 1775

Dublin, Oct. 14.
Died: yesterday morning, in an advanced age, the Right Hon. Alexander
M'Donnell, Earl of Antrim; succeeded by his only son, William Randall
M'Donnell, Lord Dunluce.

Londonderry.
The ship <u>Minerva</u>, Alexander Ewing, arrived safe at Philadelphia on Aug. 20,
in seven weeks, all well.
Married: at Straw, Co. Derry, Rev. Francis Gray to Miss Edwards, daughter of
Edward Edwards.

353 - Tues., Oct. 24, 1775

Dublin.
Died: at Newry, Rev. Mr. Seaver; Thomas Coates, surveyor; at Wyonstown, Co.
Dublin, the [wife or relict?] of Dominick M'Causland; Mrs. Mary Bacon, relict
of the late Dr. Bacon.

Londonderry.
Ads: Mary Dougherty, Derry, not responsible for her son James Dougherty,
butcher, Derry.

354 - Fri., Oct. 27, 1775

Limerick.
Catherine and Bridget Powell, church of Duntrileague, converts to the Church
of Ireland.

Dublin.
Captain Mallay, Alderman Forbes, and several ladies and gentlemen were lost
in the Friendship in a recent storm. [But see No. 355.]

Londonderry.
Died: last night, Mrs. Anne, relict of the late William Reynolds, merchant.

355 - Tues., Oct. 31, 1775

Dublin.
Those lost on the Friendship were Alderman Ferguson and two servants, Mrs.
Farrel and three daughters and a son; Daniel Byrne; a merchant of Bordeaux;
Capt. Norton of the Sixth Regiment; Mr. Cormick; Doctors Nowlan and Hanly;
and four of the ship's company; and an unknown young gentleman. (Captain
Mallay did not die.)

Londonderry.
Married: Robert Moore of this city, merchant, to Miss Nancy, daughter of
Joseph Scott of Millenium.

356 - Fri., Nov. 3, 1775

Londonderry.
The Minerva and the Hibernia were both lost off the capes of Virginia, in
September; both crews safe.
Married: Andrew Ferguson, merchant of this city, to Miss Lydia M'Clintock,
sister of Robert M'Clintock, Dunmore.

357 - Tues., Nov. 7, 1775

Londonderry.
Ads: John Stirling, Ballydivett, to sell the stock and chattles of the late
John Blair, at Ballydivett, Co. Derry. Honor Kane or Donaghy has left her
husband Arthur Donaghy, Straad, parish of Banagher.

358 - Fri., Nov. 10, 1775

Dublin.
Married: the Duke of Leinster to the daughter of Lord St. George.

Londonderry.
Died: last Sunday, Mrs. Letitia, wife of James Walker.

359 - Tues., Nov. 14, 1775

Dublin.
James Horan was elected alderman in place of W. Forbes, deceased.

360 - Fri., Nov. 17, 1775

Londonderry.
Married: at Birdstown, Richard Charleton to Miss Benson.

361 - Tues., Nov. 21, 1775

Dublin.
Died: on the 13th at Corke, Cadwallader Lord Blayney, Lt. General in the
Irish establishment.

362 - Fri., Nov. 24, 1775

Dublin.
Daniel Sullivan and Timothy Harrington, parish of Bantry, diocese of Corke, converts to the Church of Ireland.

363 - Tues., Nov. 28, 1775

Dublin.
Married: J. Hamilton, merchant, of the Linen Hall, to Miss Kirkland, Co. Longford; Capt. Jordan of His Majesty's cutter Hamilton to Miss Hind of Great George's st.
Died: Thomas Usher, surveyor of the North Wall; the wife of Alderman Sir Anthony King; the Lady of Edward Sneyd; Counsellor Cope; Bernard Kane, attorney; on the Combe, Mr. Meadows, apothecary; near Bandon, Rev. James Weeks; at Middleton, aged 80, Rev. Thomas Frankland, rector of Carrigtoohill; at Corke, Capt. Brooks; the wife of Surgeon Cunningham; Lady Parsons, relict of the late Sir Laurence Parsons, bart.; Samuel Powell, printer; the wife of Rev. Mr. Baird.

Londonderry.
Ads: Thomas Wensley, Sandville, Co. Tyrone, deceased; Thomas Chambers, merchant, executor.

364 - Fri., Dec. 1, 1775

Dublin.
Married: Caesar Colclough, Co. Wexford, to Miss Martha, daughter of Rev. John Waring of Kilkenny; John Murray to Miss Catherine Alexander, both of the parish of Fahan, Co. Derry.

365 - Tues., Dec. 5, 1775

Londonderry.
Died: Friday, at an advanced age, Mrs. Anne Caldwell, relict of the late Mathew Caldwell of this city.

366 - Fri., Dec. 8, 1775

Kilkenny.
Ambrose Power, Barretstown, Co. Tipperary, J.P., brother of Baron Power, was slain by White Boys; he had apprehended William Mackey at Feathard fair.

Dublin, Dec. 5.
In an epidemic died Monday fortnight William Meadows, apothecary; three days later his wife; next day her aunt (who lived in the same house); next day his sister; their apprentices and servants lie without hope of recovery.
Married: Thomas Palmer, Summerhill, Co. Mayo to Miss Rynd, eldest daughter of Thomas Rynd, merchant; Thomas Doran to Miss Mary Gallagher of Sligo; at Lisburn, Rev. Patrick Parker to Miss Gear.
Died: James Trant of Co. Corke; at Loughgall, John Hardy , linen draper; at Belfast, Robert Armstrong; John Gunston, upholder; George Stackpole; the Lady of Col. Gore of the Battleaxe Guards.

368 - Fri., Dec. 15, 1775

Dublin.
Reward of 1,000 pounds offered for the first and 300 pounds for each of the next twelve taken and convicted for the murder of Ambrose Power.
Died: at Six-mile-bridge, Col. Augustine Fitzgerald; Frederick Shippey; at Finea, John Hogan, aged 104 years, who lifed these fifty years on a milk diet; at Corke, Henry Sheares, banker.

Londonderry.
Ads: William M'Elwaine, eldest son and heir of John M'Elwaine, deceased, and Alexander M'Elwaine, executors of said John, vs. William Brown; to sell former lands of Joseph Brown, Ballybigly, on Lough Swilly and bordering Joseph Alexander's farm in the manor of Mount Stewart, barony of Rapho.

369 - Tues., Dec. 19, 1775

Dublin.
Mary St. John, Leighlenbridge, convert to the Church of Ireland.

Londonderry.
Ads: John M'Elwee, apprentice, has run off from William Linn.

370 - Fri., Dec. 22, 1775

Limerick.
Mr. Lamb, a Quaker near Mountrath, was attacked and killed by White Boys.

Londonderry.
Ads: Andrew Kennedy ran off from the service of Thomas D. Logan; about twenty years old; reward from T. D. Logan or Henry Patterson, Newtown Cuningham.

371 - Tues., Dec. 26, 1775

Dublin.
Died: at Ballendrate, Co. Donegal, Mr. Francis Hamilton; at Dungannon, Co. Tyrone, Oliver M'Laughlin.

Londonderry.
Ads: John M'Elwee has left William Linn because of ill treatment and will apply for justice.

372 - Fri., Dec. 29, 1775

Dublin.
Died: at Carrick-on-Suir, Mark Scott, Mohubber, brother of the Solicitor General; at Ballyclare, age 99, Charles Crimble; Thomas Murray, Killulta, linen draper; at Strabane, Miss Martha Nichol.

Londonderry.
Ads: Wallace Moorhead, parish of Ardstraw, alledgedly was murdered by John M'Laughlin of the same parish, who has absconded.

373 - Tues., Jan. 2, 1776

Corke.
Died in a storm aboard the Rockingham transport, Lt. Marst of the 32nd Foot, his wife, Ensign Sandyman, Lt. Barker's wife, and over ninety men.

375 - Tues., Jan. 9, 1776

Dublin.
Married: at the house of Sir William Montgomery, Sir John Blaquire to Miss Elinor Dobson, heiress of Robert Dobson of Ann-grove, Co. Corke; at Prospect near Carrickfergus, Charles Adair of Loughanmore to Miss Ellis, daughter of Henry Ellis; Daniel Davies, late a Captain in the 58th Foot, to Miss Baker; Roger Bristow, surveyor of Newry, to Miss Fivey, only daughter of W. Fivey of Loughadian, Co. Armagh.
Died: the wife of Major Whitlock (married for fifty years); Mrs. Ann Rolls; in the Four Courts Marshalsea, John Lawlor, attorney; at Portglenone, David Bateson; at Newtown Lemavady, John Ross, innkeeper; near Raphoe, John M'Cleery, farmer.

Londonderry.
Ads: Catharine Miller or Swan has left her husband Joseph Millar,
Ballynamoor, parish of Cumber.

376 - Fri., Jan. 12, 1776

Kilkenny.
---- Downing, alias Captain Slasher, was gaoled for the murder of Ambrose
Power.

Dublin.
John Knight was executed, after being found guilty of robbing the house of
John Jones.

Londonderry.
Married: on the 11th at Strabane, David Weir of Dublin to Miss Martha Orr,
Strabane.
Ads: Stephen Deroche, Kevan Izod, and Robert Traverse, executors of Robert
Lane, deceased, and Paul Benson, James Benson, Benjamin Vaughan the Elder,
and Ben. Vaughan the Younger vs. John Mauleverer; lands to be sold include
his interest in houses in Muff, Co. Londonderry, etc., formerly in possession
of James Huey of Muff, linen draper, the residue of a lease for life of Henry
Fox, son to Rt. Hon. Henry Fox of Holland House, Co. Middlesex; also his
interest in a farm belonging to the house of Henry Darcus of Londonderry,
formerly held by George Crookshanks and Thomas Beasley, merchant (north of
the River Foyle), bound on the east by Rev. Edward Hart's land and on the
west by Alexander Stewart's and Clotworthy Lenox's lands in the Liberties.

377 - Tues., Jan. 16, 1776

Dublin.
---- Butterly (a young woman) and ---- Hancock (a young girl) and another
girl were killed when two old houses collapsed.
Died: at Clontarf, Col. Clarke; John Echlin of Sandbrook Park, Co. Carlow; at
Lahine, Co. Leitrim, John Peyton; at Lisbon, Harding Pedder, late of Corke
and a Lt. in the 61st Foot.

378 - Fri., Jan. 19, 1776

Dublin.
William Nevil, Lisburn, Co. Antrim, bankrupt.

379 - Tues., Jan. 23, 1776

Dublin, Jan. 20.
At Clonmel, ---- Downey, alias Capt. Slasher, and William Hayes were tried,
convicted, and executed on Tuesday last for the murder of Ambrose Power.

Londonderry.
Died: on the 16th at Convoy of the influenza, Rev. David Fairly, age 96,
Dissenting Minister there for 67 years; Saturday, Mrs. Elizabeth Hope, wife
of William Hope, merchant of this city.

380 - Fri., Jan. 26, 1776

Galway.
A letter from Walter Burke, Captain of the _Julian_ of Galway, which arrived at
Baltimore before Oct. 27, 1775: "we disposed of our servants tolerably well."

Dublin.
Married: T. T. Faulkner, printer of the _Dublin Journal_, to Miss Moncrieff,
daughter of Richard Moncrieff, bookseller.

58

381 - Tues., Jan. 30, 1776

Dublin.
Letter from Clonmell: The White Boys hung were John Hayes and William Downey; they were hung "without being allowed a clergyman"; John Murphy was found not guilty but was to be tried under the White Boy act; W. Mackey and Philip Borbag were convicted under that act for burglarizing the house of John Watson, Carryganstown, and were immediately executed.

382 - Fri., Feb. 2, 1776

Dublin, Jan. 30.
Married: the Lord Mayor to Widow Howard of Enniskillen; John Wogan, Cashel, to Miss Carew; John Carven Carden, Templemore, to Miss Mary, daughter of Arthur Pomeroy, member of parliament; at Magherafelt, Co. Derry, Samuel Strean to Miss Martha Morrow, both of Magherafelt.
Died: at Waterford, Robert Dobbyn sr.; at Sligo, Mr. Dom. Hallinon, Roman Catholic clergyman; at Enniskillen, Alexander Cole, uncle of Lord Mountflorence; at Stephen's green, Daniel Deane; at Portarlington, William Slack; at Inchmore, Co. Westmeath, Thomas Stanly; at Cullen's Wood, Alderman Peter Barre; John Read, cutler; Thomas Radcliffe, LL.D., Vicar General of Metropolitical Court of Armagh and Judge of the Consistory Court of Dublin; Rev. John Bowden, D.D., vicar of Syddan; at Creville, George Frend, formerly Major of the 9th Foot; John Edmonds, apothecary; Edward Fry, druggist; Samuel Morrison, attorney; Mr. Thornton, linen draper; Capt. Robinson of the 47th Regiment; at Kilkenny, Jonah Wheeler, of Syrath.
Bankrupt: William Wightman, Lisburn, Co. Antrim, and William Sherrard, Dublin, haberdasher.

384 - Fri., Feb. 9, 1776

Dublin.
Married: Major Faviere of the 1st Horse to Miss Maria, daughter of George Despard of Donore, Queen's Co.; Dennis Daly of Castle-daly, Co. Westmeath to Miss Harriet, youngest daughter of John King of Ballylin, King's Co.; Thomas Naughton, surgeon, to Miss Higgins; at Paris, Allen O'Reilly of Milltown, Co. Meath, to Miss Norris; Robert Dillon, Clonbrock, Co. Galway, to Miss Letitia Greene, Co. Tipperary.
Died: at Coagh, Co. Tyrone, John Vance; James Kelly, fencing-master; Dominick Brown, Castle-margaret, Co. Mayo; Matthew Nesbit, Derrygaster, Co. Leitrim; Mrs. French, relict of the late Arthur French of Co. Roscommon; John Wilson of the Quit-rent Office; at Newry, William Wier and W. Hamilton, merchants; at Kilmainham Hospital, George Burston, Auditor and Register of same; Charles O'Hara, member of parliament for Armagh; at Talisho, Co. Westmeath, Richard Rochford Mervyn, brother of the Earl of Belvedere, Lt. Col. of the 39th Foot; at Tuam, Co. Galway, Richard Bodkin Blake.

Londonderry.
Married: at the seat of Theophilus Jones near Dublin, Rt. Hon. John Creighton, Baron Erne of Crumcastle, to Miss Mary Hervey, daughter of the Lord Bishop of Derry.
Ads: Debts due to the late William Patterson are to be paid to his son Robert Patterson, not to John Patterson.

385 - Tues., Feb. 13, 1776

Londonderry.
Feb. 10 was the birthday of Mrs. Elizabeth Hervey, lady of the Bishop of Derry; their son John was a naval officer.

386 - Fri., Feb. 16, 1776

Dublin.
Married: Samuel Stock, hosier, to Widow Lane, daughter of Alderman Horan;

James M'Cabe to Miss Elizabeth Reynolds; Rev. Walter Bigot to --- Cliboorn; at Loughren, William Staunton, M.D., to the Widow French.
Died: at Rowesgift, Co. Derry, the lady of John Downing; at Dun_bin, Co. Cavan, Richard Booth; at Gallo, Co. Meath, Rev. John Bomt___, rector of Radinstown; the mother of John Monck Mason; Robert Wallis, notary public; at Burton Hall, the Widow Smith; at Maghrecrigan, Co. Tyrone, John Galbraith, aged 105 years; James Stewart jr., Larne, boat-builder; at Belfast, John Leggat, age 101; Mary, wife of Armor Lowry Corry, sister of the Earl of Carrick, age 26.

387 - Tues., Feb. 20. 1776

Dublin.
Died: at Bourdeaux, the wife of Samuel Delap, merchant; Charles Meare_, attorney; Rev. Mr. Thriddle of Carlow.

Londonderry.
Died: on the 16th, John Ross, age 20 years, son of Alderman Ross; on the 18th, Miss Mary, daughter of Capt. James Mitchel.

389 - Tues., Feb. 27, 1776

Londonderry.
Died: William James, formerly a considerable dealer in this city.

390 - Fri., Mar. 1, 1776

Londonderry.
Thomas M'Closky of the parish of Banagher, Co. Londonderry, was gaoled for murder.
Died: Tuesday last at Beach Hill, Co. Londonderry, the wife of Rev. Alexander Skipton.

391 - Tues., Mar. 5, 1776

Dublin.
Married: Peter Pasmier to Miss Hamilton, daughter of the late Archibald Hamilton of Ballysatton (?), Co. Tyrone; Robert Rochfort to Miss Nugent, Clonlost, Co. Westmeath; Benjamin Chapman, counsellor at law, to Miss Louther, only daughter of John Louther, Stafordstown, Co. Meath; Charles Drumgoole, apothecary, to Miss Isabella M'Neil; Mr. Williams, apothecary, to Miss Dickenson; P. Kelly, apothecary, to Widow Graves; George Thornton, merchant, to Miss Hodginson, Lisburn; at Abbey Leix, seat of Lord Knapton, Sir Robert Staples to Miss Vesey; near Dungannon, Widow Wildman, age 65, to Mr. English, age 21.
Died: C. Fitzgerald; Joseph Ward, one of the vicars choral; at Lodge, hunting, Humphrey Nixon; at Portarlington, Mrs. Beaghan, age 10_; on the 21st near Dungannon, Terence Gallagher, age 116, who was born in the Castle of Charlemont in 1659, served at the Battle of the Boyne under King William, and at the taking of Gibralter (married four times and left two sons).

Londonderry.
Died: Saturday, Elizabeth Hogg, relict of the late Alderman Hogg of this city.
Born: a daughter to the lady of William Ross.

392 - Fri., Mar. 8, 1776

Dublin.
Ann M'Carty, church of Holycross, diocese of Cashel, convert to the Church of Ireland.
Died: at Newry, Rev. James Hacket, fifty years a curate; at Sligo, a son of Mr. Duke, apothecary; at Newtownards, Samuel Orr, merchant.

Londonderry.
Ads: Mr. Gregg, Melmount, James Blair, Camone, Robert Gray, Gortin, and
Richard Cowan, Lifford, to sell the interest of Richard Gregg, deceased, in
lands now held by George Keys and John Denning, at the house of Arthur Blair,
innkeeper, Strabane.

393 - Tues., Mar. 12, 1776

Dublin, Mar. 9.
Christopher Hawkins and John M'Daniel were executed Saturday for murder.
Married: at Blarney Castle, Dominic Trant of Dunkettle to Miss Fitzgibbon,
daughter of John Fitzgibbon, member of parliament; William Craig,
Carrickfergus, to Miss Murray, same; William Hall, Co. Westmeath, to Miss
Codd, Co. Meath.
Died: C. Simpson, inspector of the Liberty Woollen Warehouse; Robert Crowe,
sen., upholder; Rev. John Clements, Chaignean; near Castlemartyr, Edward
Supple; at Antrim, William Williamson died in an election quarrel; Richard
Cox, grocer; Philip Byrne, wine merchant; in Strabane, Mrs. Anne Law, relict
of the late Rev. Samuel Law.

394 - Fri., Mar. 15, 1776

Londonderry.
Ads: Catherine Ferguson or M'Morris has left her husband William Ferguson.

395 - Tues., Mar. 19, 1776

Londonderry.
Married: at Whitehall, Co. Antrim, Robert Delap, Rathmelton, to Miss Mary
Anne, daughter of the late James Boyle, Castlefin.
Died: on the 15th at Dromore, Co. Derry, Rev. Robert Bryan; Friday,
Elizabeth, wife of Capt. Thomas Marshall, of this city.

396 - Fri., Mar. 22, 1776

Dublin.
Thomas Grady, church of Cahircorny, Co. Limerick, convert to the Church of
Ireland.
Married: near Corke, John Pyne to Miss Davis, daughter of Archibald Davis;
Harlow Knott, Battlefield, Co. Sligo to Miss Mary, second daughter of Harlow
Phibbs, Rathmullin, Co. Sligo; at Portpatrick, Henry Walter French to Miss
Plunket, daughter of Bart. Plunket, late of Mantua, Co. Roscommon; Roger
Higginson, Lisburn, to Miss Hull of Hillsborough; at Newry, Ensign Ki_kes of
the 33rd Regiment to Miss Henderson; at Loughgall, Co. Armagh, Patrick Nat__
to Miss M'Cann.
Died: near Clonmell, Edward Manville, M.D.; at Kinsale, Baron de Courcy;
Thomas Topping, Beaulieu, Co. Louth; the widow of Christopher Irvine, Cooles,
Co. Fermanagh; at Swords, Thomas Haze; Mr. Martin, attorney; Robert Acheson,
attorney; at Moira, Miss Eleanor Berwick; Lt. Col. Chenevia, of the Royal
Artillery; at Corke, Norah Travers; at Corke, Rev. Mr. Donaghy, Roman
Catholic clergyman; Counsellor Darby; Counsellor Palmer; at Naas, Counsellor
Spring; Charles Caldwell, formerly Solicitor for the Revenue at Large;
William Bolton, attorney; Bedell Stanford, Belturbet, Co. Cavan; John Irwin,
attorney; at Loughgall, Co. Armagh, James Ashmur (?), sen.; Fielding Ould, a
high sheriff of Dublin.

397 - Tues., Mar. 26, 1776

Dublin.
Married: John Atkinson of Ballyshannon to Miss Elizabeth Hamilton, Dublin;
James Fitzmaurice to Widow Cooper of Bennekerry; Mr. Shaw to Miss Robinson.
Died: at Killongford, Thomas Walsh of Waterford; at CahirHurly, Ben. Watson
of Co. Limerick; Mr. W. Faucet of Lisbofin, Co. Fermanagh; at Johnstown, Co.

Wexford, Rev. Bart. Thomas; James Flack, attorney; John Ridge, counsellor at
law; at Tinnera_e, Co. Clare, Mr. David Bran, age 117.

Londonderry.
Ads: James Lendrum was assaulted by James Lindsay of Rathaniny (age about
24); reward for his apprehension offered by Robert M'Kerachan.

398 - Fri., Mar. 29, 1776

Dublin.
Died: David Smith, merchant; at Athy, Widow Bennett, age 109.

Londonderry.
Died: on the 22nd, at Longford, Thomas Scott, counsellor at law and Recorder
of the City of Londonderry; Mrs. Agnes, wife of Andrew Sayres, Convoy, Co.
Donegal; Wednesday, Mrs. Fanny, wife of James Major, merchant of this city.

399 - Tues., Apr. 2, 1776

Dublin.
Born: a daughter to Lady and Lord Townshend, in London.
Married: Rev. Thomas Ingliss, Co. Wicklow, to Miss Anne Major of Cherrymount,
Co. Donegal; Mr. M'Mullan, merchant, to Miss Currin, milliner.
Died: Rev. William Evelyn, D.D., Vicar of Trim, etc.; at Bath, Hugh
Carmichael, counsellor at law, crown clerk for Leinster; Mr. Hutchinson,
attorney; at Waterford, John Smith, attorney; at Waterford, David Caldwell,
age 103, veteran of Queen Anne's wars.

Londonderry.
Ads: Anne M'Connell, deceased, formerly possessed interest in a tenement now
occupied by Thomas Miles; also her household furniture etc. to be sold.

400 - Fri., Apr. 5, 1776

Kilkenny, Mar. 27.
Michael Bulger, a White Boy, found guilty of destroying the house etc. of
John Grant, Kilinogue, to be executed March 30. Edmund Butler, White Boy,
found guilty of cutting an ear off of Patrick Pigott, to be executed same.
James Kennedy, alias Capt. Madcap Setfire, of the White Boys, was arrested in
Queen's Co. by Rev. Chamberlain Walker and gaoled at Maryborough.

Dublin.
Died: at Barr, Mr. Sylvester, attorney; on Milltown road, Col. Pepper;
William Henry Delawar, native of the East Indies; at Sligo, Widow Smith; at
Lusk, Rev. John Wisdon; at Athlone, Dr. Bryan Keogh; Mrs. Ryder, wife of Rev.
Dr. John Ryder, Dean of Lismore; the Lady of Robert Hartpole, Queen's Co.; at
Ballycastle, Co. Antrim, the widow of Hugh Boyd, age 90.

401 - Tues., Apr. 9, 1776

Dublin.
Died: at Kinsale, Capt. Tryon of an East Indiaman; Thomas Stevens, merchant;
at Bath, Sir Edward Barry, bart. etc.; Eusabius Low; at London, Albert
Nesbit, merchant; George Jackson, Co. Kilkenny, of a gunshot; in Kevin's
port, John Nenoe; Benjamin Chapman, counsellor at law and member of
parliament.

Londonderry.
Died: on the 5th at Magilligan, Henry M'Neil, age 75.

402 - Fri., Apr. 12, 1776

Dublin.
Edmund Beasley was sworn in as high sheriff in place of Fielding Ould,

deceased.
Married: Samuel Davy, Sligo, to Miss Letitia, daughter of George Ormsby of Belvoir, Co. Sligo; at Derry, Mr. Parkinson, sail maker, to to Miss M. M'Laughlin.
Died: near Galway, Rev. Dr. R. Kirwan; at Kilkenny, Rev. Patrick Magennis, Roman Catholic clergyman; at Derry, Alexander Ewing, publican.

Londonderry.
At the Omagh assizes, Charles Sproul's trial for the murder of Ann Dougherty ended in a hung jury; to be re-tried. At Lifford, Richard Jones, found not guity of burning a house etc. belonging to Mr. Ferguson of Letterkenny; to be transported for stealing yarn from same. At Derry, James Holmes, found guilty of manslaughter in self defense of Dennis M'Powell; and James M'Closky found not guilty in the murder of O. M'Gilligan.
Died: Tuesday last, Miss Margaret Hunter, age 18, sister of the late John Hunter of St. Christopher's.

403 - Tues., Apr. 16, 1776

Dublin.
Married: at Limerick, Robert Molesworth, formerly a captain in the 38th Regiment, to Miss Kane; Richard Allen, Co. Meath, to Miss Featherstone, Co. Westmeath.
Died: at Naul (?), Co. Meath, Art Mervin; Dr. Michael Clancy, Master of the Diocesan School of Ossory.

404 - Fri., Apr. 19, 1776

Londonderry.
Robert Boyd, counsellor at law, was named Recorder of Londonderry in place of the late Mr. Scot.
Married: Captain Richard Hunter to Widow Godfrey, yesterday.
Ads: Margaret M'Closky alias Kelly has left her husband (not named).

405 - Tues., Apr. 23, 1776

Dublin.
Died: on the 17th, age 74, William Scott, Second Baron of the Exchequer.

Londonderry.
Ads: Margaret M'Closky (who advertised in Number 404) was the wife of Michael M'Closky.

407 - Tues., Apr. 30, 1776

Dublin.
Married: Joseph Burke to Miss Jane, daughter of Simon French. Died: near Chapelizod, Richard Reddy, M.D.

408 - Fri., May 3, 1776

Belfast.
James Hezlet or Hezley was executed at Downpatrick for burglary.
William Weldon of Gravelmount, Co. Meath and Richard and Henry Cane, converts to the Church of Ireland.
Edward Curren, a potter, died of excessive drink.

Londonderry.
Died: John Hervey of Millenan near this city; Mrs. Edmiston of Millenan, at an advanced age.
Ads: Elizabeth Craig or Hunter has left her husband Thomas Craig, Ardnamhogie.

409 - Tues., May 7, 1776

Corke.
Thomas Mead, Kilwinny, Co. Waterford, was charged with the murder of his wife.

Dublin.
Died: in London, Sir Matthew Aylmer, bart., of this city; Mr. C. Eustace, linen draper, by a fall from a horse; Thomas Ewing, bookseller.

Londonderry.
Died: Friday last, John Aiken, age 67, 24 years usher to the Free School of Derry.
Ads: The furniture of the late Alderman Charles M'Manus to be sold.

410 - Fri., May 10, 1776

Londonderry.
Ads: Andrew Irwin deserted from the 30th Regiment, now at Drogheda; native of Douglas Bridge, Co. Tyrone, aged about 22 years, a weaver; reward offered by William Knox, Killcaddon, Co. Donegal.

411 - Tues., May 14, 1776

Londonderry.
Died: Sunday, Mrs. Jane Thompson, wife of Capt. John Thompson.

412 - Fri., May 17, 1776

Dublin.
Died: Rt. Hon. Anthony Malone, former member of parliament etc.

Londonderry.
Married: Samuel Ball of Grousehall to Miss Chichester of Dresden, Co. Donegal.

414 - Fri., May 24, 1776

Dublin.
Died: Patrick Brady, attorney; Wentworth Thewles, attorney.

416 - Fri., May 31, 1776

Dublin.
Married: Henry Gore Sankey to Miss Barbara, second daughter of the late Rev. William Sneyd.
Died: at Mt. Merrion, Viscount Fitzwilliam; Rev. Mr. Matruine; Mrs. Ebery, relict of the late Rev. Dr. Ebery; Mrs. Palmer; the only son of Col. Graham.

Londonderry.
Peter Colgan and Mary Donnel, church of Carrigans, converts to the Church of Ireland.
Ads: Robert Thompson, John Cairns (innkeeper), and David Macky, executors of Moses Macky, to sell his land.

420 - Fri., June 14, 1776

Dublin.
Margaret Abbot, parish of Ettagh, diocese of Killaloe, convert to the Church of Ireland.

Londonderry.
Ads: Andrew Patton, Springfield near Letterkenny, or Counsellor Maffet, Dublin, to sell the late Andrew Murray's lands.

421 - Tues., June 18, 1776

Londonderry.
Ads: Seeking the sister of Francis Soly, who [he] went to Philadelphia with
Captain Falls.

422 - Fri., June 21, 1776

Londonderry.
Ads: Mr. Chambers, Sandhill near Strabane, has property alledgedly stolen
from John Gwynn, merchant of Strabane, found in the house of John Gormly,
Moyage, where live Alexander Hamilton (called Hamilton the Coiner), Thomas
Gallagher, Bridget Gallagher, Mary Gallagher, and Mary Morrow or Gallagher.

425 - Tues., July 2, 1776

Dublin.
Married: Henry Laws Luttrell, Lt. Col. of the Blue Horse, to Miss Boyd,
daughter of George Boyd of Abby street; Gabriel Johnston, Latin's court,
merchant, to Miss E. Nix, Co. Kildare; Rev. Thomas Smyth of Delgany, son of
the late Baron Smyth, to Mrs. Scot, daughter of John Bowes Benson, Co. Louth.

Londonderry.
Died: Rev. William Barker, Dean of Raphoe, last Thurdsay, age 62.

426 - Fri., July 5, 1776

Londonderry.
Married: in the house of Samuel Delap, Rathmelton, Robert Given jr. of
Coleraine to Miss Stevenson, daughter of the late James Stevenson of this
city, merchant.

427 - Tues., July 9, 1776

Londonderry.
Died: Sunday last, Jane, wife of Nat. Hunter of this city.
Ads: George Keys, Strabane, administrator of William Sinclair, deceased, late
of Strabane.

428 - Fri., July 12, 1776

Dublin.
Died: near Coolock, Charleton Whitelock; Alfred Howard, attorney, clerk of
the common council of this city; at Kill, Co. Westmeath, John Bonynge; at
Belfast, the wife of Rob. Smith, bookseller.

Londonderry.
Ads: John Gonne, to let a shop and house and the house in Shipquay st. where
the late Mrs. Bellew dwelt.

429 - Tues., July 16, 1776

Dublin.
Married: Mr. Phelan, malster, age 70, to Miss Downing, age 16; James Bacon,
Church st., linen draper, to Mrs. Darcy, Cork st.

432 - Fri., July 26, 1776

Dublin.
Died: Wednesday last, in Fleet st., Miss Carncart, sister of Mrs. Hamilton of
Omagh; in Corn-market, James Corbally, linen draper.

434 - Fri., Aug. 2, 1776

Dublin.
Married: Rev. Mr. Sandys jr. to Miss Tighe, Co. Wicklow; Thomas Ledwich,
counsellor at law, to Miss O'Neil of Ely Place; John Henzell, the Little
Green, to Miss Hudson, Co. Kildare; John Boucher Brampton, to Snugborough, to
Widow Carr; Rev. James Hewet, eldest son of the Lord High Chancellor, to Miss
Pomeroy, daughter of Arthur Pomeroy, member of parliament for Co. Kildare.
Died: July 4 at Westport, John Earl of Altamont, age 67; July 18 at
Castledawson, Co. Derry, age 84, Mrs. Catherine Nicolson, daughter of the
late Archbishop of Cashell; in Watling st., Mr. Flood, skinner, by a fall
from his horse; at Drumcondra, Whitfield Harvey, typographer; in Werburgh
st., John Bell, woollen factor; in Abbey st., the Lady of Capt. Ormsby.

Londonderry.
Ads: Charles Harkin, Prospect, Co. Tyrone, accused as accessory in the death
of John M'Carter, Malin, Co. Donegal, has surrendered himself to the gaoler
at Lifford.

435 - Tues., Aug. 6, 1776

Dublin.
Monday, --- Nowlan, a soldier in the 66th Regiment, was shot in Phoenix Park
for repeated desertions and robbery.

436 - Fri., Aug. 9, 1776

Londonderry.
Ads: Archibald Courrey, Belfast, Co. Antrim, accused as accessory in the
death of Jane Gormley alias Sutherland, wife of Kennety Sutherland, gardiner
in Belvoir, Co. Down, will surrender himself to the gaoler of Londonderry.

437 - Tues., Aug. 13, 1776

Dublin.
Married: Abraham Fuller, counsellor at law, to Miss Kitty Williams, Co.
Kildare; David Nixon Donellan to Miss Cullen; Edward Smith Maine, Co. Louth,
to Miss Palmer, Palmerstown; Mr. Wood, porter merchant, to Miss Paine, Meath
st.; James Fagan, merchant, Usher's quay, to Miss Coppinger of Hawkins st.;
Rev. Mr. Brady, Co. Carlow, to Miss Paine; Rev. David O'Brien to Miss
Hamilton, Co. Westmeath; Thomas St. George, member of parliament, to Miss
Acheson, daughter of Lord Gosford, at Gosford Castle, Co. Armagh; Rev.
Benedick Arthur, Scafield, to Miss Bunbury, Co. Carlow.
Died: in Leeson st., Rev. Dr. Thomson, rector of Drumcree; Charles M'Dermot,
Co. Roscommon.

Londonderry.
Died: last Friday, age 70, David Ross, many years an alderman.

438 - Fri., Aug. 16, 1776

Dublin.
Married: at Monaghan, Co. Fermanagh, John Johnston, Brookhill, Co. Leitrim to
Miss Weir, daughter of Alexander Weir; Rev. Chamberlain Walker, rector of
Rosconnel, to Miss Glascock.

440 - Fri., Aug. 23, 1776

Dublin.
Married: Rev. Alexander Downes to Miss Jessop, King's Co.; Will. M'Kay,
attorney, to Miss Culter of Summer-hill; John Carleton to Miss Hodgson of
Ship st.
Died: on Usher's island, Mr. Archbold, paper-maker; at Booterstown, Mrs.
Robert Price; in Nassau st., Master William Beaufort.

Bankrupt: William Seed, Belfast, merchant.

442 - Fri., Aug. 30, 1776

Dublin.
Mrs. Mary Johnson of Marlborough st. was murdered; accused are Mary Martin and Thomas Maguire.
Married: William Monsell, Co. Limerick, to Miss Strettle, Fleet st.; Rt. Stevenson, bookseller, to Miss Anne Cuming, both of Newry; Samuel Ryder to Miss Anne Strong, George's quay; James M'Kiernan to Miss Clarke, Co. Westmeath; C. D. Medlicot to Miss Meredith, King's Co.; R. L. Everard to Miss Cuffe; John Poe to Miss Barton.

Londonderry.
At the Omagh assizes, Charles Sproul was acquitted in the murder of Anne Dougherty. At the Derry assizes, Arch. Curry was acquitted in the death of Jane Gormley and John Gordon was acquitted in the rape of Anne Pilkington.

445 - Tues., Sept. 10, 1776

Dublin.
Patrick Lynch, Oughernone, Co. Kerry, saw an apparition in a graveyard.

447 - Tues., Sept. 17, 1776

Dublin, Sept. 14.
Patrick Buchanan was executed last Saturday for robbery; he admitted robbing Mr. Allen some time ago.

448 - Fri., Sept. 20, 1776

Dublin.
Thomas Connor, charged with the murder of ---- Howel, arrived here from England under guard.

Londonderry.
John Coningham, high sheriff of the City and County of Londonderry, was elected alderman in place of the late Alderman Ross.

449 - Tues., Sept. 24, 1776

Dublin.
Catherine Molloy, church of Mountmelick, convert to the Church of Ireland. Died: in Queen st., age 82, Dix. Coddington; at Kilkenny, Capt. Stopford of the 1st Horse; in Capel st., Michael Clarke, Examiner of Excise in the Custom House; James Jackson, age 22, a student in Trinity College; Mrs. Blakeney, wife of Charles Blakeney, Co. Roscommon; the Lady of Sir John Freke, bart., Co. Wexford; at Kerb_fe, Richard Butler; at Glasnevin, Mrs. Phepoe (?); near Wexford, Samuel Batt; Rev. Thomas Plunkett, dissenting minister of the Strand st. congregation, Wednesday, age 51.

451 - Tues., Oct. 1, 1776

Dublin, Sept. 24.
Died: Henry Kyle of Mornbeg near Omagh, of a fall from his horse; in Grafton st., Henry Graydon; at St. Catherines, Mrs. Marlay; near Cashel, Thomas Lloyd Prince; John Lawrenson, Co. Kilkenny.

453 - Tues., Oct. 8, 1776

Londonderry.
Married: at Newtonheath near Manchester, England, John Mitchel, M.D. of this city to Miss Goodyeare.

454 - Fri., Oct. 11, 1776

Dublin, Oct. 8.
Nicholas Hussey, Dublin, convert to the Church of Ireland. Mary Brien of
High st. was delivered of three boys and a girl; all were doing well.
Died: in Aire, Scotland, the wife of Rev. Mr. Hazlet of this city; in Dame
st., George Harpur, door-keeper to the House of Commons; in Kilkenny, Robert
Stotesbury; on Milltown Road, James Price, a Welsh gentleman.

455 - Tues., Oct. 15, 1776

Londonderry.
Married: Friday last, William Patterson, M.D. to Miss M'Connell, both of this
city.
Died: Friday last, Mrs. Mary Preston, relict of the late James Preston, of
this city.
Ads: John Mooney, age about 24 years, deserted from the 3rd Horse at Carlow;
born in the parish of Clonmany, Co. Donegal; his last residence was
Londonderry.

456 - Fri., Oct. 18, 1776

Londonderry.
Married: Tuesday last, John Irwin to Miss Boyd; he is a 70 year old chimney
sweep who buried his second wife six weeks ago; she is 35 inches tall and
three feet wide.
Ads: Bartholomew O'Cain warns against Mary Bar of Loughtylobe, parish of
Banagher, Co. Londonderry, who robbed her own husband's house.

457 - Tues., Oct. 22, 1776

Corke.
Gotfred Gerard Fehrman vs. William Falkiner, Charles M'Carthy, and Sam.
Phillips (government agents); for detaining his wife Mrs. Ann Fehrman for
three hours.

Londonderry.
Mr. M'Clellan, Dunduff's Fort, parish of Rye, Co. Donegal, was murdered on
the road.

458 - Fri., Oct. 25, 1776

Dublin, Oct. 12.
Married: Edward Ferguson, Co. Donegal, to Miss Anne Montgomery of same;
Benjamin Thomas to Miss Anne Redford, Co. Wexford; Capt. Simmons of the
Active to Miss Brown of Parkgate; Hugh Lynch, merchant, to Miss Connell, both
of Drogheda; John Burke, Bride st., linen draper, to Miss Cullidon; Edward
Shaw, Co. Kildare, to Miss Anne Jane M'Causland; at Downpatrick, John Speers,
apothecary, to Mrs. Webb.

Londonderry.
Ads: James Macklin not responsible for the debts of his wife, Elizabeth
Macklin or Rogers, or her mother, Sarah Rogers.

459 - Tues., Oct. 29, 1776

Dublin, Oct. 26.
Mary Martin was found guilty of the murder of Mary Johnson.
Died: Percival Hunt, the senior Alderman of this city; in Sligo, Patrick
Reilly; in Capel st., John Higgenbotham; in Kildare st., Charles Curtis; at
Glassnevin, the Lady of E. Netterville; on Ormond-quay, Thomas Finlay,
banker; at Ball's bridge, Samuel Grant, linen printer; in Chancery lane, John
Smyth, attorney, and secretary to the Lord Chancellor; at Kilkenny, Alderman
Gore; at Enniscorthy, Mrs. Clare Sutton; near Cork, Col. Whyte; at Coleraine,

Mrs. Robert Galt; in Abbey st., Mrs. Robert Mayne; Rev. Peter Chaigneay, Secretary to the Dublin Society; in Queen st., John Nugent; at Maryborough, Surgeon Despard.

461 - Tues., Nov. 5, 1776

Dublin.
George Alcock, George's Hill, was elected alderman in place of Alderman Hunt, deceased.

462 - Fri., Nov. 8, 1776

Londonderry.
Ads: Hugh O'Donnell, Comber Claudy, not responsible for debts of his brother Richard O'Donnell. William Knox, Kilcadden, acting executor of the estate of the late Charles Ramsay, Dowish, Co. Donegal. Deserted from the 3rd Foot (Buffs) at Castle Comber, Co. Kilkenny: Patrick M'Namee, age 19 years 5 months, born Carrickghan, Co. Tyrone, laborer, enlisted at Strabane April last; Michael M'Colghan, age 17, born Taughboyne, Co. Donegal, laborer, red hair, enlisted at Strabane April last; and Patrick Kelly, age 17 years 7 months, born in parish of Conwell, Co. Donegal, laborer, enlisted at Strabane April last; they all went off in their uniforms.

464 - Fri., Nov. 15, 1776

Dublin, Nov. 11.
Married: at Belfast, Mr. Rodger, book seller, to Miss Elizabeth Sloss; Capt. John Campbell to Miss Martin of Mecklenburgh st.; Mr. Perrin of Castle st., apothecary, to Miss Andrews of the Upper Coomb; Mr. Burnet, Corke, merchant, to Widow Perrier of Kevan st.
Died: Rev. Mr. Killburn, Presbyterian minister; the wife of Rev. Sam. Kearnes of Cookstown; at Monaghan, Mr. Rogers, attorney.

Londonderry.
Died: yesterday, Mrs. Margaret Scott, wife of William Scott, merchant of this city.

465 - Tues., Nov. 19, 1776

Londonderry.
Saturday evening died Mr. Patrick Bradley, publican, leaving a wife and children.

469 - Tues., Dec. 3, 1776

Dublin, Nov. 30.
Miss Martha Carrol, Kilfadda, Co. Tipperary, and Catherine M'Ilwaine, Letterkenny, converts to the Church of Ireland.

470 - Fri., Dec. 6, 1776

Dublin.
Married: John Burke, attorney, to Miss Eleanor Hampton of Capel st.; Pat. Stewart, Newry to Miss Jane Mollan, Dungannon; Garret Tyrel, Co. Westmeath to Miss Montgomery, Co. Monaghan; John Hays, attorney, to Miss Carroll, Co. Tipperary; Ed. Morris to Miss Jones, both of Co. Meath; Robert Kinnier, printer, to Miss Christian; T. Carthy to Miss Kiernan, both of Co. Cavan.
Died: in Stafford st., Mrs. Cope, sister to the Bishop of Clonfert; at Newry, Mr. Burke, broker; in Winetavern st., Mr. Larkin of the Rolls Office; in Fishamble st., Pierce Byrn, attorney; at Ricehill, William Villers, Co. Cavan; Thomas Fetherson, Co. Westmeath.

471 - Tues., Dec. 10, 1776

Castlebar, Nov. 26.
Last night the elegant house of Edward M'Donnell of Brendrem burned down (in
the loss was the entire correspondence of Bennet Lord Arlington, Secretary to
Charles II).

Londonderry.
Died: yesterday, Catherine, wife of David Ross of this city.
Ads: The still of John Floyd, deceased, at Ballycallen in Fannet to be sold
by Robert Gara and Alexander Ewing.

472 - Fri., Dec. 15, 1776

Dublin.
Married: at Cashel, Law. Clutterbuck to Miss Cooper; Ed. Beesley to Miss
Bowen; John Francis to Miss St. George.
Died: in Capel st., Rev. Dr. Townly Smith of Coollystown; in Michael's lane,
Peter Cooke, attorney; John Gibbony, age 100.

Londonderry.
Ads: James M'Clintock, Trintaugh, reward for information concerning the
murder of George M'Clellan at Garfuey, Oct. 17 last.

473 - Tues., Dec. 17, 1776

Londonderry.
Ads: Patrick Boggen deserted from the 13th Light Dragoons; age 18, left
Londonderry on Nov. 26.

474 - Fri., Dec. 20, 1776

Dublin.
Mary Donaghy and Anne Gafney, parish of Mullingar, converts to the Church of
Ireland.
Married: William Nicholson, St. Andrew st., to Miss Ryan; Rt. Rev. Bishop of
Cloyne to Miss Benton; D. Leahy, gardener, age 20, to Miss Allen, age 60; at
Newry, Mr. Moore, grocer, to Miss Boyle; William Norcliff to Miss English;
James Bird, Drogheda, to Miss Taaffe.
Died: Rev. Mr. Thornton, Co. Louth, of a fall from a horse.

Londonderry.
Married: yesterday, Paul Tharp to Miss Phillis Tharp, eldest daughter of the
late Michael Tharp, merchant, of this city.

475 - Tues., Dec. 24, 1776

Londonderry.
Married: Thursday at Buncrana, John Hart, son of Rev. Edward Hart of
Linsfort, to Miss Fairly, daughter of Alderman Fairly of this city; at
Lifford, Will. M'Farlane, merchant, to Miss Frances Millar, daughter of the
late James Millar, attorney.
Died: Sunday, John Gonne, tobacconist of this city; Mrs. Hunter, wife of
Capt. Richard Hunter; at Isla, Scotland, Capt. George Murrin.
Ads: George M'Clellan of Dunduff's Fort, Co. Donegal, farmer, was found dead
at Garfuey on Oct. 17; reward for conviction of culprits offered by Tho.
Bateson, John Lamy, Rob. M'Clintock, James Paterson, Hugh Hill, Rob. Gamble,
and Rob. Alexander.

477 - Tues., Dec. 31, 1776

Londonderry.
Ads: Thomas M'Guigan, Londonderry, wigmaker, vs. Neal Carlon, same, wigmaker,
for libel; denies sale of second-hand wigs; mentions George Cary, deceased,

who never wore a wig but always his own hair; and Edward Lynchaghan, butler
to Col. Knox; M'Guigan has a wife and five children, the eldest not quite 13
years old; deposition before Thomas Bateson, mayor. John Dudy, Muff,
butcher, was murdered by Patrick Begley of Muff, who is age 48, has ruddy,
red beard, etc.; reward for his capture offered by Martha Dudy alias M'Namee.

478 - Fri., Jan. 3, 1777

Londonderry.
Died: Mrs. Marshall, wife of Rev. Mr. Marshall of Fahan, and sister of Col.
Knox of Prehen.
Ads: Hugh Hill and Will. Lecky, executors of the estate of Will. Hogg,
deceased, and Will Ross (Lecky and Ross heirs of Hogg) vs. Isaac Read, Mary
his wife, George Hart (only son of Elizabeth Hart, deceased) (Mary Read and
George Hart being heirs of Charles M'Manus, deceased); land to be sold.

479 - Tues., Jan. 7, 1777

Dublin.
Thomas Lee, former employee of the General Post Office, was gaoled for murder
of his wife.

Londonderry.
Ads: Mary Begly declares her husband's innocence of murder in the death of
John Dudy on Dec. 13.

481 - Tues., Jan. 14, 1777

Dublin.
Married: at Brussels, John Thomas Foster, Co. Louth, member of parliament, to
Miss Hervey, second daughter of the Bishop of Derry; Rev. Mr. Jameson, St.
Mary's parish, to Miss Ellis, Stafford st.; at Newry, Francis Evans to Miss
Alice, daughter of William Ogle; James Quin to Miss Greer, both of Newry; in
Queen st., Rev. Mr. Rogers to Miss Taylor; Thomas M'Dermott to Miss Molloy,
Co. Roscommon; John Kilpatrick, member of parliament, to Miss Rochfort; Rt.
Hume, Co. Cavan, to Miss Keogh, Co. Sligo.
Died: Sir Henry Cavendish, bart.; at Carlow, John Tench, Register of the
Diocese of Leighlin; Ed. Mansergh of Cook st., paper maker; William Massy,
brother to Lord Massy; at Portarlington, John Fields, age 90, both born and
died on Christmas day; in Trinity lane, Richard Partridge, merchant, of
London.

Londonderry.
Ads: Deserters from Capt. D. Honywood's recruiting party at Strabane (3rd
Foot): Richard Bartly, Thomas Clark, James Swing, William Jacob, Henry
M'Guigan, John Scott, William Drennon, Roger M'Clousky, Alexander Craig,
Barny Ryley, William Glaughan, Arthur Trenner, John M'Aulister, James M'Nabb,
and Patrick Cole.

483 - Tues., Jan. 21, 1777

Londonderry.
The Jane, Capt. M'Causland, of Derry, was taken by an American privateer but
the ship was returned to Derry by Mr. Bachop, formerly of Derry, whom the
Americans had placed in command.

484 - Fri., Jan. 24, 1777

Dublin.
Married: at Strangfield, Co. Louth, Richard Sheridan, barrister, to Miss
M'Neal; John Beaty, book seller, Skinner row, to Miss Isa. Turvey of Leixlip.
Died: at Belfast, the wife of Henry Joy, printer; at Wexford, Rev. Nicholas
White, Roman Catholic clergyman; in Ashe st., Rev. Mr. Dignam, Roman Catholic
clergyman.

485 - Tues., Jan. 28, 1777

Londonderry.
Died: yesterday, Dr. William Scott, of this city.

486 - Fri., Jan. 31, 1777

Dublin, Jan. 28.
Married: William John Arabin to Miss Molyneux, daughter of Sir Capel
Molyneux; W. Cod, attorney, to Miss Tyrrell.
Died: in Grafton st., H. Minchin; in Leinster st., Owen Lloyd jr.; in Granby
row, the Lady of Clot. Rowley, member of parliament.

Londonderry.
Married: yesterday, Matthew Rutherford, late high sheriff for this city, to
Miss Reynolds of this city.
Died: yesterday, Mrs. Peter M'Donagh of this place.

487 - Tues., Feb. 4, 1777

Dublin.
John Mauleverer, City of Londonderry, merchant and dealer, bankrupt.

488 - Fri., Feb. 7, 1777

Dublin.
Married: Rev. Mr. William Craddock, Dean of St. Patrick's, Dublin, to Mrs.
Newburgh of Co. Cavan; Mr. Homan, Francis st., woollen draper, to Miss
Sto___, Essex Bridge; Mr. Dick of Magherafelt to Miss Ann Buckley; Mr. Crowe
to Miss Morton of Arran quay; Capt. Simon Pepper, 14th Lt. Dragoons, to Miss
Eleanor, daughter of John Andrews of Fermount, King's County.
Died: in Prussia st., John Conyngham, late a Captain of the 29th Foot; at
Agher (the seat of Samuel Winter), Mrs. Reynell, lady of the Rev. Edward
Rynell.

489 - Tues., Feb. 11, 1777

Londonderry.
Mr. Daniel gave a ball at the Town Hall in honor of Mrs. Hervey's birthday
yesterday.

491 - Tues., Feb. 18, 1777

Limerick, Feb. 3.
Last week Mrs. Michael Barey of Mellogh, in the west of Co. Clare, aged 62
years, was delivered of twins.

Dublin.
Mrs. John English, Kilkenny, age 47, twice a widow, was delivered of her
first child, a son.
Married: Rev. John Baldwin, curate of Bossenalis, to Miss Elizabeth Baldwin
of Maryborough, Queen's County; Bryan Kelly, Kilmainham, miller, age 82, to
Miss Ann Murphy, same, age 21; Mr. Bozier, native of France, age 94, to Miss
Jane Williams, age 15; John Wightman to Miss Kennedy, both of Lisburn; Mr.
Dillon, Pill lane, linen draper, to Miss Burn of New row, Thomas st.; Mr.
Perrin, attorney, to Miss Braddle.
Died: in Fishamble st., Joshua Kimster, printer; in Digges st., Rev. Henry
Clark, D.D., formerly Vice Provost of Trinity College.

Londonderry.
Ads: Mary Callaghan alias Deyermort has left her husband William Callaghan of
Garfuey.

492 - Fri., Feb. 21, 1777

Belfast.
The lawsuit between Archibald M'Neil and his brother over the estate of
Ballylessen was settled.

493 - Tues., Feb. 25, 1777

Dublin.
Married: Richard Martin, Co. Galway, member of parliament, to Miss Vesey of
Lucan; Abraham Rider to Miss Harrison, both of Athy; at Derry, Capt. M'Intire
to Miss Binning.
Died: at Caledon, Co. Tyrone, Mrs. Sarah Bringle; Robert Ramsay of Lissnenan
near Letterkenny.

494 - Fri., Feb. 28, 1777

Londonderry.
Died: Wednesday last, John Read, near Rathmelton, farmer, aged 105 years.
Ads: Adam Cruthers of Burt, recruit for the 3rd Horse, is missing.

496 - Fri., Mar. 7, 1777

Londonderry.
This morning died Rose, wife of the late James Harvey of this city, merchant.

497 - Tues., Mar. 11, 1777

Dublin.
Died: Robert Sandford, Governor of Co. Roscommon; in Great George st., Mr. G.
Rowland, printer; in Newgate, Mr. Lee, formerly of the post office; in
Marrowbone lane, aged 80, Mr. Lawrence, gardener; and a few days previously
his wife (they had been married 60 years) at Rapho, Co. Donegal, Jane, wife
of William Colhoun, innkeeper.

498 - Fri., Mar. 14, 1777

Dublin.
Died: a child of Mr. Farrington, age about seven weeks.
Married: Cornet Bever of the 2nd Horse to Miss Watts, Co. Tipperary; Rev.
Dean Ryder to Miss Blackwood, daughter of Sir John Blackwood, Co. Down; Rt.
Rev. Dr. Charles Jackson, Bishop of Kildare, to Mrs. Cope, widow of the late
Rev. Anthony Cope, Dean of Armagh; Benjamin Whitely to Mrs. Dowker.

Londonderry.
Died: yesterday, Mary, wife of Mr. Parkinson, sail-maker in this city.

499 - Tues., Mar. 18, 1777

Dublin.
---- Biggar, a young man, was pursued by a press gang and drowned.

500 - Fri., Mar. 22, 1777

Dublin, Mar. 18.
James Mathews and ---- MacGowan were executed Wednesday for street robbery.
They said they had also robbed James Lowry and the four previously executed
were innocent of that crime.
William Rol, Dublin, grocer, bankrupt. John Holmes, Dublin, merchant,
bankrupt. James Reilly, Armagh, printer, dealer, bankrupt.

Londonderry.
Married: Wednesday last in the Cathedral, George Kennedy to Miss Sarah
M'Causland.

Died: Edward Edwards, Straw, Co. Derry; last Wednesday, the wife of Capt.
M'Connell of this city.
Ads: James Blair, Rapho, apothecary, formerly of Dublin. John Miller, age
19, born in the parish of Glendermot, Co. Derry, a weaver, deserted from a
recruiting party of the 3rd Horse.

502 - Fri., Mar. 28, 1777

Dublin.
Bankrupt: Patrick M'Mahon, Dublin, merchant and trader.

503 - Tues., Apr. 1, 1777

Dublin.
Married: John Stratford, second son of the Earl of Aldborough, to Miss
Hamilton, daughter of Rev. Frederick Hamilton; at Newry, Thomas Benson,
Lieutenant in the Black Horse, to Miss Jane, daughter of Willim Ogle of
Newry; Robert Parson, Belfast, apothecary, to Miss Shanks of Lisburn.
Died: Rev. William Babington, rector of Bellaghy and Kilmacrenon; at Newry,
age 81, Rev. James M'Mahon, titular [i.e. Roman Catholic] parish priest of
Iniskeen.

Londonderry.
Ads: Mary Bradley, innkeeper, will continue the business of her late husband.

504 - Fri., Apr. 4, 1777

Dublin, Apr. 1.
Died: Sunday last, James Crawford of Crawford's burn near Belfast; near
Wexford, Sir John Freke, bart., member of parliament; at Portarlington,
Edward Nugent, brother to the Earl of Westmeath; in Great Britain st., John
Halpin, herald painter; by a fall from a horse, the son of Rev. Dr. Walsh of
Newry.

Londonderry.
Ads: John Campbell, saddler, former apprentice of his uncle Lodowick Kirk;
has wrought in London and Dublin; new shop on Bishop st. opposite the Fish
Market, in John King's former residence.

505 - Tues., Apr. 8, 1777

Dublin.
Thomas Kelly, Co. Longford, convert to the Church of Ireland. Bankrupt:
James Candy, Church st., Dublin, tavern keeper.

506 - Fri., Apr. 11, 1777

Londonderry.
At the Lifford assizes, Charles Mullen was found guilty of stealing linen; he
is to hang.

507 - Tues., Apr. 15, 1777

Londonderry.
Ads: Mary Lockhart, Iskaheen, parish of Templemore, Co. Donegal, deceased;
Victor Robinson, Drumscallan, and William Houston, Ardmore, executors.

508 - Fri., Apr. 18, 1777

Londonderry.
Ads: The house in Shipquay st. and furnishings of the late Mrs. Harvey,
deceased, to be sold. Rev. Ben. Span, deceased, Ballymacool near
Letterkenny, furniture etc. to be sold.

509 - Tues., Apr. 22, 1777

Dublin.
Married: Mr. Magee, bookseller, to Miss Stevenson, Great George's st.; Mr. Buckey, Co. Kildare, to Miss Truelock, Dame st.
Died: in Bishop st., Tho. Hughes, clerk in the War Office; at Gray hill, Mr. Bradley, and next day Mrs. Bradley, who had been married sixty years; Mrs. Ferguson and her child, at Longford.
Bankrupt: Charles Smith and Bartholomew Goulding, merchants; John Andee, High st., woollen draper; James Bacon, Church st., merchant; Robert Johnson, Greek st., merchant; William Fallon, Galway, merchant.

510 - Fri., Apr. 25, 1777

Clonmel.
At the assizes, C. Laughlin, for stealing, was to be executed; Ed. Grady, hanged last spring for the rape of Mary Donohy at Nenagh but afterwards came back to life, to be executed; Pat. Kelly, for rescuing a deserter, was to be whipped.

512 - Fri., May 2, 1777

Dublin.
Miss Mary Colclough, Clonegal, and Mr. Mullowney, Ballybarny, converts to the Church of Ireland, church of Maycomb, diocese of Ferns.
Married: Mr. Ravenhill, Mullingar, to Miss Price, Nicholas st.
Died: at Moorfield, Co. Tyrone, Rev. Tho. M'Donnell, D.D., S.F.T.C.D., rector of Dromore in the Diocese of Clogher; Rev. Alexander Colvill, M.D., in his 78th year, Dissenting minister of Dromore for 54 years; Mrs. Waddell, relict of R. Waddell, Islanderry; at Belfast, old Laird M'Neil.

513 - Tues., May 6, 1777

Londonderry.
Ads: William Scott, merchant, vs. Martha Cowdon, James Cowdon, Reb. Stevenson, Robert Given, and Catherine Given otherwise Stevenson his wife, Sarah Stevenson, and Elizabeth Ross; tenement in Londonderry and other land to be sold.

514 - Fri., May 9, 1777

Dublin, May 6.
Saturday se'nnight, John Hurlay, otherwise Capt. Fearnot, and Owen Sullivan, otherwise Capt. Thunderbolt, notorious White Boys, were executed near Roscarberry, Co. Corke, pursuant to their sentence.

Londonderry.
Ads: Hugh Hill and William Lecky, executors of William Hogg, deceased, and William Ross (William Lecky and William Ross being heirs of William Hogg) vs. Isaac Read, Mary Read otherwise M'Manus his wife, George Hart, only son of Eliz. Hart otherwise M'Manus, deceased, and Meredyth Workman, only son of Jane Workman otherwise M'Manus, deceased (Mary Read, George Hart, and Meredyth Workman being heirs of Charles M'Manus, deceased); D. Ross, deceased, late executor of William Hogg; lands lately held by Charles M'Manus to be sold; rent roll is with Aeneas Murray, plaintiff's attorney.

515 - Tues., May 13, 1777

Londonderry.
Ads: James M'Cormick ran away from the service of Hugh Lecky, Agivy.

520 - Fri., May 30, 1777

Dublin.
Married: William Woolsey to Miss Belsingham of Co. Louth; Mr. Hutchinson, King st., linen-draper, to Miss Humphrys; Capt. Douglas Campbell to Mrs. Gray; Rev. Mr. Kearns to Miss Clements, both of Stewartstown, Co. Tyrone; Robert Read, Bray, to Miss Huggins of Dungannon.
Died: Nat. Clements, Deputy Vice Treasurer of Ireland; at his seat of Dundrum, Co. Tipperary, Lord De Montalt; in Cavendish row, Mrs. Meade, aunt to Lord Clanwilliam; in Dawson st., age 55, James Moutray of Killybrick, Co. Tyrone; at Sligo, Mr. Isaac Powel; at Armagh, Francis Houston, late of Tullydowey.

Londonderry.
Married: on the 17th at London, Archibald Buchanan, watchmaker, native of Londonderry, to Miss Sarah, daughter of Mr. Dutton, watchmaker, of Fleet st.

521 - Tues., June 3, 1777

Dublin.
Charles O'Neill was named the new Port Surveyor of Coleraine in place of Mr. Steel, deceased.
Nathaniel Clements's remains were interred in St. Michan's Church.
Bankrupt: Isaac Middleton, Dublin, grocer; Henry Dea, Dublin, woollen draper; Jonathan Waller, Capel st., linen draper; and Patrick Curley, Galway, grocer.

Londonderry.
Ads: Mrs. Rebecca Hamilton, widow, Ballindrate, tenement etc. to let; James Porter, Ballindrate, and William Keightly, Rapho, agents. Cicily Smith or Linch has separated from her husband, Henry Lynch, Carnamoyle.

522 - Fri., June 6, 1777

Londonderry.
Married: at Rapho, Thomas Venables to Miss King, daughter of Rev. Dr. King, Dean of Rapho.

523 - Tues., June 10, 1777

Belfast, June 3.
Married: Saturday last, Joseph Fulton, Lisburn, to Miss Graham, Belfast.

Dublin.
James Osborne, native of Belfast, captain of the American sloop _Active_, was taken by his crew and sent into Kinsale.

Londonderry.
William M'Grorty, his wife, and two children were drowned when their boat overturned near Dunylong.
Ads: Dan Smyth, breeches maker, who formerly carried on the business for the late John Smyth, continues to carry it on for the widow, at the Sign of the Buck and Breeches, outside Ferryquay gate. Margaret Donichy, wife of Will. Donichy, Rossnagallagh, parish of Glendermot, Liberties of Londonderry, has left him.

524 - Fri., June 13, 1777

Londonderry.
Ads: William M'Crackin, peruke maker, Londonderry, newly arrived from Paris.

525 - Tues., June 17, 1777

Londonderry.
Married: yesterday, Robert Martin to Miss Galbraith, both of this city.

Died: yesterday, Mrs. Lenox, wife of Clotworthy Lenox of this city; Michael
Owens, tidewaiter in this port, leaving a widow and eight children.

527 - Tues., June 24, 1777

Dublin.
Died: in her carriage coming to town, the Lady of Sir William Montgomery.

Londonderry.
Died: Wednesday last, George Church, the Grove, Co. Derry, by a fall from his
horse (a few days earlier, his brother S. Church had a leg amputated and is
despaired of); Friday last, Andrew Stewart, a young merchant some time since
in Maryland, by a fall from a horse in Ards, Co. Donegal; Friday last, Mary,
wife of Andrew Bond, at the Waterside.

528 - Fri., June 27, 1777

Londonderry.
Ads: All debtors of James and William M'Connel, both late of Lustycal, parish
of Taughboyne, are to pay Mrs. Jane Marshall, otherwise M'Connel, Manor
Cuningham, administrator by appointment of the court of Raphoe.

530 - Fri., July 4, 1777

Londonderry.
Died: last Sunday, Alexander Work, late schoolmaster in the parish of Movill;
Mr. Cololly (?) was found dead on Monday.

531 - Tues., July 8, 1777

Londonderry.
Married: at Strabane, Robert Irvine to Miss Mary, daughter of Alexander
Sinclair.
Died: Samuel M'Crea, dealer in this city, leaving a widow with ten children
and carrying the eleventh.

532 - Fri., July 11, 1777

Dublin.
James Bruce, a soldier in the 67th Regiment, was found guilty of the murder
of John Carter in King st., Oxmantown green.
Died: the Earl of Alderborough; Neal Segrave, Co. Dublin; on the 29th,
William Newburgh, Drumcairn, Co. Cavan, age 78; at Bath, Lady Crofton of Co.
Roscommon; the Lady of Ponsonby Moore.

Londonderry.
Ads: Dan Chambers or John Kennedy, Seneschal of the Manor of Lismonaghan,
have two horses thought to have been stolen; James Boyle (abt. 25 years) and
Patrick Davitt (abt. 35 years), the suspected thieves, were rescued from the
constable on the road from Letterkenny to Raphoe.

533 - Tues., July 15, 1777

Dublin.
The two M'Cuorkans or Corkrans lately apprehended in London arrived in
Dublin; they are charged with the murder of a barber near Monaghan some time
ago; had been living with their father, who kept a beer house in London. [See
number 551.]

535 - Tues., July 22, 1777

Dublin.
Married: Mr. Brown, son of Lord Kenmare, to Miss Dillon, daughter of Lord
Dillon; in London, John Forster [sic], eldest son to Sir Nicholas Foster

[sic] of Tullaghan, Co. Monaghan, to Miss Winch, daughter of Gov. Winch; John M'Causland to Miss Pilkington and Claud. M'Causland to Miss Maxwell, all of Omagh; Alex Cochran jr., linen merchant near Derry, to Miss Roden of Dublin.

Londonderry.
Ads: Margaret Huston has left her husband James Huston of Drumraw, near Omagh.

537 - Tues., July 29, 1777

Dublin, July 26.
Wednesday ---- Duffy was executed for robbing the mail; the young man maintained his innocence.

538 - Fri., Aug. 1, 1777

Sligo.
Capt. Parkinson, captain of the American privateer Polly, was born in Londonderry; his crew is mostly French.

Dublin.
Married: Lord St. Lawrence, eldest son of the Earl of Howth, to Lady Margaret Birmingham.
Died: the Earl of Inchiquin; Arch. Hamilton, fellow of the College of Physicians.

Londonderry.
Married: William Glen, merchant, to Miss Hope, millner, both of this city.

541 - Tues., Aug. 12, 1777

Dublin.
Chevalier Jaques Bartheme de Lamote, convert to the Protestant church, parish church of Finglass.

Londonderry.
Died: James Fisher, formerly an innkeeper of this city; the wife of John Cairns, publican.
Ads: The late Neal Campbell's interest in the house and adjoining concern, where George Campbell, baker, now dwells, near Bishop's gate, to be sold. Francis M'Collum, Pat M'Carren, and Daniel Boyle, accused in the murder of Robert M'Cormick at the Old Town of Letterkenny, will surrender themselves to the sheriff of Co. Donegal.

543 - Tues., Aug. 19, 1777

Cork.
Capt. Cleland of the Sally was killed by a broadside from a privateer.

Londonderry.
Died: at Letterkenny, Henry Gamble, formerly of this city.
Ads: Debts owed to the late Robert Ramsay of Lisnenan, Co. Donegal, are to be paid to John Ramsay of Londonderry or James King, Trimra near Letterkenny. Deserted from the 3rd Horse or Carabineers on July 16: James Dougherty, age 18, born at Drumquin, Co. Tyrone, former schoolmaster at Letterkenny; and Robert M'Kim, age 20, born near Lettekenny, labourer; they had been enlisted at Derry by Lt. Daniel.

544 - Fri., Aug. 22, 1777

Dublin.
Married: Col. Sandford to Lady Rachel M'Donnel, sister of the Earl of Antrim; Chevalier Betheme de la Mothe, of France, to Miss Flood of Co. Kilkenny.

Died: Maj. Richard Temple; James Pettigrew, age 89, formerly a linen
merchant; in Castle st., John Armstrong, ribbon weaver.

545 - Tues., Aug. 26, 1777

Dublin.
Died: Alexander Galbraith, of burns received while endeavouring to extinguish
the fire in his house.

546 - Fri., Aug. 29, 1777

Londonderry.
Married: yesterday, William Hope, merchant, to Widow Moore of Butcher st.;
Sam. Tagert, merchant, Strabane, to Miss Armstrong of Magwire's bridge.

547 - Tues., Sept. 2, 1777

Londonderry.
Ads: Matthew Kirwan is to carry on his late father's jewellery and engraving
business.

548 - Fri., Sept. 5, 1777

Londonderry.
Ads: Sally Harkin otherwise Kelly and her husband John Harkin have agreed to
separate; parish of Culdaff, Co. Donegal.

549 - Tues., Sept. 9, 1777

Dublin.
Mention of the bequests left by Mrs. Margaret Algoin, late of this city.

550 - Fri., Sept. 12, 1777

Dublin.
Married: Col. Calendar to Lady Elizabeth M'Donald, sister to the Earl of
Antrim; Rev. Mr. Morgan, rector of Clonuff, Co. Down, to Miss Moore; Charles
Townshend to Miss Smyth; at Ballykelly, James Phillips, bailiff, age 93, to
Isabella Canning, age 19.

Londonderry.
Ads: Michael Dermot, native of Derry, yarnmaker, deserted from the 6th or
Inniskilling Dragoons. Charles Higgins, weaver, age 26, is accused of
robbery by his former employer, Moses M'Kean Ballyskeagh, parish of
Leckpatrick, Co. Tyrone.

551 - Tues., Sept. 16, 1777

Monaghan, Sept. 8.
At the assizes which ended Saturday, Michael Quorkan, who was transmitted
here from London with his two sons, was found guilty of the murder of Arthur
Woods of Ballymackey, near Carrickmacross; to be hanged etc. on the 16th.
Hugh Quorkan, for being an assistant in the murder, to be executed on Nov. 15
next. John Watson, for horse-stealing, to be executed Nov. 15. Bryan
Connelly, for felony, to be whipped. Elinor Smyth, for felony, to be
privately whipped.

553 - Tues., Sept. 23, 1777

Dublin.
Died: in Bride st., William Crookshank, attorney; in the Custom House, George
Shannon, formerly Cashier of Excise; in Britain st., Capt. Richardson; in
Cavendish row, Art Magan; at Drumcondra, Tristram Swettenham; Ed. Murphy of
the Black Rock; in Kildare st., Mrs. Gamble, sister to the late Provost; in

the Custom House, William Hulbertson, Deputy Receiver General of the Port; at
Belfast, Alexander Legg.

Londonderry.
Last Wednesday, ---- West, a labouring man, hanged himself.
Died: Michael Priestly, architect.
Ads: Debtors of James and William M'Connell, both late of Lustycal, parish of
Taughboyne, are to pay James Brown jr. of Manor Cuningham and Samuel M'Cay,
Moyle, executors of Jane Martha otherwise M'Connell, administratrix of said
James and William, deceased.

554 - Fri., Sept. 26, 1777

Londonderry.
At the Lifford assizes, ---- Monaghan was found guilty of the murder of her
own child; she is to be hanged.

555 - Tues., Sept. 30, 1777

Londonderry.
Married: John Johnston to Miss Gamble; Mr. Campbell, saddler, to Miss Hay.
Died: the wife of Henry Darcus; Robert Smily, Cams near Strabane.

556 - Fri., Oct. 3, 1777

Dublin.
Died: at Spa on the 11th, Philip Tisdall, Attorney General, Judge, etc.

Lifford.
---- Monaghan, for the murder of her child, was executed Tuesday.

Omagh.
At the assizes, Robert Nethry, was found guilty of the murder of his brother-
in-law John Cook; he is to be executed.

Londonderry.
Ads: Creditors of James Porter, late of Claudy, deceased, are to notify Will
or James Porter, Claudy, executors.

557 - Tues., Oct. 7, 1777

Dublin.
Patrick Campbell and Sara M'Ilhone, parish of Artrea, and Elinor Byrne,
parish of Clonlusk, converts to the Church of Ireland.

Londonderry.
Ads: John Drue, apprentice to Thomas Andrews, Ardstraw, whitesmith, has left
his master.

558 - Fri., Oct. 10, 1777

Dublin.
Died: at Sligo, Lt. Cox of the 1st Horse, an Englishman; at Bristol, Capt.
Cummin of the 1st Horse; at Ballycastle, George Straughton, M.D.

Londonderry.
Married: yesterday, William Ross of Newtown Lemavaddy to Miss Elizabeth
Stewart of Londonderry.
Died: this morning, the daughter of Alderman Kennedy, a young lady.

562 - Fri., Oct. 24, 1777

Londonderry.
Ads: Deserters from the 3rd Horse or Carabineers: David Sheerert, age about

26, born at Ballykelly near Newtown Lemavady, Co. Derry, enlisted 11 Sept.,
1776, deserted 23 April 1777; John Graham, age about 24 years, native of the
parish of Camus near Strabane, wheelwright, enlisted 24 July 1776, deserted
from Kilkenny 11 July 1777; Robert M'Kim, age about 22, born parish of
Templemore near Derry, enlisted 2 Sept. 1776, deserted from Kilkenny 16 July
1777; and James Dougherty, age about 19, born parish of Longfield near the
market town of Drumquin, Co. Tyrone, schoolmaster, enlisted 7 Sept. 1776,
deserted from Kilkenny 16 July, 1777.

563 - Tues., Oct. 28, 1777

Bailyborrow.
John Blessing, a woman posing as a man since the age of 14, baker, was
delivered of a son; mentioned: Mrs. Porterfield, midwife, and Dr. Wright.

Kilkenny.
William Collier, age about 18, servant to Darby Brenan, merchant of this
city, was robbed and murdered.

Dublin.
Died: the Lady of Theophilus Clements; in Frederick st. Counsellor Lord;
Jeffery Symes, Co. Wicklow; Kedagh Gahagan, Co. Westmeath; in Dame st., Mr.
Is. Middleton, grocer; Francis Piers, Co. Wexford.

Londonderry.
Died: William Moore, formerly a merchant in Kilkenny.

565 - Tues., Nov. 4, 1777

Londonderry.
Ads: Elizabeth Hamilton, Ballindrate, Co. Donegal, spinster, died intestate;
Edward Finney warns all her debtors not to pay until an administrator is
appointed.

566 - Fri., Nov. 7, 1777

Londonderry.
Married: yesterday, John Ewing of this city, merchant, to Miss Alexander,
daughter of Peter Alexander, merchant.

568 - Fri., Nov. 14, 1777

Londonderry.
Died: a few days ago, Frederic William Hamilton, son of Cl. Hamilton,
accidentally shot; a few days ago, at Rathmelton, Alexander Nesbit, merchant;
at Castlefin, Mrs. Ralston, wife of Mr. Ralston, merchant.

573 - Tues., Dec. 2, 1777

Londonderry.
Died: at Omagh, Surgeon Maxwell; at Newtown Lemavaddy, Henry Osborn.

574 - Fri., Dec. 5, 1777

Dublin.
Married: Robert Mayne, Dromore, Co. Monaghan, to Miss Waller, Meath; at
Clonmell, William Coppinger of Barry's court to Miss M'Mahon of Clare; at
Belfast, John Brown, age 96, to Mrs. Dunkin, age 83; Alexander Graham to Miss
Donaldson.
Died: at Enniscorthy, Daniel Kelly, attorney; in New st., ---- Woodward, Mus.
Doct.

Londonderry.
Ads: Martha Todd otherwise Marshall, wife of George Todd, Lisnacreve near

Fintona, Co. Tyrone, is unlawfully detained by Allen Marshall; Mr. Todd will
not pay her accounts.

577 - Tues., Dec. 16, 1777

Londonderry.
Married: Rev. David Young, Dissenting Minister, to Miss Gordon.
Died: in Dublin, William Ross of this city.

578 - Fri., Dec. 19, 1777

Londonderry.
Ads: William Maxwell, Omagh, to sell furniture etc. of the late James Maxwell
of Omagh, deceased.

580 - Fri., Dec. 26, 1777

Londonderry.
Married: Rev. John Law, Banagher, to Miss Kilpatrick, Derry.

581 - Tues., Dec. 30, 1777

Londonderry.
Died: in Dublin, the Lady of James Alexander, member of parliament for this
city; near Birr, Claudius Cathcart, former officer of the 50th Regiment; Mrs.
Sloan, wife of Mr. Sloan, attorney.

582 - Fri., Jan. 2, 1778

Londonderry.
Married: Alexander Fletcher, merchant of this city, to Miss Patterson,
daughter of William Patterson; Thomas King of Newtown Limavady to Miss Glen
of Derry; William Stewart to Miss Shannon.
Died: at Gibralter, Lt. Joseph Swettenham of the 12th Foot.

583 - Tues., Jan. 6, 1778

Dublin.
Married: at Taplow Court, London, Hon. Thomas Fitzmorres to Hon. Lady Mary
O'Brien, only child of the Countess of Orkney and of Morough Earl of
Inchiquin; the Earl of Glandore to Mrs. Ward, niece of Hon. Agmundisham Vesey
and first cousin to Lord Viscount de Vesci; at the Earl of Bute's house,
London, ---- Dawson, Irish member of parliament, to Caroline Stuart, daughter
of Lord Bute; Archibald M'Donald, member of parliament, to Lady Louisa
Levison Gower, daughter of Earl Gower; Lt. Barry of the 2nd Regiment to Miss
Stout, daughter of Mr. Stout, hatter.

584 - Fri., Jan. 9, 1778

Londonderry.
Ads: The household furniture of the late Mrs. Crigan (now Mrs. Inns) to be
sold at her shop in Butcher st.

585 - Tues., Jan. 13, 1778

Dublin.
Married: Samuel Strean of Magherafelt to Miss Crawford of Tullyhog, niece to
Rev. James Lowry; Robert Hamilton, Newry, to Miss Kean, Narrow-water.
Died: at Mooretown, Co. Tyrone, Hodgson Gage of Bellarena (buried at the old
church yard in the parish of Magilligan); at Lisburn, Mrs. Heron, wife of Mr.
Heron, attorney; at Newry, Mr. Drumgool, apothecary; near Omagh, Andrew Scot;
at Belfast, Ed. Bailey of Joy, Co. Down; at Mountmelick, Adj. Hemphill of the
4th Horse.

Londonderry.
Died: Sunday last, Capt. John M'Clure of this city.

587 - Tues., Jan. 20, 1778

Londonderry.
Married: John Balfour, M.D. to Miss Moore, both of this city.
Died: Miss Alexander, eldest daughter of Alderman Alexander.
Ads: Robert Clark, Collaghymore near Rapho, will not be responsible for debts
of his wife Jane Clark otherwise Porter.

588 - Fri., Jan. 23, 1778

Dublin.
James Egan, a journeyman shoemaker in Armagh, having a wife and seven
children, was a lottery winner.

589 - Tues., Jan. 27, 1778

Londonderry.
Ads: George Hart, Derry, has separated from his wife Winnefred Hart or Mahon
and children George Hart and Ann Humphrys.

590 - Fri., Jan. 30, 1778

Londonderry.
Ads: David Shearer, deserted from the 3rd Horse (Carabineers); age 29, ship
carpenter, born in Ballykelly, Co. Derry; has a wife and family now at
Drumraighlin near Ballykelly.

591 - Tues., Feb. 3, 1778

Londonderry.
Ads: Debtors of Rev. Dr. Theaker Wilder, Grovehall near Ramelton, deceased,
to pay Letitia Wilder, his widow.

592 - Fri., Feb. 6, 1778

Dublin.
John Craddock (or Captain Slasher), a White Boy, is to be hanged on Stephen's
Green on the 7th for the murder of Ambrose Power of Barretstown, Co.
Tipperary.
Married: John Crawford, Castle Dawson, Co. Derry, to Miss Hamilton of
Monaghan; Mr. Dick, Co. Derry, to Miss King, Mary st.; R. Gage, Stewartstown,
to Miss Wier, Drumkern; Capt. Burrows to Miss Farrell, daughter of Dr.
Farrell.
Died: near Rathmelton, Co. Donegal, Rev. Dr. Wilder; near Newtown Stewart,
James Fitzsimons; at Mountmelick, Lt. Piget of the 4th Horse; Col. Wyne,
member of parliament and Governor of Corke; in Peter st., William Lane,
attorney; in Armagh, Miss Greaves; near Stewartstown, Mrs. James Richardson;
in Ely Place, the widow of Robert Leslie, Co. Monaghan; near Limerick, Rev.
Dr. Kearney, titular [Roman Catholic] Bishop of Limerick.

Londonderry.
Died: at Welshtown, Co. Donegal, Francis Gallaugher, age 107 (he fought for
Berwick at Derry and for James at Aughrim; was discharged in 1715).
Ads: Creditors of the late Robert Coleman, Donaghmore, deceased, are to apply
to John Patton jr., Castlefin.

593 - Tues., Feb. 10, 1778

Londonderry.
On Jan. 26, the brig Ebeneezer of Openrade, Denmark, was driven onto Ardmalin
head, Co. Donegal, and the master, ---- Maire, died.

Died: Robert King, merchant, Ballybofey.

594 - Fri., Feb. 13, 1778

Dublin.
Died: Rev. Dr. Isaac Weld, near fifty years minister of Eustace St. Meeting House.

596 - Fri., Feb. 20, 1778

Londonderry.
Died: Tuesday last, Capt. Patrick Miller; in Moville parish, Inishowen, Mrs. Mary Dobbin, aged 111 years (her descendants including great-great-grandchildren attended her funeral).

597 - Tues., Feb. 24, 1778

Dublin.
Died: in the Kingdom of Grenada, in his 85th year, Don Richard Wall, native of Ireland, Lt. General in His Catholic Majesty's service, formerly Ambassador Extraordinary from the King of Spain to Great Britain; at his house in Eustace St., Rev. Dr. Richard Stewart, Dean of Leighlin.

Londonderry.
Ads: The house in Bishop St. where the late Miss Kirkpatrick lived to let by Jonathan Nicolls.

598 - Fri., Feb. 27, 1778

Dublin.
Died: at Killfaddy, Co. Tyrone, John Elliot Cairns sr.; near Callan, Michael Scot, brother to the Attorney General; in Moor St., Colonel Roberts; in Lurgan St., Col. John Cuningham; at Rapho, Dr. Porter; near Letterkenny, Mr. M'Nutt.

599 - Tues., March 3, 1778

Londonderry.
Ads: Donald and Shane Cramshy, charged with plundering a ship on the coast of Co. Donegal [near Malin head] on Feb. 25, have escaped from Lifford gaol; reward offered by John Boyle, gaoler.

600 - Fri., March 6, 1778

Dublin.
Captain Davis, returning home to recruit, died when the Sir William Erskine, from Halifax to Glasgow, was driven on shore near Sligo.
Died: near Omagh, Rev. Mr. M'Cawell, parish priest of Drumraw and Capagh; at Lisburn, Mr. Fra. Burden, linen draper; at Gloucester, England, Robert M'Lean, aged 142.

Londonderry.
Ads: Edward M'Groary, accused of the murder of Bryan Coyle of Carland, will surrender himself for trial to the High Sheriff of Donegall.

601 - Tues., March 10, 1778

Dublin.
John Mullan and Farrel Harding, parish church of Ballyclog, converts to the Church of Ireland.
Died: Lt. Gen. Gisborne, Governor of Charlemont, member of parliament, and Colonel of the 16th Foot; in Granby Row, Ralph Gore, member of parliament; Rt. Hon. Mr. Dawson, son of Lord Dartry; in Britain st., Lady Doneraile; in Bedford Row, John Carrick, printer; Hulton Bradley, formerly of Dame st.;

Bryan Higgins, M.D., Co. Sligo; in Hoey's court, Mr. Bourns, taylor; on the
Blind quay, William Darquier, merchant; on the Inns quay, Thomas Egan,
merchant; the Lady of Arthur French, Co. Roscommon.

Londonderry.
Ads: William Mulhern, charged with the murder of William Allen, Three Trees,
will surrender himself for the Lifford assizes.

605 - Tues., March 24, 1778

Londonderry.
Died: Friday, James M'Elwee, watchmaker.
Ads: Debts due the late James M'Elwee are to be paid to Mary M'Elwee or to
James M'Elwee at his shop.

606 - Fri., March 27, 1778

Londonderry.
Ads: John M'Closky, Dungwillan, was deserted by his wife Catherine M'Closky
or Dudy.

607 - Tues., March 31, 1778

Londonderry.
Ads: Abraham M'Causland and James Thompson offer a reward for the
apprehension of George Moore, John Dougherty, or Owen Divlaghan of the Lower
Liberties, who are "compleat rogues."

608 - Fri., April 3, 1778

Londonderry.
Ads: Matthew Mains, Gartnarney, parish of Balteagh, Co. Londonderry, has left
his wife Prudence Mains or Hopkins.

609 - Tues., April 7, 1778

Londonderry.
Married: at London, William, son of Alderman Kennedy of this city, to Miss
Parkinson, only daughter of Thomas Parkinson.
Died: at Ballybofey, Mr. G. Basil.

610 - Fri., April 10, 1778

Dublin.
J. Martin, a poor, industrious chairman, was shot dead in a riot at the opera
house in Smock alley; he left a wife and four children. Bridget Higgins and
her daughter, of Lissanaha near Leitrim, are accused of the murder of her
sister.
Died: near Carrickmacross, Rev. Dr. O'Reily, titular Bishop of Clogher; at
Enniskillen, William Carleton; on Temple-bar, Mr. James Parker, comedian; in
Sycamore alley, Mr. P. Fitzgerald, printer.
Bankrupt: John Hoop, Springfield, Co. Down, linen draper; Mathew Small,
Shonetaken, Co. Armagh, linen draper.

Londonderry.
Married: Wednesday last, Peter M'Donagh, attorney, to Miss Falls.

611 - Tues., April 14, 1778

Londonderry.
Died: Mrs. Patterson, wife of James Patterson, shoemaker.

612 - Fri., April 17, 1778

Londonderry.
Died: yesterday, Elizabeth, wife of Capt. James Millar.
Ads: The house where the late Rev. Mr. Humble lived in Newtown Stewart to be sold.

613 - Tues., April 21, 1778

Dublin.
Died: Mrs. Ann Davis, sister to the Countess Dowager of Granard; in Trinity st., Mrs. Jane, relict of the late Ralph Spence of Co. Donegal.

Londonderry.
Died: Sunday last, aged 91 years, William Folliot, oldest member of the Corporation of Derry.

614 - Fri., April 24, 1778

Dublin.
Bankrupt: Hugh Henry Mitchel, banker, broker, and dealer in exchange.

Londonderry.
Ads: William Coningham and Jane his wife vs. Rev. Andrew Ferguson and others, for debts (in the form of liens on the estate of John Hamilton, late of Castlefin, Co. Donegal, deceased, prior to his Deed of Settlement of 1 and 2 June, 1757), lands in the Manor of Castlefin to be sold.

615 - Tues., April 28, 1778

Dublin.
Died: in College green, Mrs. Knox, relict of the late Andrew Knox of Prehen; in Paris, Lady Viscountess Mountgarret; Miss Armstrong, daughter of A. Armstrong of Gallen; Rev. Dr. Bligh, Dean of Elphin; in Capel st., Capt. Thomas Edwards; aged 76, Mrs. Reily, printer; aged 99, Mrs. Nugent, Co. Westmeath; in Henry st., Lady Elizabeth Parsons.

Londonderry.
At the Omagh assizes, Miles M'Grory was found guilty of murdering his wife and is to be hung on the 30th; Charles Kerr, for stealing cloth, to be executed May 7. At the Londonderry assizes, ---- O'Freel, for stealing sheep, to be transported.

618 - Fri., May 8, 1778

Dublin.
Married: John Franks, Skinner row, to Miss Jane Bellew of Londonderry; James Anderson, Fintona, to Miss M'Comb of Omagh; John Hogarty, age 20, to Mrs. Flood, age 86, Co. Dublin; William Barry to Miss Lord, Dame st.
Died: at London, Lord Archer; at Ennis, Thomas Maunsel; at Framemount, Co. Monaghan, Charles Mayne; at Dungannon, Mrs. Higgins; at Darvystown, Co. Westmeath, Francis Hopkins; in Molesworth st., the Lady of Francis Smith; the Lady of Rev. Mr. Hewit; Mr. Clements, deputy surveyor of Ringsend; in Hume st., George Mears; near Loughrea, aged 100, Rev. Dr. Donnellan, fifty years titular Bishop of Clogher.
Bankrupt: Francis Fetherston, merchant; James Maguire, Co. Cavan, shopkeeper.

621 - Tues., May 19, 1778

Londonderry.
Died: at Coleraine, Hugh Lyle; at Muff, Co. Derry, the wife of Rev. James Dunn; at Strabane, Mr. S. Jenkins; at Derry, Mr. L. Benson.

622 - Fri., May 22, 1778

Londonderry.
Died: Samuel Moore, Convoy, Co. Donegal.
Ads: James M'Farland, Teaboe, parish of Donaghedy, Co. Donegal, offers reward
for the location of Robert M'Farland, age about 30, late of same, accused of
stealing two of James's heifers.

624 - Fri., May 29, 1778

Dublin.
Wednesday evening, the youngest daughter of the Earl of Antrim was publicly
baptized, and was named Charlotte, after Her Majesty, by the Lord Primate.
Married: Boyd Maxwell to Miss Margaret Gray, both of Omagh; Capt. Mackenzie
of the 68th Regiment to Miss Trail of Rockmount.
Died: in Aungier st., St. George Caulfield, formerly Lord Chief Justice of
the Court of King's Bench; near Londonderry, Paul Bromhall.

630 - Fri., June 19, 1778

Dublin.
Died: at Brest in France, Lt. Dobbs, of wounds received in the engagement
between the _Drake_ and the _Ranger_; in England, the Lady of John Cowan of
Lifford, Co. Donegal.

632 - Fri., June 26, 1778

Dublin.
Married: Sir Cornwallis Maude, bart., to Miss Isabella Monck.
Died: near Inistioge, Sir William Fownes, bart., member of parliament; in
Bolton st., Redmond Kane, attorney.

633 - Tues., June 30, 1778

Londonderry.
Ads: Hamilton Stuart and Andrew Hannagan, both of the parish of Burt,
apprentices to Capt. S. Hurry of the ship _Amity_, have deserted his service.

634 - Fri., July 3, 1778

Dublin.
Rich. Heron is appointed to the office of searcher, packer, and gauger of the
port of Corke in place of Sir William Fownes, deceased.

635 - Tues., July 7, 1778

Dublin.
Married: in Henry st., Robert Bryan, Co. Derry, to Miss Butler, sole heiress
of the late Richard Butler of Co. Kilkenny.

636 - Fri., July 10, 1778

Belfast.
A letter from Robert M'Clelland, a young seaman, to his mother here, relating
how he and his comrad Robert Horseman recaptured their brig, the _Loyalty_,
Capt. Campbell, from a French privateer prize crew.

Dublin.
Married: Rev. Mr. Burgoyne to Miss Miller, both of Lifford, Co. Donegal; Rev.
Mr. Ryan of Trinity College to Miss Eliza Crosdale of Duke st.; Thomas Lyons
of Belfast to Miss Armstrong, Bolton st.

637 - Tues., July 14, 1778

Londonderry.
Ads: Deserters from the 6th (Inniskilling) Dragoons: Michael Dermot, age 25,
yarn maker, lurking in Inishowen; Will Coots, age 20, Glentymont, parish of
Urney, Co. Tyrone; Hugh Slaven, age 22, of same; John Lecky, age 18, parish
of Glendecky, Co. Donegal; Thomas Charlton, alias M'Cauly, age 20, glasier,
travels in the country and often resides at Muff; Arthur M'Cormick, lower
Behallen, parish of Templemore.

638 - Fri., July 17, 1778

Londonderry.
Died: Tuesday last, Miss Caldwell, daughter of William Caldwell of this city;
at Strabane yesterday, Thomas, son of Robert Porter, merchant.

639 - Tues., July 21, 1778

Londonderry.
Ads: Hugh M'Ginnis, Gortnavana, parish of Tully Aughnish, Co. Donegal,
charged with the murder of Bryan Coyle, Catland, Co. Donegal in January or
February last, will surrender himself for the assizes.

640 - Fri., July 24, 1778

Dublin.
Married: Robert Montgomery to Miss Frazer, Co. Monaghan; Rev. Hugh Owen to
Miss Wilkinson; James Wilson to Miss Faulkner, Co. Dublin; Counsellor
Crawford to Mrs. Barry, the celebrated actress; at Derry, Mr. Ewing, land
surveyor, to Miss Hood, daughter of Mr. Hood, land surveyor.
Died: Lady Elizabeth Fownes, relict of the late Sir W. Fownes and daughter of
the late Earl of Besborough; the wife of Rev. J. Nixon, Co. Fermanagh; in
Suffolk st., Miss Dunkin, daughter of the late Rev. Dr. Dunkin; in Moore st.,
Mr. Moore, attorney; at Donaghmore, Rev. D. Noonan, parish priest; near
Stewart's town, Rev. Andrew Irvine.

"At a burying place called Ahedy in the county of Donegal, there was lately
dug up a piece of flat stone about three feet by two, the device on which was
a figure of Death with a bow, shooting at a woman with a boy in her arms; and
underneath was an inscription in Irish character, of which the following is a
just translation:
'Here are deposited, with a design of mingling them with the parent earth,
from which the mortal part came, a mother who loved her son to the
destruction of his death. She clasped him to her bosom with the joy of a
parent, the pulse of whose heart beat with maternal affection; and in the
very moment whilst the gladness of joy danced in the pupil of the boy's eyes,
and the mother's bosom swelled with transport -- Death's arrow, in a flash of
lightning, pierced them both in a vital part, and totally dissolving the
entrails of the son without injuring his skin, and burning to a cinder the
liver of the mother, sent them out of this world at one and the same moment
of time in the year of Christ 1343.'"

641 - Tues., July 28, 1778

Dublin.
Judith Shiel, Dungannon, was attacked while returning from a fair in
Virginia, Co. Cavan; her life is despaired of.

642 - Fri., July 31, 1778

James Buchanan, Charles Harding, and Edward Kelly were apprehended near
Clones, Co. Monaghan, and charged with the murder of George William Frazer of
Inverlochy in the Highlands of Scotland, some time in August, 1774; they had
been soldiers in a Scottish regiment and quartered at his house and had

deserted after robbing and murdering him; they were to be sent to Scotland for trial.

643 - Tues., Aug. 4, 1778

Londonderry.
Died: last Tuesday at Castle Coole, the seat of Armar Lowry Corry, Thomas Gladstone of Ahenis, Co. Tyrone; at Bath, Mrs. Blacker, wife of William Blacker of Carrick, Co. Armagh, sister of Edward Cary.

644 - Fri., Aug. 7, 1778

Dublin.
James Bourke, country school-master, convert to the Church of Ireland, parish church of Clonmusk, Co. Carlow.

Londonderry.
Died: Miss Stewart, daughter of Charles Stewart, Hornhead, age 14 years.
Ads: by Elizabeth Magill, setting forth that three houses in Wapping advertised for sale as property of William M'Kean are the property of William Magill, late of Raphoe, now of America.

646 - Fri., Aug. 14, 1778

Londonderry.
Died: Wednesday last, Mrs. M'Laughlin, at the Ship Quay.
Ads: Thomas Major claims that the crop and stock of Rossnagallagh, advertised to sell by his mother, Widow Major, is his and will not be sold.

648 - Fri., Aug. 21, 1778

Londonderry.
Ads: Matt. Kirwin, jeweller and engraver, Ship Quay, Londonderry, just arrived from Dublin.

649 - Tues., Aug. 25, 1778

Londonderry.
Ads: Charles Gobbon and George M'Ilheney fled from Kirkeedy after stealing sheep.

651 - Tues., Sept. 1, 1778

Dublin.
Died: yesterday, Miss Hornidge, age 17, of Francis st., of a gun accident.

654 - Fri., Sept. 11, 1778

Londonderry.
Died: a few days ago near St. Johnston, Anthony Thompson; Wednesday last, Mrs. Hannah Ramage, wife of Capt. James Ramage.
Ads: Creditors of Ann Miller otherwise Orr of Gallbally near Omagh are to furnish John Orr of Omagh with an account of her debts. Deserters from the 30th Foot, from their camp near Clonmell: Charles Kelly, age 18, born Rathmelton, flax dresser, whose parents now live at Donylong Ferry; Samuel Rogers, 22, born parish of Glendermot, Co. Derry; James Rogers, 18, born in the lower part of Faughan, Co. Derry; Thomas Quin, 19, born Crossmalane, Co. Mayo; Francis Dougherty, 28, born Milltown of Burt, Co. Donegal; Walter M'Farland, 21, born Liscleen near Dunnymana, Co. Tyrone, weaver; Henry M'Gill, 20, born Moville, Co. Donegal, weaver, formerly at Derry; Thomas Armstrong, 18, born Enniskillen, Co. Fermanagh, weaver; John M'Donald, 15, born at Gortree, Co. Donegal, weaver; Samuel Culbertson, 17, born Glendermot, Co. Derry, weaver; all had been enlisted by Ensign Alexander Hewey at Londonderry.

655 - Tues., Sept. 15, 1778

Belfast.
Died: Monday the 7th, at Manor Pottenger, Mrs. Savage.

Dublin.
Married: on the 6th, William Knox, Kilcadden, Co. Donegal, to Miss Elizabeth, only child of Charles Nesbit of Scurmore, Co. Sligo; Edward Fitzgerald, member of parliament for Co. Clare, to Miss Burton, daughter of Major Burton.

656 - Fri., Sept. 18, 1778

Londonderry.
Died: Wednesday last, James M'Ilwaine, aged 84, of Burt, for many years an eminent linen draper.

657 - Tues., Sept. 22, 1778

Londonderry.
Died: Friday morning last, James Miller, merchant of this city.

658 - Fri., Sept. 25, 1778

Dublin, Sept. 19.
Died: Thursday, Mr. Worthington, Ringsend, in a boating accident.

659 - Tues., Sept. 29, 1778

Dublin.
Bankrupt: Richard Nesbit the younger, now or late of Rathmelton, Co. Donegal, shopkeeper.

Londonderry.
Died: Thursday last, the wife of Robert Hart of Cashel.
Ads: Michael Spence, Donaghmore, warns against Alexander Bradburn who deserted his service as a huntsman after going to Derry upon pretense of his wife's death; Bradburn has no right eye.

660 - Fri., Oct. 2, 1778

Londonderry.
Married: Rev. Harrison Balfour, Derry, to Miss Magawly, Ballycastle; Dr. Mungan, Ballyshannon, to Miss Price, Enniskillen.

661 - Tues., Oct. 6, 1778

Londonderry.
Ads: The stock of the late Anthony Thompson, deceased, to be sold at Summerhill; also his interest in Marymore and Creeve Glebe.

662 - Fri., Oct. 9, 1778

Dublin.
Married: at Strabane, Rev. William M'Ghee to Mrs. Murray.

666 - Fri., Oct. 23, 1778

Dublin.
Died: Charles Dunbar, member of parliament for Blessington; in Nassau st., Mrs. Coote, aunt to the Earl of Bellamont; Andrew Devoy, professor of music.

672 - Fri., Nov. 13, 1778

Londonderry.
Married: Alexander Daniel of this city to Miss Cust, daughter of Henry Cust
of Magilligan.

673 - Tues., Nov. 17, 1778

Dublin.
Died: in Dawson st., Richard, Earl of Cavan etc.; in Jervis st., Mrs.
Elizabeth Ferguson, relict of the late Dr. Ferguson and mother to the Lady of
Sir Edward Loftus, bart.

Londonderry.
Died: yesterday, Mrs. Rev. Mr. Torrens.

676 - Fri., Nov. 27, 1778

Londonderry.
Ads: Mark Ker O'Neill offers a reward for apprehension of Robert Kirk or
Kirkland or Kirkwood or Church, age about 19, who ran away from his service
as postilion; he was from the parish of Moville, near the sea, his mother a
widow, his uncle a miller; he formerly lived with Sir Robert Pynsent.

677 - Tues., Dec. 1, 1778

Londonderry.
Married: at Summerset, Co. Derry, James Stewart, eldest son of Sir Annesley
Stewart, bart., to Miss Whaley, daughter of the late Richard Chappel Whaley.

678 - Fri., Dec. 4, 1778

Londonderry.
Married: at Rathmelton, Rev. John Rankin to Miss Patterson.
Died: at Letterkenny, Tues. last, Rev. John Whittingham, Rector of Conwell,
diocese of Rapho.

679 - Tues., Dec. 8, 1778

Londonderry.
Ads: George Keightly, Rapho, is to receive the debts etc. due to the
partnership of Ann and William Keightly, late deceased.

681 - Tues., Dec. 15, 1778

Dublin.
Died: at London, Benjamin Victor, Poet Laureat of this kingdom; yesterday, at
the palace in Kevin st., Rt. Rev. Dr. John Cradock, Archbishop of Dublin.

687 - Tues., Jan. 5, 1779

Dublin.
Died: at his house in Cavendish Row, David Macbride, M.D.; in Dame st., Mr.
T. H. Powell, printer of the Dublin Evening Post; at Tullagh, barony of
Inishowen, George Dogherty, gent.; Alderman French of this city; near
Downpatrick, Rev. Dr. M'Cartin, titular Bishop of Down & Conor; on Pimlico,
Rev. Mr. Shaw, a Romish clergyman; at Newry, Thomas Carrol, formerly an
eminent mathematician in that town.

689 - Tues., Jan. 12, 1779

Londonderry.
Ads: The executors of the late John Beatty, deceased, are to sell his farm in
Drumhagart.

690 - Fri., Jan. 15, 1779

Londonderry.
Ads: Deserted from the 3rd Horse (Carabineers) at Athy, Dec. 15, 1778,
William King, aged about 22 years, born in Newtown Lemavady, enlisted at
Newtown Lemavady on July 27, 1776.

691 - Tues., Jan. 19, 1779

Dublin.
James Lawder, Kilmore, Co. Roscommon, was slain by armed thieves.

695 - Tues., Feb. 2, 1779

Dublin.
Died: at Sans Souci, Rt. Hon. Brinsley Butler, Earl of Lanesborough; in Abby
st., John Sheene, former examinator of the hearth-money accounts; at Steven's
hospital, Surgeon Mitchel.

696 - Fri., Feb. 5, 1779

Londonderry.
Died: James Vanneck.

697 - Tues., Feb. 9, 1779

Dublin.
Died: at her house in Frederick st., the relict of Henry Cary (interred in
Dungiven, Co. Derry); James Squire, Co. Fermanagh; at his seat at Monivae(?),
Co. Galway, Robert French, member of parliament.
Bankrupt: John Morgan, stone cutter; Henry Hart and John Hart, merchants.

698 - Fri., Feb. 12, 1779

Londonderry.
Married: yesterday, Charles Gray of this city, merchant, to Miss Miller,
eldest daughter of Capt. James Miller.

700 - Fri., Feb. 19, 1779

Londonderry.
Died: Anne, wife of Thomas Davis sr. of Manor Cuningham.

701 - Tues., Feb. 23, 1779

Londonderry.
Ads: George Hogg offers a reward for the apprehension of William Paxton of
Rathmullan, who bored holes in the sloop Betty; age about 40 years, a Scot,
speaks English "with a very oily tongue."

702 - Fri., Feb. 26, 1779

Dublin.
Died: Edmund Butler, Viscount Mountgarret; Thomas Smith, Yeoman Usher of the
House of Lords, etc.; in St. Andrew st., James Anderson, clerk of the
Appearance...Exchequer; in Abby st., R. M. Johnston.

705 - Tues., Mar. 9, 1779

Londonderry.
Died: Samuel Henderson, Rathmullan.

706 - Fri., March 12, 1779

Dublin.
Rev. Charles Farrel, convert to the Church of Ireland, at the parish church
of St. Michael.

Londonderry.
Ads: John Black, Butcher st., will discharge the debts of his father, John
Black, Brayhead. Deserters from the 6th (Inniskilling) Dragoons: James
Robinson, age 21, born in the parish of Clonish, Co. Monaghan, laborer; John
M'Fall, age 19, laborer; Michael M'Dermot, age 20, born in the parish of
Derry, yarn maker; Daniel Tole, age 26, born in the parish of Drumel, Co.
Tyrone, farmer; John Lucky, age 18, born in the parish of Glendaghy, Co.
Donegal, laborer; Patrick Geerin, age 18, born in the parish of Arknish, Co.
Donegal, tailor; Thomas Charlton, age 19, born in parish of Killen, Co.
Donegal, glazier; David Park, age 20, born in the parish of Rye, Co. Donegal,
weaver; Michael Morgan, age 20, born in the parish of Clanoff, Co. Down,
weaver.

708 - Fri., March 19, 1779

Dublin.
Died: Robert Gamble; in Abbey st., Richard Underwood, member of parliament;
in Clare st., John Chaigneay, Treasurer to the Ordnance; at Dunshaghlin, Co.
Meath, Patrick Supple; at Summerhill, Mrs. Rowley; at Chapel-izod, Mrs.
Dawson and the next day her daughter, Miss Dawson; in Francis st., Mr.
Reynolds, mercer.

Londonderry.
Ads: Hugh Muckerlane, Bellaghmedan, was deserted by his wife, Anne M'Intire
or Muckerlane.

709 - Tues., March 23, 1779

Dublin.
Bankrupt: Richard Underwood, dealer in exchange.

713 - Tues., April 6, 1779

Dublin.
Died: Mrs. Verpyle, wife of a stone cutter in Batchelor's walk, by falling
from a window; last Saturday at Dundalk, Thomas Tennison, justice of the
Court of Common Pleas; in Stafford st., Ed. Forster, M.D.; in Cellbridge,
Sylvan Conyngham, son of the late Rev. William Conyngham of Newtown Lemavady,
Co. Derry.
Married: Wybrants Olphert to Miss Smith; Mr. Wier, attorney, Co. Sligo, to
the widow Farrel of Sligo.

Londonderry.
At the assizes, Denis Kane was found guilty of breaking into the house of
David Read, near Garvagh, Co. Derry; to be executed Saturday next.

714 - Fri., April 9, 1779

Belfast, Apr. 6.
Died: yesterday, Rev. George Kennedy, dissenting minister of Lisburn;
Thursday last, John Spratt of this place, merchant; at Bray, John Holmes, age
77, married three days previously to a widow at Stewartstown.

Dublin.
John Johnson of Farncassidy, James Johnson of Maghermona, and three others
drowned on Lough Erne above Belleek.

Londonderry.
Thursday last, William Blacker, convicted in Co. Tyrone of burning the house of James Heathers near Moy, was hanged and beheaded at Omagh.
Died: Mr. S. M'Farland; the wife of Paul Tharp, merchant.

715 - Tues., April 13, 1779

Londonderry.
Denis O'Kane was executed pursuant to the sentence for breaking into the house of David Reed of Moyltragh near Garvagh.
Died: at Omagh, Rev. William Pilkington.

716 - Fri., April 16, 1779

Dublin.
Rev. Peter Roe, parish priest of Riddenstown, Co. Meath, convert to the Church of Ireland.

718 - Fri., April 23, 1779

Londonderry.
Ads: James Parkinson, sail maker, Derry, is going to settle abroad.

719 - Tues., April 27, 1779

Corke.
In a duel between Lt. Dixon of the navy and Dr. Newtown of this city, surgeon and apothecary, the latter died.

Dublin.
Married: James Colhoun, Co. Tyrone, to Miss Coghlan of Capel st.; Mr. Carey to Miss Grayson; Rev. Mr. Daniel, Co. Meath, to Miss Fortescue; Rev. Mr. Moore to Miss Verner of Churchill.

Londonderry.
Married: George Lenox of this city to Miss Hamilton, daughter of the late Counsellor Hamilton.

720 - Fri., April 30, 1779

Dublin.
Richard Talbot, Mallahide, convert to the Church of Ireland.

721 - Tues., May 4, 1779

Dublin.
Rev. Barnabas O'Farrel, a Capuchin Friar, convert to the Church of Ireland, at the church of St. Michan.

724 - Fri., May 14, 1779

Londonderry.
Ads: Mary Limerick vs. James and Margaret Gourney and Mary Limerick vs. James, Joseph, and Margaret Guerney; John Darcus and Matthew Rutherford, late Sheriffs of the City and County of Londonderry are to sell the Gourneys' interest in a tenement at the Waterside in Derry and part of the Termon or Errenagh Lands of Clooney, formerly occupied by John Read, deceased.

725 - Tues., May 18, 1779

Londonderry.
Married: Alexander Lecky, Capt. in the 1st Horse, to Miss Cottingham, daughter of Rev. Mr. Cottingham, Co. Cavan.

Died: at Rapho, the wife of Rev. Mr. Greenfield; in this city, Mrs. Pye, wife of Mr. Pye, comedian.

727 - Tues., May 25, 1779

Limerick, May 10.
Saturday last, Thomas Lloyd, Cloverfield, brother of doctor Lloyd of this city, was killed by a bull. Sarah Crofts, convert to the Church of Ireland.

Londonderry.
Died: Sunday last, Mr. Edward Schoales of this city.

729 - Tues., June 1, 1779

Dublin.
Died: in Co. Galway, Patrick Hamilton; at Loughrea, Nicholas Lynch; at Birr, Francis Rolleston; in Co. Longford, Mrs. Denny, aged 102 years; at Sligo, Mr. Hartley, aged 96 years; at Belfast, Mr. Noseda, instrument maker; at Favour Royal, Co. Tyrone, John Moutray; at Shamsany, Co. Monaghan, the wife of James Corry; on Summer hill, John Read; in King st., Eatton Stannard, student of Trinity College; in Hanover lane, Mrs. M'Cullogh, aged 102 years; in Capel st., Cornelius Wynne, bookseller.

730 - Fri., June 4, 1779

Belfast, May 28.
Died: Monday last at Newry, Rev.James Moody, for 40 years dissenting clergyman of that place.

Dublin.
Timothy Tracy, convert to the Church of Ireland at the parish church of Monnkstown.
Died: the Archbishop of Cashel.

Londonderry.
Married: Capt. Andrew Miller to Miss Finlay, both of this city.

733 - Tues., June 15, 1779

Limerick.
Mr. Kennedy O'Kennedy and Margaret his wife, converts to the Church of Ireland, at the Cathedral.

Dublin.
Bankrupt: Paul Benson, Corke; James Doyle, Dublin; Thomas King, Newtown Lemavady.

Londonderry.
Died: in Dublin, George Cary, age 21, of Redcastle (body was returned to Redcastle for burial).

734 - Fri., June 18, 1779

Londonderry.
Died: Tuesday, Mrs. Anne, wife of John Kinnear of Greenfield.

736 - Fri., June 25, 1779

Londonderry.
Married: yesterday, Mr. Stevens, sugar merchant of this city, to Miss Gray, daughter of Hugh Gray of Burt.

737 - Tues., June 29, 1779

Dublin.
Married: James Scot, son of the late Baron Scot, to Miss Leslie, daughter of
the late Bishop of Limerick; John Scot, the Attorney General, to Miss
Lawless.

743 - Tues., July 20, 1779

Londonderry.
Married: at Letterkenny, John Hunter to Miss Groves; Mr. Sayers of Convoy to
Mrs. M'Clenachan of Strabane.
Died: at Rathmelton, Henry Patterson; at Lifford, Surgeon Gillespy.

745 - Tues., July 27, 1779

Kilkenny.
Pat Duffy of near Kellymount was slain by White Boys.

747 - Tues., Aug. 3, 1779

Dublin.
Died: at his house in Gloucester st., Col. Arthur Browne, brother of the Earl
of Altamont, member of parliament, age 47; at his house in Henry st., of a
dueling wound, William Henry Wall; on Temple bar, Thomas Euart, book binder.

Londonderry.
Ads: Mrs. Jane Thompson, widow, of Summer Hill near St. Johnston, stock,
crops, and furniture to sell.

751 - Tues., Aug. 17, 1779

Londonderry.
Ads: Jean Montgomery has left her husband Samuel Montgomery.

752 - Fri., Aug. 20, 1779

Londonderry.
Ads: Thomas Strawbridge and Will Scot, executors of the late James M'Cleary,
deceased, are to set his farm in Tartnakelly, parish of Ballykelly.

753 - Tues., Aug. 24, 1779

Londonderry.
Dan. Gallagher and Pat. Johnson, condemned at the Tyrone assizes for robbing
the house of Mr. Harper near Derge, were executed at Omagh.
Died: yesterday, the wife of William Deering, surveyor of excise.

755 - Tues., Aug. 31, 1779

Londonderry.
Died: yesterday in Ferryquay st., Miss Martha Young.

756 - Fri., Sept. 3, 1779

Limerick, Aug. 2_.
At the assizes, Margaret M'Coy, for destroying her new-born infant, was
sentenced to be strangled and burned next Saturday.

Dublin, Aug. 31.
Died: at Swadlinbar last Sunday, William Henry Viscount Carlow, aged 67.

759 - Tues., Sept. 14, 1779

Limerick, Aug. 30.
Last Saturday, Margaret M'Coy was hanged and burned at Gallows green.

Kilkenny.
At the assizes at Maryborough, Catharine Parkinson, for the murder of her
husband James Parkinson, was to be burned alive, Sept. 16; Daniel Daly, for
the murder of Michael Conrahy by cutting his throat in the jail of
Maryborough, was to be drawn, hanged, and quartered on Sept. 9.

760 - Fri., Sept. 17, 1779

Belfast.
Thomas Allen, grenadier in the 30th Foot, was killed by Antonio Dies Monte, a
Portugese sailor.

761 - Tues., Sept. 21, 1779

Dublin.
Married: George Bateson, London, to Miss Prudence, daughter of Edward Brice,
Belfast.
Died: Rt. Rev. Dr. Richard Chenevix, Bishop of Waterford; near Waterford,
aged over 100 years, Widow Sheafts, commonly called the Queen of Creaden;
near Dromore, Rev. John Cochran, a young dissenting minister.

762 - Fri., Sept. 24, 1779

Londonderry.
Ads: Jane Martin, daughter of the late Catherine Martin, Freeschool lane,
will continue her mother's cake-making business.

765 - Tues., Oct. 5, 1779

Dublin.
Married: at Moore hall, Co. Down, John Elliot Carns of Saville lodge, Co.
Tyrone, to Miss Moore.

Londonderry.
Ads: John Tyrrell, Strabane, and Charles Gallagher, Letterkenny, to let the
house and tenement in Letterkenny lately possessed by Rev. Dr. Whittington,
deceased.

767 - Tues., Oct. 12, 1779

Londonderry.
Ads: Thomas Bateson to set the house in which the late Matt. Kirwan lived.

768 - Fri., Oct. 15, 1779

Corke.
After a duel between Athenasius Nagle and Maur. Courtney, the former is not
expected to survive.

Londonderry.
Catherine Dermot, servant to a farmer near this city, was missed on October
4; her body was found in the river near the Ferry Quay on Sunday last; she
was pregnant; two men were confined on suspicion.
Married: yesterday, Will. Walker, lately returned from the East Indies, to
Miss Curry, daughter of Sam. Curry of this city.
Died: near Rapho, Samuel Knox; Rev. John Elder, aged 8_ years, over fifty
years dissenting minister at Aghadoey, Co. Derry.

772 - Fri., Oct. 29, 1779

Dublin.
Edmond Ryan was found guilty of the murder of William Wall (in a duel, July last).

773 - Tues., Nov. 2, 1779

Londonderry.
---- Dougherty has given evidence regarding the murder of Catherine Dermot; Mr. and Mrs. Buchanan, with whom she lived as a servant, have been gaoled.

784 - Fri., Dec. 10, 1779

Londonderry.
Died: Wednesday last, Rev. Thomas Torrens, master of the Free School of this city; Thomas Moody, merchant.

787 - Tues., Dec. 21, 1779

Londonderry.
Ads: W. Babington offers a reward for capture of James Clark, aged about 20 years, who ran away from his service.

788 - Fri., Dec. 24, 1779

Londonderry.
Rob. M'Cay, Derg, was attacked and fatally shot on his way to the fair of Drumquin.

789 - Tues., Dec. 28, 1779

Dublin.
Died: in Nicholas st., Andrew Mackelwain, attorney and barrack-master of Derry; at Drumcondra, aged 79 years, Mrs. O'Callahan.

790(2) - Tues., Jan. 4, 1780

Londonderry.
Died: last Thursday, James Galbraith, for many years an eminent school master in this city.

791 - Fri., Jan. 7, 1780

Londonderry.
Ads: James Ramsay, Culkenagh, not responsible for his wife Anne, who has left him.

793 - Tues., Jan. 11, 1780

Sligo.
The following were gaoled for plundering a ship aground at Mullaghmore: Patrick Conway, Daniel Conway, Denis Gallagher, Conell Connor, Martin Gilgan, James Judge, Anthony Burke, Bartly Burke, John Coman, John Conaughan, John Harly, and John Finly.

794 - Fri., Jan. 14, 1780

Dublin.
Bankrupt: Rev. Wm. Rynd, late of Ballynaleck, Co. Fermanagh, clerk, dealer in exchange.

795 - Tues., Jan. 18, 1780

Sligo.
James Millian, Arthur Millian, and Owen Geoghegan, converts to the Church of
Ireland, at the parish church of Ahamlish.

797 - Tues., Jan. 25, 1780

Clonmel.
Catherine Bohilly, only daughter of James Bohilly, Abbea near Clonmel, was
carried off by armed men.

798 - Fri., Jan. 28, 1780

Londonderry.
Rev. James Scot of Omagh was murdered.
Died: John Ellis, formerly of the navy.

799 - Tues., Feb. 1, 1780

Londonderry.
Married: John Chambers of this city, merchant, to Miss Cowan, daughter of
Richard Cowan of Lifford.
Died: Friday last, aged 85 years, John Ewing; the wife of Capt. Johnson.
Ads: A deed to 130 acres in Kent Co., Maryland and other articles were stolen
from James Foster, Bogside.

800 - Fri., Feb. 4, 1780

Dublin.
Born: a son and heir to Mrs. Anne Lunell Cary, relict of George Cary of Red
Castle, Co. Donegal; a daughter to the Lady of the Bishop of Waterford.

801 - Tues, Feb. 8, 1780

Mullingar.
John Gibbs was fatally shot in an accident; he left a wife and six small
children.

803 - Tues., Feb. 15, 1780

Londonderry.
Died: Thursday last, James Mahon, leaving a wife and seven children, a member
of one of the Volunteer companies.

805 - Tues., Feb. 22, 1780

Dublin.
Married: at Rapho, Mr. Feloon to Miss Foster.

Londonderry.
Died: Capt. Fred. M'Causland, Thursday last.

806 - Fri., Feb. 25, 1780

Londonderry.
Ads: J. Macklin will prosecute Charity Coyle, who eloped from his service.

808 - Fri., March 3, 1780

Belfast, Feb. 29.
The Amazon privateer went to pieces in a bay near Bangor in the storm Friday
night last; Capt. Colville, five men, four boys, and seven others perished.

809 - Tues., March 7, 1780

Londonderry.
Died: at Rapho Sunday last, the Lord Bishop of Rapho; Tuesday last near
Dungiven, the wife of Audley Fanning.

810 - Fri., March 10, 1780

Londonderry.
Died: Wednesday last, William Deering, surveyor of excise in this city; on
the 5th at Rapho, Rt. Rev. Dr. John Oswald, Bishop of Rapho.

811 - Tues., March 14, 1780

Londonderry.
Died: in England, Miss Patterson, daughter of Daniel Patterson of this city.

812 - Fri., March 17, 1780

Dublin.
Married: at the Castle, Armar Lowry Corry, a knight of the shire for Co.
Tyrone, to Lady Harriot Hobart, eldest daughter of the Lord Lieutenant.

813 - Tues., March 21, 1780

Londonderry.
Ads: Joseph Smith and Pat Glen, accused of being accessory to the murder of
John Kelly, late of Aughill, parish of Tamlaghtard, Co. Derry, will surrender
themselves for the next assizes.

815 - Tues., March 28, 1780

Sligo.
Robert Bunton and Mich. Rorke, found guilty of the murder of James M'Gaurain,
were to be hanged and quartered on Saturday, May __.

Londonderry.
At the Omagh assizes: Joseph Bell was acquitted of the murder of Rev. Mr.
Scot; John and Charles Ross, found guilty of manslaughter in the death of ---
- Wilson, to be imprisoned twelve months; James Williams was to be executed
for horse stealing.

816 - Fri., March 31, 1780

Londonderry.
The noted M'Cue, with five of his gang (who have, for a long time past,
infested part of the counties of Tyrone and Fermanagh) were taken near
Enniskillen by Volunteers, after robbing the house of Mr. Armstrong near that
place.
At the Lifford assizes, ---- Hamilton, for burglary, to be executed Tuesday
next; ---- Monachan, for stealing yarn, to be executed; Richard and Catherine
M'Dead, for robbing Martha James, to be executed.
Ads: James Smith, Cross, to sell the horse Sir Richard, formerly the property
of Samuel Smith, deceased.

817 - Tues., April 4, 1780

Dublin.
A letter from Enniskillen, March 23, describing the capture of M'Cue, called
Francis Dough, after robbing the house of James Armstrong of Lisgool and
retreating past Pettigo into Co. Donegal.

Londonderry.
---- Miller, found guilty of breaking into a house and carrying off a young

woman, was to be executed.

818 - Fri., April 7, 1780

Limerick, March 27.
John Hennesy was executed last Saturday for running away with Martha Chapman.

Dublin.
A shorter account of the taking of Francis M'Cue by the Enniskillen
Volunteers under the leadership of James Armstrong jr., whom they had
wounded. The graves of Margaret Ringrose or Armstrong, Ballyannan, and of
Jacob Ringrose her son, at the church of Moynoe, near Scarrefin, Co. Clare,
were disturbed for unknown reasons.

Londonderry.
At the Lifford assizes: John Hamilton, for breaking into the house of Mr.
Boyle near Killygordon, was executed on the 4th; ---- M'Fadian, for burglary,
to be executed on the 11th; Richard M'Dead and Catherine M'Dead, for robbing
Mr. James, to be executed on the 11th.
At the Londonderry assizes: David Miller, for house breaking and kidnapping,
to be executed May 6; Anthony Dougherty, for theft, was sentenced to three
years in prison or naval service; Henry Atkin, for stealing, sentenced to
three years hard labor or naval service; Thomas Metham, for theft, sentenced
to five years hard labor or naval service; Thomas Rea or Gilmour, for cow
stealing, was sentenced to same; William Dougherty, J. O'Hara, W. Finigan,
and M. Finigan, sentenced to find 100 pounds security or enter naval service.

819 - Tues., April 11, 1780

Dublin.
An account of the recapture of the ship Lively from Frenchmen by apprentice
boys John Warneck and William Nicolson of Whitehaven and William Carton, age
16, of Drogheda.

Londonderry.
Ads: The household furniture of the late Widow Henderson, Ferryquay st., is
to be sold.

820 - Fri., April 14, 1780

Dublin.
John Hird, Belfast, gardener, employed by Francis and John Mankin near
Belfast forty years ago, described the cultivation of tobacco; Mr. George
Mankin lived twelve years in Virginia and introduced the culture of tobacco
here.

822 - Fri., April 21, 1780

Londonderry.
Respites were given to David Miller, who was under sentence of death at
Derry, and to two men and the woman under similar sentences at Lifford.

824 - Fri., April 28, 1780

Londonderry.
Married: near Letterkenny, Rev. Mr. Barr to Miss Taylor.
Died: at Linsfort, aged 59 years, the wife of Rev. Edward Hart.

825 - Tues., May 2, 1780

Londonderry.
Died: in Ferryquay st., Mrs. Law.

827 - Tues., May 9, 1780

Eniskillen, May 2.
At special assizes, the following were found guilty of robbing James
Armstrong of Liscoole: Francis M'Cue or Prances Dough, Captain of the gang;
Richard Monkham, Patrick Corrigan, James M'Cabe, Alexander Wright, and Bryan
M'Alin.

829 - Tues., May 16, 1780

Sligo, May 5.
Wednesday last, a mob freed Robert Burton and Michael Rorke from the gaol
(both under sentence of death). [See number 835.]

Dublin.
Married: at Limerick, Rev. C. Smith, Prebendary of Croagh, to Mrs. Dancier;
in Pill lane, James Stewart to Mrs. Darley.

830 - Fri., May 19, 1780

Drogheda, May 12.
Soldiers fired on the people and killed five, including Samuel Woodhouse.

Londonderry.
Ads: Andrew Sproul warns against Edward Mullan, a bleacher, who ran away from
his service; he was bred near Cumber Claudy.

831 - Tues., May 23, 1780

Londonderry.
Died: aged 70 years, Mrs. Mary Fulton, Drumbarnet, near this city.

833 - Tues., May 29, 1780

Londonderry.
Died: Sunday last, Mrs. Gordon, relict of George Gordon, apothecary.

834 - Fri., June 2, 1780

Belfast, May 20.
Died: Tuesday last, Henry Show of this town, a respected young man; at
Ballyclaif Wednesday last, Dr. Murray of Glenvany.

Londonderry.
Died: yesterday, George Kirk, aged 79 years, for many years surveyor of
excise in this city.

835 - Tues., June 6, 1780

Dublin.
Two of the three escapees from Sligo were captured in Co. Donegal by
Volunteers. [See number 829.]

836 - Fri., June 9, 1780

Dublin.
An anecdote of Francis M'Cue, lately executed at Enniskillen.

841 - Tues., June 27, 1780

Londonderry.
Died: at Carn in Inishowen, Mrs. Catharine Murray.

844 - Fri., July 7, 1780

Londonderry.
Deserters from the 1st Horse, at Belturbet, June 14: David Fulton, age 23,
born Donahedy, Co. Tyrone; John M'Crab, age 19, born Altaugderry, Co.
Donegal, connected in some measure with Capt. Robert M'Clintock.

845 - Tues., July 11, 1780

Belfast, July 7.
Tuesday last died James White, Surveyor of Larne, by the bursting of a gun
which was being fired to salute him.

Dublin.
Married: Hugh Auchenleck, Strabane, to Miss Stewart, Pill lane; Charles
Clark, Pill lane, to Widow Maguire.

847 - Tues., July 18, 1780

Londonderry.
Ads: John Gallagher, Stradeigh, parish of Glendermot, not responsible for
debts of his wife Martha Gallagher, alias Carswell, who left him July 3.

850 - Fri., July 28, 1780

Dublin.
---- Fleming, wire drawer, Mary's lane, died of food poisoning; his wife and
four children were saved.

852 - Fri., Aug. 4, 1780

Dublin.
Died: Sir Robert Walter, a commissioner of the Revenue.

853 - Tues., Aug. 8, 1780

Londonderry.
Died: Friday at Birdstown, near Londonderry, Mrs. Benson, relict of Peter
Benson sr., of Birdstown, aged 69 years, sister of Sir Henry Hamilton, bart.

855 - Tues., Aug. 15, 1780

Londonderry.
Died: John Hamilton of this city, aged 6_ years.
Ads: James Johnston and Samuel Johnston, both of Lisnagril, Co. Londonderry,
farmers, charged with the murder of Benjamin Lindsay, late of Derrymore, Co.
Londonderry, will surrender themselves for the next assizes; Jeremiah Lindsay
is the father of the deceased.

858 - Fri., Aug. 25, 1780

Dublin.
Died: last Sunday at Cloyne, Rt. Rev. Dr. George Chinnery, Bishop of Cloyne.

859 - Tues., Aug. 29, 1780

Londonderry.
Died: lately in England, Mrs. Susanna Nesbit, daughter of William Patterson
of this city; Saturday, Mr. Pat. Toy, for many years sexton of the cathedral
church of the See of Derry.
Ads: Thomas Jackson, accused in the murder of Philimy M'Cluskey, late of
Culnafuliagh, Co. Derry, will surrender himself for the next assizes.

861 - Tues., Sept. 5. 1780

Dublin.
Died: near Clontarf, Thomas Lord Viscount Southwell; in Camden st., Rev. R.
C. Grange; near London, Sir Patrick Hamilton, an alderman of Dublin.

Londonderry.
Ads: Mary Toy, widow of the late Patrick Toy, will carry on her husband's
glazing business with the assistance of his workmen.

863 - Tues., Sept. 12, 1780

Londonderry.
Died: yesterday, Mrs. Samuel Curry.

865 - Tues., Sept. 19, 1780

Dublin.
At Galway, ---- Mousley, a deserter, was tried and convicted of murder and
robbery of a peddler and murder of his own wife and child.
Died: in Hume st., James St. John Jefferys.

Londonderry.
At the Omagh assizes: Stephen Loughman, for stealing cows etc., was to be
executed on the 28th. At the Lifford assizes: ---- Bradley, for horse
stealing, was to be executed.

873 - Tues., Oct. 17, 1780

Dublin.
At Attyrory, Co. Roscommon, near Ballinasloe, an armed mob went to the house
of Malacky Fallon and there shot and killed Adam Sharpy of Knockhall and John
Gordon, a servant of Mr. Fallon (and mortally wounded others). Patrick Down
and John Flanagan were apprehended at Grangemore near Ballinasloe and gaoled
in Loughrea; they were to be taken to Galway.

874 - Fri., Oct. 20, 1780

Dublin, Oct. 17.
The Aurora, Simmons, from Dublin to Liverpool, was driven ashore on the coast
of Wales yesterday fo'night; Capt. Cooke (owner of the vessel), a Mrs.
Shannon, the mate, and two boys were among the dead.

875 - Tues., Oct. 24, 1780

Dublin.
The body of Edward Dwyer, revenue officer, was found near the Custom house;
he had been missing for fourteen days after a disagreement with the captain
of a Portugese vessel.

876 - Fri., Oct. 27, 1780

Kilkenny, Oct. 18.
At the assizes: Gerald Byrne, Patrick Strange, and James Strange were found
guilty of carrying away Miss Catherine and Miss Ann Kennedy, with the intent
that Byrne and James Strange should marry them; they were to hang on December
2. [See No. 888.] Michael Blenham, for stealing a bullock belonging to John
Lalor, to hang Dec. 2. John Mullowney, for killing and skinning a calf, to
steal the skin, to hang on Nov. 10. Patrick Kelly, guilty of a felony on the
White Boy act, to hang Nov. 10.

Dublin.
Died: at Ballynakill, Queen's Co., John Woodworth, aged 112; at Belaghy, Co.
Derry, Capt. Rankin.

877 - Tues., Oct. 31, 1780

Dublin.
Margaret Reilly, convicted of robbery of Mr. Shields, silver smith, Ormond
quay, is with child.
Died: Rt. Rev. Dr. Samuel Hutchinson, Bishop of Killala and Athenry.

878 - Fri., Nov. 3, 1780

Dublin.
The excommunication of Francis Freeman, late of Co. Dublin but now of Tuck
Mill, Co. Wicklow, who apostacized to the Church of Ireland, was pronounced
by Rt. Rev. Philip Dunn.

Londonderry.
Died: in Persia, George Abraham, son of the late Thomas Abraham of this city;
in England, Joseph Duprey, former Governor of Madra__ in the East Indies,
brother-in-law of Alderman Alexander of this city; in London, William, son of
Alderman Kennedy of this city; at Strabane, James Eaton; near St. Johnston,
Mrs. Cary.

Cork.
---- Gerran of near Castletown-Roche was murdered on Oct. 21 by his wife and
servants.

879 - Tues., Nov. 7, 1780

Dublin.
At Clonmel, Thomas Kyte, shoemaker, a young man, was murdered by five
soldiers of the 12th Regiment on Oct. 15. [A different account is given in
No. 880.]

884 - Fri., Nov. 24, 1780

Sligo, Nov. 14.
Last Saturday Mary M'Dermotroe or Lynch was murdered by her husband, Michael
M'Dermotroe, her brother, and others; the accomplices were caught but the
husband escaped. [See No. 888.]

Londonderry.
Ads: Reward offered for apprehension of Michael M'Dermotroe, aged about 24
years, who murdered his wife Mary near Boyle, Co. Leitrim.

887 - Tues., Dec. 5, 1780

Londonderry.
Ads: John Dougherty, about 21 years of age, a native of the parish of
Ardstraw, Co. Tyrone, deserted from the 3rd Horse at Dublin, Nov. 24, 1780.

888 - Fri., Dec. 8, 1780

Dublin.
The Stranges and Byrne were executed at Kilkenny on December 2. [See No.
876.] "M. Dermotroe" and his mother, sister, and two brothers were captured
at Carrick and taken to Roscommon. [See No. 884.]

Londonderry.
Ads: A reward is offered for the apprehension of John Porter jr. of
Buncranna, who enlisted as a trooper in the 3rd Horse.

889 - Tues., Dec. 12, 1780

Londonderry.
Died: at Whitehall, Co. Antrim, Samuel Delap of Rathmelton, Co. Donegal.

893 - Tues., Dec. 26, 1780

Londonderry.
Married: at Kingston, Jamaica, Lt. Johnston of the 88th Regiment to Miss Boggs, formerly of this city.

895 - Tues., Jan. 2, 1781

Dublin.
Walter Byrne, Kilcullen bridge, convert to the Church of Ireland at the parish church of Carnallaway, diocese of Kildare.

897 - Tues, Jan. 9, 1781

Londonderry.
Ads: George Fulton, about 27 years of age, born at Newtown Stewart, deserted from the 3rd Horse on Dec. 24 and is supposed to have gone to near Omagh, where he has some relations.

899 - Tues., Jan. 16, 1781

Londonderry.
Ads: William Dunn, age about 20, born in the parish of Ballyachran near Coleraine, Co. Derry, deserted from the 3rd Horse on furlough.

900 - Fri., Jan. 19, 1781

Tralee.
The following soldiers of the 52nd Regiment were gaoled by Richard Blenerhasset, coroner, for murder: John M'Laughlin, Hugh Waters, John Duke, Peter O'Neal, Thomas White, Henry Doherty. Those murdered were Florence Sullivan, Danny Sullivan, Denis Sullivan, Daniel M'Carthy, and Florence M'Gillicuddy, all of Kilgarven in Glenerough, on December 20. Sergeant Bell and private David White escaped.

901 - Tues., Jan. 23, 1781

Dublin.
Married: Fred. Geale to Miss Brady, co-heiress of the late P. Brady of Co. Cavan; at Thomas Conolly's by the Dean of Clogher, Rev. Samuel Little to the Countess Dowager of Granard.

904 - Fri., Feb. 2, 1781

Londonderry.
Died: Friday last, Mary, relict of Patrick Toy, late of this city.

905 - Tues., Feb. 6, 1781

Londonderry.
Married: near St. Johnston, Tristram Cary, aged 70, to Widow Woods, aged 75; John Kinnear to Miss Rankin; at Strabane, John Keys to Miss Hays; at Omagh, Denis Gallagher, Drumrah, to Miss M'Evoy.

906 - Fri. Feb. 9, 1781

Londonderry.
Ads: Margaret Coyle alias Gallagher, wife of James Coyle of Taughboyne, has left him.

907 - Tues., Feb. 13, 1781

Londonderry.
Married: Friday last at Strabane, James Orr to Catherine Smily.

909 - Tues., Feb. 20, 1781

Londonderry.
Ads: Stephen Butler, age 27, born Clanmally, Co. Donegal, deserted from the
1st Horst at Belturbet.

910 - Fri., Feb. 23, 1781

Dublin.
Letter from Castle Dawson, Co. Derry, Feb. 11: two young brothers named
Otterson, sons of a farmer, died in a field near their home yesterday. John
and Ann Quinlan and family, converts to the Church of Ireland, parish church
of Cloghan, near Swords. Mr. Lynch of Bray was robbed and shot dead on the
road.

Limerick.
Rev. Patrick Mullconry, convert to the Church of Ireland, at the cathedral of
Killaloe.

Londonderry.
Adam Schoales, Josiah Marshall, and Roger Blackall offer a reward for the
apprehension of Hugh M'Swine, accused of robbing his late employer, Mrs. Mary
Bradley, widow.

914 - Fri., March 9, 1781

Londonderry.
Died: at Bristol, England, Miss Isabel Harrison.
Ads: A reward is offered for the apprehension of Nicholas and Charles O'Kane
of Dreen, parish of Banagher, Co. Derry, who are accused of murdering Patrick
Divin of Stroanbrack, parish of Donaghedy, Co. Tyrone on December 14; their
ages are about 40 and 36 years. Offered by Thomas Bond, Robert Galbraith,
Robert Woods, James Lighton, William Jack, Charles Ramsay, Samuel Lighton,
William Hamilton, William Divin, Patrick Trenor, Henry Donaghy, Charles
Gormley, John Divin, and Widow Divin.

915 - Tues., March 13, 1781

Londonderry.
Ads: Neal Devlin, Aughabane, charged with the murder of Owen Martin on April
11, 1780, will surrender himself at the Co. Tyrone general assizes.

918 - Fri., March 23, 1781

Londonderry.
Died: at Elogh, John Hanagan; the wife of William Stewart of this city.

919 - Tues., March 27, 1781

Londonderry.
Died: Saturday last, Miss Major, daughter of James Major, merchant.
Yesterday the remains of the late Miss Harrison were brought from a Bristol
vessel and interred in the Cathedral churchyard of this city.

920 - Fri., March 30, 1781

Dublin.
John Judge, Peter Martin, and Anne Wilkinson, converts to the Church of
Ireland at the parish church of Cloghran, diocese of Dublin.

922 - Fri., April 6, 1781

Londonderry.
A letter from James M'Ghee, Curate of Faughanvale, verified by Har. Balfour,

Curate of Derry: Tuesday night last a fire consumed the house of Alexander
Ewing in the parish of Faughanvale; he and a grandchild died; his daughter
and son-in-law and five children escaped.

923 - Tues., April 10, 1781

Londonderry.
Ads: The goods of the late Francis Hicks are to be auctioned.

924 - Fri., April 13, 1781

Dublin.
Born: a son to the Lady of Alexander Crookshank, in French st.

925 - Tues., April 17, 1781

Londonderry.
At Carrickfergus Tuesday last, William Fairchild was found guilty of robbing
the bleach green of Mr. Allen of Drumdaragh, his employer; he is to be
executed at Ballymena on the 8th.

926 - Fri., Apr. 20, 1781

Londonderry.
Died: at Ross, Co. Waterford, Nat. Hunter of this city; Tuesday last, Mary,
wife of Stephen Bennet sr., aged 84 years.

927 - Tues., Apr. 24, 1781

Londonderry.
Died: Daniel Swiney of this city.
Ads: John Church of Coleraine (and others, not named) offer a reward for the
apprehension of Robert Jack, Bernard Dogherty, John M'Cay, James Maskimmen,
John Maskimmen, Bryan M'Nogher, and/or Patrick Cushaglen, who are accused of
murdering John Kelly in the parish of Magilligan, Co. Derry.

930 - Tues., May 8, 1781

Belfast.
William Fairchild died two hours before his appointed execution.

Londonderry.
Ads: At Moyle near Newtown Stewart, the furniture of the late Dr. Pelessier
is to be sold. Mrs. Swiney is to carry on the business of her late husband,
merchant Daniel Swiney.

932 - Tues., May 22, 1781

Londonderry.
Died: at Bath, in an advanced age, Mrs. Isabella Forward, relict of William
Forward late of Castleforward, Co. Donegal; her only daughter is the Lady of
Baron Clonmore.

936 - Tues., June 19, 1781

Londonderry.
Died: on Tuesday the 5th, Rev. Andrew Welsh, dissenting minister of Ardstraw,
aged 70 years.
Ads: Mary Agnew and her sister Henrietta Agnew have a new mantua-making ship
in the Cross lane joining Shipquay street; Mary served as apprentice in Derry
and Henrietta served four years to Miss Prentice, who wrought for Mr.
Brownlow and the people of Armagh.

937 - Tues., June 26, 1781

Londonderry.
Died: Wednesday last, John Porter of Burt, gent., Lieutenant of the Burt
Foresters [Volunteer Company].

939 - Tues., July 10, 1781

Londonderry.
Died: Saturday last, Alexander Cummin, cabinet maker of this city, a member
of the Fusileer Company.
Ads: Those indebted to Arthur Vance, late of Dominica, at the time of his
decease, are to pay Montgomery and Gamble, merchants of this city.

940 - Tues., July 17, 1781

Londonderry.
Married: Edward Ross of Newtown Lemavady to Miss Gara of Fannot.
Died: the wife of W. Mountgarret of Kittyban; the wife of Mr. D. Dunbar.
Ads: Deserters from His Majesty's Independent Companies of Foot commanded by
Capt. Bleaket Meares: Peter M'Cavill, age 20 years, native of the parish of
Clogher, town of Newton Saville, laborer; Edward Quin, age 20, native of the
parish of Cappagh, laborer; Charles Dawley, age about 28, native of Strabane
or vicinity, breechesmaker; Owen M'Kever, age about 28, born in the parish of
Drumra, laborer; Thomas Eakins, age about 30, born near Clogher, laborer;
Michael Rielly, age 25, born in the parish of Clogher, laborer; William
Colhoun, age 22, native of Tullymuck, parish of Ardstraw, weaver; Charles
M'Guire, age 20, native of Drumra, weaver; William M'Colgan, age 20, native
of the parish of Rapho, Co. Donegal, laborer; George M'Conkey, age 20, native
of the Milltown of Rapho, laborer; Neal Lafferty, age 18, from the parish of
Cappagh, Co. Tyrone, laborer; Edward Monaghan, age 17, native of the parish
of Drumra, taylor and fifer; Cornelius M'Anulty, age 30, formerly servant to
Capt. Lawson, near Newtown Stewart.

942 - Tues., July 31, 1781

Londonderry.
Ads: The furniture etc. of the late John Tyrrell is to be sold at his house
in Strabane.

943 - Tues. Aug. 7, 1781

Londonderry.
Ads: John Brown and Jenny Brown, Lettermire, have separated. Hugh M'Bryan,
Eskragh, parish of Clogher, is not responsible for his wife Alice M'Bryan or
M'Williams, who has left him.

944 - Tues., Aug. 14, 1781

Londonderry.
Died: Monday the 6th, at Coleraine, the Lady of Richard Jackson.

946 - Tues., Aug. 28, 1781

Londonderry.
Ads: Deserted from the 14th Light Dragoons, at Bandon, Aug. 12, 1781: Daniel
O'Creely, age 19, born two miles from Maghera, Co. Londonderry, enlisted
February last, laborer; and Joseph Nelson, age 19, laborer, born and enlisted
as O'Creely above.

947 - Tues., Sept. 4, 1781

Londonderry.
Married: Mr. Todd, Ballykelly, to Miss Miller.

948 - Tues., Sept. 11, 1781

Cork, Aug. 27.
On the 4th, Margaret Collins was murdered at Gurrane, near Dunmanway, Co. Cork, by her husband John Collins.

Londonderry.
Married: at Newtown Lemavady, Capt. M'Causland to Miss M'Causland, daughter of Marcus M'Causland; James Ross to Miss Ogilby.

949 - Tues., Sept. 18, 1781

Londonderry.
Died: on the 30th, aged 18 (?) years, Miss Mary Stewart Mortimer, youngest daughter of William Mortimer, Rathmelon, Co. Donegal.

950 - Tues., Sept. 25, 1781

Londonderry.
Died: the wife of Mr. Joseph Baxter, Omagh.

951 - Tues., Oct. 2, 1781

Londonderry.
Married: on the 18th at Fort Stewart, Co. Donegal, John Moore, eldest son of John Moore of Drumbanagher, Co. Armagh, to Miss Stewart, only daughter of Sir Annesly Stewart, bart.

952 - Tues., Oct. 9, 1781

Londonderry.
Ads: John Davis, Manor Cuningham, to let farms which are the property of Mrs. Catherine Porter, widow and administratrix of John Porter, Bohillan, in Burt. Susan Speer or Murray, wife of John Murray of the parish of Taughboyne, has left him.

953 - Tues., Oct. 16, 1781

Dublin.
Last week the wife of Rev. Mr. Fay was delivered of three daughters and a son.

Cork, Oct. 4.
On Monday last Lt. Hickson of the 5th Regiment killed George Brerton in self defense.

Limerick, Oct. 1.
On Saturday last were executed Edmund Fivir (for the rape of Catherine Kennedy) and Mary Welsh (for the murder of her husband).

Londonderry.
On Thursday the 27th at Cleagh, barony of Inishowen, Frederick Doyle or Doak killed Patrick Gill; Doak is a blacksmith, aged around sixty years.

954 - Tues., Oct. 23, 1781

Londonderry.
Married: John Allen, Springmont, Co. Antrim, to Miss Stewart of this city.
Died: Richard Raby, merchant; yesterday, Mr. Henry Swan, attorney.

955 - Tues., Oct. 30, 1781

Kilkenny.
Mention is made of the wishes of the late Henry Eccles regarding his burial.

956 - Tues., Nov. 6, 1781

Dublin, Nov. 1.
Yesterday were interred the remains of Richard Reynolds, D.D., Vicar General under the titular [Roman Catholic] Archbishop of Dublin, upwards of thirty years parish priest of Lazer's hill chapel.

Londonderry.
Married: Robert Holland to Miss Margaret, daughter of Doctor Scott of this city.

957 - Tues., Nov. 13, 1781

Londonderry.
Died: Rev. John Stokes, D.D., Prebendary of Ray and Rector of Clondehurka, Diocese of Rapho.
Ads: George Kennedy, merchant, vs. Alexander Hawes, Jane Hawes or Davis or Boyd his wife, and others; a tenement in Manor Cuningham etc. formerly possessed by John Davis and the ground under the kiln of Mathew Rogers of Manor Cuningham held by lease from James Irwin, deceased, to be sold.

958 - Tues., Nov. 20, 1781

Dublin.
Thomas O'Flaherty of Co. Kilkenny was alledgedly murdered by poison on June 28, 1778 by his wife (who absconded) and by Thomas Lonnergan, a tutor in the family; Lonnergan was tried at the Court of King's Bench and found guilty.

959 - Tues., Nov. 27, 1781

Dublin.
Mrs. "Lenargan," wanted for poisoning her late husband, is a cousin of the infamous Capt. Donellan (?), lately executed in England for poisoning his wife's brother. The unfortunate Mr. O'Flaherty was a relation of Mr. O'Malley, who lately died in the Marshalsea and for whose sudden death Mrs. O'M. took her trial along with Counsellor B.

Londonderry.
Ads: Stock of the late Annesly Gore, deceased, to be sold at Ballyshannon.

960 - Tues., Dec. 4, 1781

Dublin.
Thomas Lenergan was executed Saturday; he was son of Edward Lenergan, a respectable baker of Kilkenny. He was 26 years old, a Roman Catholic, and maintained his innocence.

962 - Tues., Dec. 18, 1781

Londonderry.
Ads: Debts due to the late Hugh Grier of Letterkenny are to be paid to his widow and administratrix, Mildred Grier, who carries on the grocery and cloth shop as usual. Mrs. Boggs, Mall Wall, lease of a garden to be sold, late in the possession of Henry Sloan, deceased, opposite the Bishop's garden.

963 - Tues., Dec. 25, 1781

Londonderry.
Elizabeth Stevenson or M'Kinla has left her husband John Stevenson.

966 - Tues., Jan. 15, 1782

Dublin.
The privateer Captain Kelly or Grumly, a native of Rush, was captured. [Two articles.]

967 - Tues., Jan. 22, 1782

Dublin, Jan. 17.
Monday last died Dr. William Clement, Vice Provost of Trinity College and member of parliament.

968 - Tues., Jan. 29, 1782

Londonderry.
Born: a son last Wednesday to the Lady of Lt. Col. Bateson [of the Volunteers].
Died: in Dublin, Claudius Hamilton of Beltram, Co. Tyrone.
Ads: Rebecca Cummin, widow of Alexander Cummin, cabinet-maker, has entered a partnership with Edward Doherty, her late husband's former apprentice, and will carry on the business at the Mahogany Warehouse in Rosemary lane.

969 - Tues., Feb. 4, 1782

Dublin.
Letter from Magherafelt: Henry Kane and his associates in arms, who have long braved the laws of this country, were taken by the high sheriff and a company of Volunteers near Maghera.

Londonderry.
The estate of the late Claudius Hamilton of Co. Tyrone devolves upon his son-in-law, Hon. Arthur Cole, now Hon. Arthur Cole Hamilton.
Died: Friday last, aged 27 years, Gard. Gates, M.D., only son of George Gates; Sunday last in Bishop st., Mrs. Margaret Patterson, aged 87 years.

970 - Tues., Feb. 12, 1782

Dublin, Feb. 7.
Yesterday during an assembly held to nominate for parliament, the floor of the hall gave way; among the dead was Mr. Byron, jr. and Mr. Taylor of High st. was said to have died.

971 - Tues., Feb. 19, 1782

Dublin.
Died: of the hurts they received at the collapse of the floor of the Music hall, Fishamble st.: Mr. Pemberton sr., Fleet st.; Mr. M'Mahon, Abbey st.; Robert Deey, attorney, Chancery lane; Mr. Johnson, shoemaker, Cutpurse row; and Richard Shaw, Essex bridge, sword cutter.

Londonderry.
Married: at Newtown Lemavady, William Creighton (?) to Miss Mar___.

972 - Tues., Feb. 26, 1782

Londonderry.
Married: Oliver L___, merchant, to Miss Isabella Crompton, daughter of Heape Crompton.

973 - Tues. March 5, 1782

Dublin, March 2.
John Doyle, a watchman at St. Andrew's parish, was executed yesterday for the robbery of Henry Draper.

Married: Rev. Alexander Hurst to Miss Summer, daughter of Rev. James Taylor, Smallbrook, Co. Tyrone.
Died: March 1, at his house in Leinster st., aged 74 years, Rt. Rev. Dr. John Garnett, Lord Bishop of Clogher since 1758; yesterday at his house in Abbey st., Francis Fetherton, nearly twenty years an alderman of this city; in Joseph's lane, John Scott, barber, of the injuries received in the Music hall.

Londonderry.
Died: in Dublin, Richard Dobson of Capel st., from a broken leg suffered in the Music hall.

974 - Tues. March 12, 1782

Londonderry.
Ads: Rewards are offered by Michael Ross and William Lenox, sheriffs, for the apprehension of the following, who escaped March 5 from the Londonderry gaol: Bernard Dougherty, shoe maker, charged with murder, formerly resided at Newtown Lemavady, about 35 years old; Patrick Dickey or Dickenson or Murren or McMullen, formerly lived in the Meentoghs near Black Water Ford in Co. Armagh, aged about 32 years; Alexander Martin, formerly lived in Newtown Lemavady, aged about 35 years; John Murray or Magraw, born Lisburn, Co. Down, aged about sixteen years; Ezekiel Davis Cross, formerly a servant, about 55 years old; William King, born at Newtown Lemavady, about 24 years old; James Holmes, about 25 years old; and Elizabeth Dermot or M'Dermot, about 24 years old.

976 - Tues., March 26, 1782

Londonderry.
Ads: Claimants on the estate of the late Tristram Cary of Rushfield are to notify George Cary, White Castle.

977 - Tues., April 2, 1782

Belfast.
At the Downpatrick assizes, ---- Kelly, found guilty of stealing a horse and mare in Co. Meath in February last, was to be executed April 30. At the Carrickfergus assizes: John Campbell, found guilty of the murder of Joseph Barton near Roughtorch, Co. Antrim, August last, is to die April 6; Richard Kennedy, found guilty of stealing a gold watch of Richard Maunsell from the house of David Burchell of Nineteen Mile House in Co. Kildare May last, to die April 6.

Londonderry.
At the Omagh assizes: Owen and Michael M'Carrol, brothers, found guilty of the murder of Pat. M'Bride at Ballygawly in 1779, are to die April 4.
At the Derry assizes, William Gibson, sergeant, and Peter Ryan, private, of the marines, were found guilty of extorting money from Nola Farren, wife of Dennis Farren, who had enlisted in said corps.

978 - Tues., April 9, 1782

Londonderry.
Married: at Castleton near Strabane, John Coningham of this city to Miss Elizabeth Campbell, sister of the late Robert Campbell of Isla [Scotland].

979 - Tues., April 16, 1782

Dublin, April 11.
Wednesday fortnight ended the assizes at Armagh; Alexander and James Toulerton, father and son, were found guilty of the murder of John Maneely

and were to be executed Monday next near Lurgan; Alexander Toulerton is Captain Firebrand.

981 - Tues., April 30, 1782

Londonderry.
Married: Tuesday last, Joseph Curry of this city to Miss Ann Richardson, and ----- Richardson of Dungannon to Miss M. Richardson, both daughters of David Richardson of Drum, Co. Tyrone; Mr. T. Fulton, merchant, to Miss Fulton of Newtown Lemavady.
Died: at Portumna Castle, Co. Galway, the Earl of Clanrickard; James Gamble of this city, glazier.

983 - Tues., May 14, 1782

Londonderry.
Died: Friday last, Rev. Maxwell Kennedy; at Warrington Academy, England, Will. Reynolds of this city.

986 - Tues., June 4, 1782

Londonderry.
Married: George Woods to Miss Wilson; Jo. Miller of the Trench to Miss Buchanan of this city.

987 - Tues., June 11, 1782

Londonderry.
Married: in Dublin, Samuel Madden, formerly of this city, to Miss Eliza Allen of Cu____ st.; Sam Cochran of Glendermot to Miss Sarah Gale of Co. Mayo.
Died: at Newtown Lemavady, William Bacon; the wife of James Mackey of Gallagh near this city.

989 - Tues., June 25, 1782

Dublin.
Died: John Dennis Baron Tracton; the Archbishop of Tuam.

Londonderry.
Married: John Kelso, Maghrecrigan, to Miss Jane Scott, Ballyorr.
Died: near St. Johnston, James Woods, Captain of the Taughboyne Volunteers.

990 - Tues., July 2, 1782

Londonderry.
Died: Miss Martha Ross, youngest daughter of the late William Ross; in Dublin, Rev. Edward Ledwich, LL.D., Dean of Kildare and Rector of Cumber.

991 - Tues., July 9, 1782

Londonderry.
Died: at Bath, Sir Henry Hamilton, an alderman of this city.
Ads: James M'Pherson will not pay debts contracted by his wife Isabella M'Pherson alias Johnston.

992 - Tues., July 16, 1782

Dublin.
Two young men bathing in Lough Erne a little below Enniskillen, named Soden and M'Guire, drowned on June 27; Soden had served an apprentice-ship in the wine business in Dublin; M'Guire was a tradesman.

Londonderry.
Married: at Dublin, William Hamilton, attorney, to Miss Collins of Bride st.;

Rich. Coningham to Miss Mary Gay, both of Burt near this city; Thomas Betagh, watch maker, to Miss Culbert.

995 - Tues., Aug. 6, 1782

Londonderry.
Died: on passage from Jamaica, Robert Delap, barrister at law.

996 - Tues., Aug. 13, 1782

Londonderry.
Ads: Mrs. Rachael Martin, widow and executrix of John Martin, deceased, to lease part of the quarter of Carrymena in Myro, Manor of Limavady, Co. Londonderry, on the sea shore. Deserted July 28 from a recruiting party of the 11th Foot: Con O'Neal, born in the parish of Ardstraw, Co. Tyrone, and Hugh M'Conway, born in the parish of Drumachose, Co. Derry, aged about 21 years.

998 - Tues., Aug. 27, 1782

Londonderry.
Ads: Creditors of the late David Denny of Omagh, deceased, are to notify executors Henry Gwin and James Prerin of the Parish of Cappagh.

999 - Tues, Sept. 3, 1782

Londonderry.
At Lifford, ---- M'Fadden was found guilty of house breaking and is to be executed on Sept. 10.
Died: at Newtown Lemavady, John Martin, apothecary; yesterday, aged 17, J. Adams, son of Delap Adams of this city.

1000 - Tues., Sept. 10, 1782

Londonderry.
Married: Thursday last, John M'Clintock to Miss Alexander, both of Bishop st.; William Ross of Strabane to Miss Sayers of Convoy.

1001 - Tues., Sept. 17, 1782

Dublin.
Andrew Johnston who murdered shoemaker William Lidford of Ballyshannon last March 14, was apprehended and lodged in Newgate.

1002 - Tues., Sept. 24, 1782

Dublin.
Died: John Dillon, Earl of Roscommon; Pat. Blake, Lt. Col. of the Galway Volunteers; at Moira, Sam. Blacker, counsellor at law; at Kilkenny, Robert Blake, counsellor at law.

Londonderry.
Married: George Gledstane to Miss Swettenham; Mat. Phillson of Letterkenny to Miss King of Ballybofey.
Ads: William Murray, administrator of Catherine Murray, deceased, to sell a farm in Carnshanagh, Inishowen.

1004 - Tues., Oct. 8, 1782

Londonderry.
Married: Joseph Sayers of C----, linen merchant, to Miss M. Clenachan, daughter of C. M. Clenachan of Strabane.
Died: at Letterkenny, the Lady of Lt. Roch of the 49th Regiment; at Castlehill in Burt, William Patterson.

George Hamilton warns that he will contest John Fairly's pretended interst in a moiety of the profits of a lease of the Ferries of the city, advertised for sale, which belonged to his father, Will. Hamilton.

1005 - Tues., Oct. 15, 1782

Dublin.
Bankrupt: James Morrow, Ballybofey, Co. Donegal, shopkeeper.

Londonderry.
Died: in England, Mrs. Mortimer, relict of the late William Mortimer of Ramelton (?), Co. Donegal.

1007 - Tues., Oct. 29, 1782

Dublin, Oct. 26.
James Malone, aged 14, son of Joseph Malone of Rogerstown in King's County, was leading a horse belonging to his grandfather Saturday when the horse took fright and killed him.

1008 - Tues., Nov. 5, 1782

Londonderry.
Married: Rev. Jo. Marshall of Fahan to Mrs. Stewart, widow of the late George Stewart.

1009 - Tues., Nov. 12, 1782

Londonderry.
Ads: A lease of the tenement and land of the late Mrs. M'Crea, Rapho, to be sold.

1010 - Tues., Nov. 19, 1782

Dublin, Nov. 14.
On Monday the 28th, a Scottish boat, Duncan Campbell, master, was wrecked in a storm near Coleraine; only one crewman saved himself by swimming.

Londonderry.
Died: Sunday, aged 26, Mrs. Mary Ross, daughter of the late John Knox of this city.

1014 - Tues., Dec. 17, 1782

Dublin.
Married: Henry Grattan, member of parliament for the borough of Charlemont, to Miss Fitzgerald of Dawson st.; John Fitzpatrick of More, Queen's County, to Miss D. Fitzgerald of Grafton st.; Counsellor West of Frederick st. to Miss Hutchinson, daughter of Dr. Hutchinson of Stafford st.

1015 - Tues., Dec. 24, 1782

Dublin.
On Nov. 20, Francis Lendram of Beagh, Co. Tyrone, while on his way to Fintona in the townland of Carnugal was robbed and shot; he survived but a few days.

Londonderry.
Died: Saturday last, aged 71, James Stirling of Wallworth near Newtown Limavady.
Ads: A mare was stolen from the stable of the Widow French near Randalstown, Co. Antrim; reward offered by the Widow, William, John, Henry, John, James, and Robert French; return to John French or T. M'Alley of Randalstown.

1016 - Tues., Dec. 31, 1782

Dublin.
Died: on Dec. 15 at Garden hill near Enniskillen, the wife of Alexander
Young, of Snow hill, Co. Fermanagh.

1017 - Tues., Jan. 7, 1783

Dublin.
On Dec. 26 a duel was fought at Longford between R. Moffat, Rynn, and his
brother-in-law, Mr. Furry; the former was killed; the marriage had been
celebrated on the 16th.

Londonderry.
Married: Mr. John Ross of Newtown Limavady to Miss Kane of Maghera; Andrew
Cochran of Glendermot to Miss Cochran of Coleraine.
Died: at Green hill near Rapho, Nicholas Spence; Saturday at his house in
this city, William Patterson of Foxhall, Co. Donegal.
Ads: Rob. Fairly, mayor, offers a reward for the apprehension of William
Keatten, apprentice of Robt. Fisher, cooper. Martha M'Morice or Dougherty
has separated from Joseph M'Morice, parish of Cumber.

1018 - Tues., Jan. 14, 1783

Dublin, Jan. 9.
Saturday, Patrick Lynch was executed at the New Prison, having been convicted
of firing a pistol at and wounding Mr. Dowling of the Coombe; his body was
taken to the College for dissection.
At Cork, ---- Dwyer was executed by a firing squad for desertion.

1019 - Tues., Jan. 21, 1783

Londonderry.
Married: James Smith of Ramullen to Miss Smith of Glendermot.
Died: at Dunfanaghy, Co. Donegal, William Babington; at St. Johnstown, Mrs.
Bond, wife of Rev. Thomas Bond; at Strabane the wife of James Orr.
Ads: The executors of the late James Henderson are to sell furniture, crops,
and lease of a house and land at Dungiven. Sarah Bell otherwise Colhoun has
left her husband Jeremiah Bell, Birdstown.

1020 - Tues., Jan. 28, 1783

Dublin.
Saturday last, James Kennedy, Patrick Farrell, and David Gaynor were executed
at Kilmainham gaol, having been convicted of robbing the house of Surgeon
Daunt at Harold's Cross.

Londonderry.
Married: Andrew Alexander, Newtown Limavady, to Miss Stewart, daughter of the
late Col. Stewart of this city.
Died: Mrs. Bellew, relict of the late Mr. M. Bellew of this city; Mrs. Bond,
reported in the last issue, has not died.

1021 - Tues., Feb. 4, 1783

Londonderry.
Died: in Pump st., Mrs. Johnston; in the Cross lane, Mrs. Hart; at
Magherafelt, Mrs. Patterson, wife of H. Patterson.

1022 - Tues., Feb. 11, 1783

Londonderry.
Died: Mar. M'Causland, of Daisy hall near Newtown Limavady; Wednesday last,
aged 13, D. H. Ferguson, son of John Ferguson of this city.

1023 - Tues., Feb. 18, 1783

Londonderry.
Married: Tuesday last at Prehen, the seat of George Knox, near this city,
David Ross to Miss Mahon, sister of M. Mahon, member of parliament for Co.
Roscommon; Mr. Rich. Hunter to Widow Law.

1024 - Tues., Feb. 25, 1783

Londonderry.
Married: Rev. James Magee of Muff to Miss Blackall of Derry; near Newtown
Limavady, Jacob Forsythe of Artikelly to Miss Haslet of Clooney.
Died: William Kennedy, for many years an alderman of the Corporation of this
city; at Convoy, the wife of James Moore; at Gort in the parish of
Kilcronachan, the wife of Rev. Clotworthy Soden.
Ads: Sam. Montgomery to sell Richard Baker's interest in Dristernan or
Dristrien in the parish of Culdaff, barony of Inishowen, which was granted by
the Earl of Donegal to George Chilick, deceased, now in possession of Richard
Baker and his undertenants (Baker resides there).

1025 - Tues., March 4, 1783

Londonderry.
Ads: The ship Mary, Arch. Stevenson, for Newcastle and Philadelphia May 1;
William Hope, William Glen, and Tho. Chambers, merchants, Londonderry,
owners; 350 tons.

1027 - Tues., March 18, 1783

Dublin, May 15.
Died: James Given, linen factor; C. Foster, Captain in the 55th Regiment; at
Strabane, Mr. W. Perry.
On March 9 the Two Friends, Carnitch, sailed from Cork for New York and
Philadelphia. A few days ago the Success sailed from Belfast for Virginia.

Londonderry.
Ads: Nicholas O'Kane will surrender himself at Omagh for the next assizes; he
is charged with the murder of Pat. Divin; notice to John Divin, Sary Divin,
widow, Hen. M'Donagh, Cha. Divin, Bridget Divin his wife, and Cha. Divin of
Belnamalagh.

1028 - Tues., March 25, 1783

Londonderry.
Died: at Fahan near this city, John Gregory, son of the late celebrated Dr.
Gregory of Edinburgh; Mrs. Gregg, wife of Mr. A. Gregg of Ballyarnet; Mrs.
Elizabeth Ross, aged 81 years, relict of the late Rev. Mr. Ross, dissenting
minister of this city.

1029 - Tues., April 1, 1783

Belfast, Mar. 25.
Sunday last the Washington sailed for Liverpool and America; yesterday the
Friendship, Thomas, sailed for Baltimore.

1030 - Tues., April 8, 1783

Dublin.
Married: Mr. Cherry to Miss Knipe, both of Mr. Atkins's company of comedians
now at Belfast.

Londonderry.
Died: Saturday, Sam. Motherel of Burt; Saturday, his daughter, Mrs. M'Crea,

wife of James M'Crea of Donaghedy; Sunday at Burt, Hugh Gay, aged 77 years;
James Osborne, innkeeper, Bishops gate.

1031 - Tues., April 15, 1783

Belfast, Apr. 11.
At the Down assizes: Pat. Gordon or M'Gurnaghan is to be executed Thursday
the 17th next at Drumbridge; Stephen Gordon or M'Gurnaghan is to be executed
at Castlewellan on Monday next, the 14th, both for stealing linen; George
Brown is to be executed at Down in June for stealing linen; John Wright is to
be executed at Banbridge for stealing linen cloth there; John Holmes (?) is
to be executed at Downpatrick on July 11 for receiving stolen goods; Edward
Higgins and Ross Slatford (?) are to be executed at Downpatrick for burglary.

Londonderry.
At the assizes here, William M'Mahon was found guilty of stealing a web of
linen from a shop in this city and is to be executed on July 2; during the
trial is wife and brother were detected picking pockets.
Died: yesterday, Alexander Major, Tullybrislan, near Muff in Co. Derry.
Ads: The brig Congress, William Chevers, from Newry for Philadelpha,
passengers are to board the 25th.

1032 - Tues., April 22, 1783

Londonderry.
A man named Porter, his two sons, and his brother were killed by a party of
soldiers when he tried to recover his illegal still which they had taken,
between Killygordon and Convoy in Co. Donegal. His brother-in-law and cousin
were among the wounded. Later, near Strabane a man named Dougherty was
seized by a mob and thrown into the river several times, as an informer
against illegal stills in the neighborhood.

1033 - Tues., April 29, 1783

Dublin, April 26.
Died: William Cleghorn, M.D. and lecturer in anatomy; Mr. Alley, gun maker,
by a fall from a horse; Adjutant Booth of the 67th Regiment; Rev. Mr. O'Mara
of Mary's lane chapel; F. Gilbert, attorney; Daniel Reney, physician; at
Drumcork, Co. Tyrone, John Martin.

Londonderry.
Died: at Ballybofey, ---- Basil; Saturday, in Widows' row, Mary, relict of
the late Rev. Mr. Gwyn, curate of the parish of Urney.
Ads: The brig Providence, James Fisher, 220 tons, at the Ship quay for
Newcastle and Philadelphia June 1.

1035 - Tues., May 13, 1783

Dublin.
On Sunday the ship Emelia of Belfast sailed for Philadelphia. May 10, Owen
Carroll, James Kelly, and Pat. Kane were executed at the front of Kilmainham
gaol for robbery.

Londonderry.
The ship Mary, Arch. Stevenson, for Newcastle and Philadelphia, is delayed on
her voyage from Norway.
Married: Thursday last, Robert M'Intire to Miss Boggs; Rev. Mr. Cairns to
Mrs. Smith.
Died: at Newtown Limavady, Thomas Coningham; near Muff, William Gillespy.

1036 - Tues., May 20, 1783

Dublin, May 17.
On Tuesday the 6th sailed the Congress, William Cheevers, 250 tons, from

Newry for Philadelphia; and on Wednesday the 7th sailed the <u>Hibernia</u>, Thomson, for same.

Londonderry.
Died: at Craig near this city, David Harvey, age 75.

1037 - Tues., May 27, 1783

Londonderry.
Died: Rev. John M'Gaoghy, age 93, dissenting minister of Fannet for over 54 years.
Ads: George Widerow will not pay debts contracted by his wife, Jane Widerow otherwise Farren.

1038 - Tues., June 3, 1783

Londonderry.
Died: at Magilligan point, Perrot Ennis.

1039 - Tues., June 10, 1783

Dublin, June 3.
Sunday sevennight the <u>Irish Volunteer</u>, Peter Dillon, sailed from Larne for Philadelphia with passengers.
Yesterday Charles Spaulding of Edinburgh and his assistant, Ebenezer Watson, suffocated in the harbor while using a diving bell.

Londonderry.
Died: in Dublin, Rev. James Caldwell of Usher's quay Meeting House; Rev. Mr. Turbet of Donahedy; near Coleraine, Abram Brown; near Coleraine, Miss Cuppage; near Malin, Miss Harvey; in Strabane, William Mease; in Stewartstown, Mr. White, Adjutant to the Killymoon Battalion [of Volunteers]; at the Ferry quay, Noble Caldwell.
Ads: Charles Byne warns tenants on the estates of the late Edmond and George Basill in Co. Donegal not to pay their rents to Samuel Hayes; he [Byne] is entitled to an undivided one-third of the estates in right of his wife, Frances Byne or Basill.

1040 - Tues., June 17, 1783

Dublin.
The <u>Darragh</u>, Capt. Boyne, from Dublin, arrived in New York on May 2.

Londonderry.
Ads: The new brigantine <u>America</u>, Charles Forrest, 250 tons, is at Warren Point (Newry) for Philadelphia and New York July 1.

1041 - Tues., June 24, 1783

Londonderry.
Married: at Rapho, Andrew Stephenson to Miss M. Laird.
Ads: The brig <u>Nancy</u>, Joseph Curry, 200 tons, for Newcastle and Philadelphia about 10 July, Samuel Curry, merchant, agent.

1042 - Tues., July 1, 1783

Belfast.
Died: 23 June at White Abbey near Belfast, Richard Bateson, son of Thomas Bateson of Orange field, Captain of the White-house Corps (interment at Newtown Breda).

Londonderry.
Died: at London, J. S. Delap; near Donegal, Thomas Young of Loughesk; at Stranorlan, Mrs. Love, wife of Rev. Mr. Love; at Castlefin, Mrs. Scott.

Ads: The ship _Liberty_, William Barclay, 300 tons, six years old, for
Newcastle and Philadelphia July 20; Thomas Gonne, propreitor.

1043 - Tues., July 8, 1783

Dublin.
Thursday sevennight John Lowry, Killinshy woods near Killileagh, Co. Down,
was killed in his bed by a shot through his window.
Married: Friday last, Hon. Maj. Gen. Stopford to Miss Letitia, daughter of
William Blacker, by Rev. Dean Stopford at the house of Rt. Hon. Edward Cary
in Marlborough st.

Londonderry.
Died: Saturday last, Mr. R. Beishane (?), member of the True Blue Volunteers.

1044 - Tues., July 15, 1783

Londonderry.
Ads: The snow _Mary_, John Ross, 240 tons, is expected from London, will sail
for Newcastle and Philadelphia by 12 August.

1045 - Tues., July 22, 1783

Londonderry.
The ship _Three Brothers_, James Gillis, 400 tons, from Belfast to Philadelphia
and Charlestown in early August.
Ads: The brig _Duke of Leinster_, Peter Devereu, 350 tons, now in Dublin, for
Newcastle and Baltimore, will stop at Culmore on her way; redemptioners and
servants are encouraged.

1046 - Tues., July 29, 1783

Dublin.
Curious advertisements are copied from the Belfast paper, according to which
Agnes Park of Larne was delivered of a male child on May 25, which she
exposed; she claims the father is William Taylor, Larne, apothecary.

Londonderry.
Died: Miss Jane Major, daughter of James Major, merchant; at Malin, Rev. D.
Walker, dissenting minister.
Ads: James Foster, Bogside, to sell his interest in a lease of a house etc.,
formerly occupied as a tanyard by the late Mr. M'Connell, in the Long
Bogside.

1047 - Tues., Aug. 5, 1783

Londonderry.
Ads: The ship _Washington_, Rob. Suter, arrived at Newry; for Philadelphia on
Aug. 5.

Londonderry.
On Friday the _Mary_, Stevenson, sailed for Philadelphia; this and the brig
Providence which sailed about three weeks ago carried over six hundred
emigrants.

1048 - Tues., Aug. 12, 1783

Londonderry.
Married: Rev. Mr. Christy to Miss Wilson.
Died: the Lady of Thomas Bateson; at Ardkill, Mrs. Thompson; at the Cross,
Miss Smith.
Ads: The ship _Liberty_, at Londonderry, for Philadelphia Aug. 26. The snow
Mary, Capt. Ross, at Londonderry, for Philadelphia Sept. 1.

1049 - Tues., Aug. 19, 1783

Belfast.
A letter from Baltimore: Major James M'Hendry, secretary to General
Washington, was the son of a grocer who lived some years in Belfast.

Dublin.
---- Burgess and ---- Godfrey were executed by hanging at the New Prison.
Died: Miss Beresford, daughter of Rt. Hon. John Beresford.

1051 - Tues., Sept. 2, 1783

Belfast, Aug. 26.
Yesterday sailed the Philadelphia Packet, Capt. Torrens, for Philadelphia
with linens etc. and 250 passengers.

1052 - Tues., Sept. 9, 1783

Londonderry.
Died: Mr. J. M'Clenaghan, Convoy.

1053 - Tues., Sept. 16, 1783

Cork, Sept. 1.
Last night Lt. Wilson of the 32nd Regiment was killed by Lt. West, who has
fled.

Dublin.
On Aug. 28 the ship Lord Templetown, Capt. M'Tier, sailed from Larne for
Philadelphia with 200 passengers and linen.
Died: at the Hot Wells, Bristol, Rev. George Cary Hamilton, D.D., his estate
in Counties Kildare and Tipperary devolving upon his brother, Rt. Hon. Edward
Cary.

1054 - Tues., Sept. 23, 1783

Londonderry.
Sailed Friday the snow Mary, Capt. Ross, for Philadelphia with Irish
manufactures and 170 passengers.
Married: George Cary of White Castle to Mrs. Cary of Red Castle.
Cleared: the Liberty, Bartley, for New York.

1056 - Tues., Oct. 7, 1783

Belfast, Sept. 26.
Tuesday last sailed the Three Brothers for Philadelphia with 240 passengers.
Dublin, Oct. 4.
Wednesday last at Armagh died Rt. Hon. W. H. Burgh, Lord Chief Baron of the
Exchequer.

Londonderry.
At the Omagh assizes, Bryan Quin, for breaking into the house of Mr. Maxwell
at Caledon and taking linen, was sentenced to be executed on the 20th;
William Cavenagh, for the rape of Ann Moor of Auchnacloy, age 8 years, to be
executed on the 20th.
Died: at Enniskillen, Hon. Godfrey Lill, Second Justice of the Court of
Common Pleas; John Sheil, one of His Majesty's Council at Law; William
Auchinleck, Mulvin near Strabane; the Lady of James M'Clintock of Trintagh.

Ad: Placed by the passengers of the brig Franklin, Capt. Arch. M'Combe, from
Newry who arrived at Philadelphia Aug. 3, 1783, signed by:

| William Dunlap | Joseph Atkinson | John Clarke | Tho. Fleming |
| Tho. Greason | Rob. Cochran | Geo. Guthrie | James Garland |

Rob. Mitchell	Philip Hearn	A. Greer jr.	Wm. Johnston
James M'Cabe	P. Warren	James Caffry	Nath. Allen
James Sampson	N. Farrell	John Douglas	Pat. Todd
Hugh Johnston	Joseph Dainty	Alex. M'Kay	Geo. M'Clune
Fran. M'Morran	Wm. Lockhart	Jos. Newton	Wm. Moore
James Henrey	John Little	John Moore	John Audrey
Bar. Dickson	Bryan Higgins	Wm. Miligan	John M'Conne
Tho. M'Whinnery	Tho. Quigly	Jer. M'Murry	Wm. Thrimble
James Dawson	John Neilson	Sam. Dobbin	Alex. Mullin
Jn. Williamson	James Kennedy	James Woods	John M'Quoid
Joseph Dickson	John Emery	James Kelly	Wm. Laverty
Wm. West	Solemon Stewart	Henry Falls	Briship Morrow
Alex. Shiell	Mich. Fitzsimons	Matt. Maclean	John M'Gaheron
Fran. Watkins	Joseph Dickson	Prussia Maclean	Edw. M'Partlan
Hugh Black	Rob. Johnston	Alex. M'Donnell	Ham. Maclean
Wm. Pettigrew	D. Somerville	Tho. Farley	John Marshall
John Cumming	S. Somerville	Bernard Wood	James Black
Hin. Wright	Wm. Law	Tho. Faris	James Moore
John Carothers			

1057 - Tues., Oct. 14, 1783

Londonderry.
At the Derry assizes: Thomas Good, for horse stealing, and Pat Doogan (alias Kane alias Dougherty), Mich. M'Pherson, and J. Steel, for cow stealing, are to be executed on Nov. 5.
Married: Roger Murray to Miss O'Hara.
Died: Rev. Roger Blackall.

1058 - Tues., Oct. 21, 1783

Londonderry.
Died: on the 15th, Mrs. Houston, wife of Robert Houston of this city; Saturday last, Captain Campbell.

1059 - Tues., Oct. 28, 1783

Dublin, Oct. 25.
Died: Wednesday last at his house in Stephen's green, Rt. Hon. Joseph Leeson, Earl of Milltown, age 83, succeeded by his eldest son Rt. Hon. Lord Rosborough; in Sackville st., Sir William Osborne.

Londonderry.
Died: Saturday last, Thomas Gonne, a young man.
Ads: A list of goods, supposedly stolen, confiscated from Elizabeth Steele, wife of James Steele who is to be executed for cow-stealing; contact Bartholomew M'Naghten or James Black in Coleraine.

1060 - Tues., Nov. 4, 1783

Londonderry.
Died: Tuesday last, Mrs. King; Sunday, William Caldwell, merchant.

Ads: Iron to be sold at the warehouse of the late Adam Maitland on the Canal quay, Newry. A reward is offered for the apprehension of Beather King, John King, Michael Breeson, and John M'Gonagle, who assaulted High Sheriff John Hart on October 27 at Mulkeeragh, Co. Londonderry.

1062 - Tues., Nov. 18, 1783

Dublin.
Died: Rt. Rev. James Tra (?), Lord Bishop of Down & Conor; in Henrietta st., the Lady of Rt. Hon. Luke Gardiner.

1063 - Tues., Nov. 25, 1783

Londonderry.
Ads: Thomas Strawbridge of Bellykelly warns not to extend credit to Mary
Strawbridge of same.

1065 - Tues., Dec. 9, 1783

Londonderry.
Died: the wife of James Burnside, merchant; Mrs. James Cahey.

1066 - Tues., Dec. 16, 1783

Londonderry.
Married: George Hart, Capt. in His Majesty's Royal Navy, to Miss Patterson,
sister of Walter Patterson, Governor of the Island of St. John; Dr. Crawford
of Lisburn to Miss Smily of Strabane.
Died: Miss Swettenham, daughter of Jo. Swettenham.

1067 - Tues., Dec. 23, 1783

Londonderry.
Married: Friday last, Thomas Abraham of this city to Miss Boyle, daughter of
James Boyle, Kirlish, near Drumquin, Co. Tyrone.
Died: Wednesday last, aged 62, John Hood, Moyle, mathematician and land
surveyor.

1068 - Tues., Dec. 30, 1783

Londonderry.
The ship _Liberty_, William Bartley, arrived at Philadelphia in six weeks and
three days from Londonderry, passengers all well; also the ship _Mary_, Capt.
Stevenson, arrived safely at Philadelphia.
Ads: Debtors owing Samuel Mothriel, late of Bowhillan, Co. Donegal, deceased,
are to pay John Mothriel of same, executor.

1069 - Tues., Jan. 6, 1784

Dublin.
Died: at the Bath, John M'Mollan, one of his Majesty's Council at Law.
Ads: The brig _Grace_, Rob. George, 140 tons, for Baltimore Feb. 10, can
accomodate a few passengers; owners Peter Alexander, John Ewing, and Robert
George; servants are encouraged.

1070 - Tues., Jan. 13, 1784

Londonderry.
Married: W. M. Kirk to Miss Bateman, daughter of John Bateman.
Born: a son to the Lady of General Gledstane of Daisy Hill, Co. Tyrone.
Ads: The brig _Peggy_, George Stewart, 200 tons, three years old, for Newcastle
and Philadelphia March 1; George Brown and William Cudbert, proprietors.

1071 - Tues., Jan. 20, 1784

Londonderry.
Died: at Letterkenny, Red. Conyngham; at Brookhall, ---- Wray, formerly a
major in His Majesty's service.
Ads: Charles and Margaret Gray, administrators of James Miller, deceased, vs.
Fred. Hamilton; sheriffs to sell his right to three houses on the Gaol Wall.

1072 - Tues., Jan. 27, 1784

Dublin.
The _Philadelphia_ packet, Capt. Torrens, from Belfast with 250 passengers on

Aug. 25, went ashore twenty miles south of Cape Henlopen [the southern entrance to the Delaware]. All the passengers got ashore, but about seventy hired a schooner to take them to Philadelphia and it sank and all of them perished.

Londonderry.
Two men named Baird, in the parish of Ardstraw, perished in the snow while returning from a mill. The snow Mary, Capt. Ross, arrived safe at Philadelphia on Nov. 16, all passengers well.
Ads: The goods and crop of the late John Witherow to be sold at Ballymagrorty for rent and arrears due Mrs. Mary Lecky. The ship Neptune, now in London, will leave Londonderry for Philadelphia in the spring; for passage apply to Capt. James Mitchell or his son H. Mitchell. The ship Alexander, W. Pinkerton, 500 tons, for Newcastle and Philadelphia April 10. The brig Mary, Sam. Hetterick, 260 tons, for Baltimore Feb. 15; Sam. Curry, prop.; a few passengers can be accomodated.

1074 - Tues., Feb. 10, 1784

Londonderry.
Married: Mr. Pue of County Mayo to Miss Park near St. Johnstown.
Died: Rev. William Stewart; Mr. John Count; at Coleraine, ---- O'Dougherty, said to be 118 years old.
Ads: The Minerva, 500 tons, for Newcastle and Virginia April 1.

1075 - Tues., Feb. 17, 1784

At Ballygawley, Co. Tyrone, on Jan. 31 Mr. Brady, surveyor of excise of Dungannon, with Mr. Walker, a gauger, and 26 men found a still there at the house of George Mains; Walker was shot and killed and others were wounded.

1076 - Tues., Feb. 24, 1784

Londonderry.
Died: Rev. G. Gifford, rector of the parish of Badoney, diocese of Derry; Hugh Wilson, overseer of the poor house of this city.

1077 - Tues., March 2, 1784

Londonderry.
Married: James Ramage jr. to Miss Moore, daughter of Capt. James Moore.
Ads: A farm in Mongavlin formerly held by William Doyle, deceased, to be sold. The brig Grace, Rob. George, for Baltimore by Feb. 20. The brig Mary, Jos. Curry, for same by March 10.

1078 - Tues., March 9, 1784

Londonderry.
Died: at Fahan, Miss Bar; at Dromore, Mr. John Morrison.

1079 - Tues., March 16, 1784

Londonderry.
Married: Rob. Tate, Kilfannan, to Miss Lydia Ross, Ballyowen.
Ads: Reward offered for the apprehension of William Coyle, who on the 28th beat and abused William O'Donnell, assistant to coast officer John Montgomery, who was seizing private stills near Three Trees, barony of Inishowen. The ship St. Patrick, Arch. M'Ilwaine, 500 tons, for Newcastle, Pennsylvania and Petersburgh, Virginia, Apr. 16; Dickson Conyngham and Venables and Crawford, proprietors; two years old, formerly advertised as the Minerva. The snow Buckskin, James Smith, 200 tons, for Newcastle and Philadelphia Apr. 20; John Ewing, merchant, agent; owned in Philadelphia.

1080 - Tues., March 23, 1784

Dublin.
Saturday last, the ship <u>Three Friends</u>, Capt. Stute, sailed for Baltimore.
Yesterday the <u>Earl of Charlemont</u>, Capt. Watson, sailed for same.

Londonderry.
Ads: The ship <u>Stewart</u>, Joseph Haynes, 300 tons, for Newcastle and Rhode
Island, to sail May 15; apply to Mr. A. Stewart or Mrs. H. Miller, near the
Ferry quay; Mr. Stewart, born near Ballintoy, Co. Antrim, has been in America
for 22 years.

1081 - Tues., March 30, 1784

Dublin.
Eleven thousand have embarked for America since the peace.

Londonderry.
Died: the Lady of John Ferguson of this city.
Cleared: the <u>Mary</u>, Curry, for Baltimore with linen etc.
Ads: The partnership of John and William Coningham is dissolved; William
Conigham is departing from the Kingdom to settle in business elsewhere.
James Smith will not be responsible for Elizabeth Jamison otherwise Smith.
Ann Ward, at the Seven Stars and Salmon, No. 40 Nicholas st., Dublin,
continues her late husband Benjamin Ward's silk business in his former
dwelling house.

1083 - Tues., April 13, 1784

Dublin.
Died: Rt. Hon. John Gore Lord Annaly, etc.; at Springfield, Co. Derry,
William Conyngham.

Londonderry.
Ads: The ship <u>General Montgomery</u>, Caleb Trowbridge, 400 tons, for Newcastle
and Philadelphia, to sail May 20.

1084 - Tues., April 20, 1784

Londonderry.
At the assizes, Edward Malone, for murder of John Barclay near Moy, to be
hanged on April 24; Charles Hagarty or M'Laughlin and James Mullan, for horse
stealing, to hang on May 13.
Ads: The ship <u>Faithful Steward</u>, Joseph Haynes, 300 tons, for Newcastle and
Rhode Island May 15.

1085 - Tues. April 27, 1784

Belfast.
Died Thursday the 8th in Monaghan, Michael Dougherty, aged 83. "He was one
of the companions of the unfortunate M'Naghten, at the time Miss Knox was
shot, for the apprehending of whom a considerable reward was offered; since
which period he has travelled about, disguised as a begger, and named himself
John. - He has left in safe hands, papers of consequence to his family, and
as we are at a loss where to apply, it is requested thais paragraph may be
copied into other prints."

Londonderry.
Cleared: the <u>Hibernia</u>, George, for Baltimore with candles.

1086 - Tues. May 4, 1784

Philadelphia, March 2: the brig <u>Liberty</u>, from Dublin, with passengers, is
lost in the Chesapeake and thirty perished; the others (100) are saved.

Londonderry.
Married: at Belfast, Dr. Holmes to Miss Joy, daughter of Mr. H. Joy, printer; at Strabane, James Orr to Miss Sarah Feter.
Died: at Castlefin, John Johnston.
Cleared: the Peggy, Stewart, for Philadelphia, in ballast.
Ads: The ship Congress, Francis Knox, 600 tons, for Newcastle and Philadelphia June 1; Capt. Knox is a Derry man and served his apprenticeship in this city in the passenger trade.

1087 - Tues. May 11, 1784

Belfast, May 7.
Tuesday last, Mrs. Lemmon, wife of William Lemmon, guager of this town, was delivered of a girl and a boy.

Londonderry.
Married: Samuel Curry to Mrs. Civil; at Tullydoney near Dromore, Co. Down, Rev. Robert Black to Miss Margaret Black.
Ads: The brig Jenny, Capt. Mackay, for Norfolk, Va.; passengers to board on May 17. The passengers are to board the ship St. Patrick, Capt. M'Ilwaine, on May 25.

1088 - Tues., May 18, 1784

Londonderry.
Cleared: the Mary, Ross, for Philadelphia, with Irish goods.

1089 - Tues., May 25, 1784

Londonderry.
Ads: Passengers are to board the Faithful Steward at Culmore this week. The brig William, 200 tons, for Newcastle and Philadelphia on July 10. William Delap, surgeon and apothecary; former apprentice to Surgeon Maxwell of the Tyrone Infirmary and then of Dublin and later on a Ship of the Line in His Majesty's service, has opened a shop in Rathmelton.

1090 - Tues., June 1,1874

Belfast.
A letter from Neal M'Colgan and Grizey M'Colgan, dated Hanover Township, Sept. 15, 1783: she emigrated to America before the War; writes greetings to her sister in Belfast, parents, sisters, brothers; warns not to come to America as servants but any should come if they can pay the passage.

Londonderry.
Died: James Mitchell, former Captain of several vessels in the American trade.
Cleared: the Alexander, Pinkerton, for Philadelphia with passengers; the Buckskin, Smith, for same.

1091 - Tues., June 8, 1784

Dublin, June 3.
Bankrupt: John Tunnadine, a Master of the High Court of Chancery.
Tuesday last the Earl of Inchiquin, Capt. William Gafney, 250 tons, with Irish wares, sailed from Berehaven for Newcastle on the Delaware; on board were over 100 passengers, mostly tradesmen from Cork and Waterford.

Londonderry.
Blair M'Clenaghan, native of Ireland, twenty-five years a citizen of America, invited the people of Derry to breakfast and a dance on his ship, the Congress. The Alexander and the Buckskin carried over 800 passengers.
Married: at Strabane, Mrs. James M'Clenaghan to Miss Blair (?).
Died: Rev. Edward Kelly, late ---- of the parish of Longfield.

Cleared: the Jenny, Macky, for Virginia with merchandise.
Ads: The brig Rebecca, Marcus M'Causland, 150 tons, for Newcastle and
Philadelphia June 15; Abraham M'Causland, agent.

1092 - Tues., June 15, 1784

Dublin.
Lewis Chapiliere, Kilkenny, lately deceased, left charitable bequests in his
will. Mr. Stack is elected a junior Fellow of Trinity College in place of
Rev. Dr. Richardson, deceased.

Londonderry.
Cleared: the St. Patrick, M'Ilwaine, for Phladelphia with passengers; the
Faithful Steward, M'Causland, for same.
Ads: Sam Hunter, indentured servant of R. Holland, has deserted his service.

1093 - Tues., June 22, 1784

Londonderry.
Since our last, the St. Patrick and the Faithful Steward have sailed, having
about one thousand passengers on board.
Married: John Alexander of Lifford to Miss Orr of Strabane.
Died: Miss Falls, Free school lane.
Ads: The brig Nancy, Sam Hetterick, 250 tons, for Newcastle and Phladelphia
10 July. The new brig Culmore Packet, Micah Campbell, 260 tons, for same
Aug. 1; passengers, redemptioners, servants apply to Ab. M'Causland,
merchant, Capt. Con. M'Causland, Streeve hill, or Rob. M'Causland, Coleraine.

1094 - Tues., June 29, 1784

Dublin, June 26.
A four-year-old son of Mr. Taylor, William st., fell from a garret window and
died.

Londonderry.
Married: Roger Harrison to Miss Elisia Boyd.

1095 - Tues., July 6, 1784

Monaghan, June 25.
One hundred families from this quarter have gone to view lands in Connaught;
the lands are held out for the linen trade by Mr. Fitzgerald.

Dublin.
Married: Capt. Mussom Gamble to Miss S. Ellwood.
Two vessels here for Philadelphia and Baltimore will sail with cabin
passengers only; no more redemptioners will be received in the American
states, it is said.

Londonderry.
Died: at Mattsmount, near Dungiven, Audley Fanning, Esq.
Ads: The brig Mary, Capt. Curry, sailed from here April 1 and arrived at
Baltimore in five weeks; soon will return and sail again; Sam. Curry,
merchant, agent.

1098 - Tues., July 27, 1784

Dublin.
---- Keenan was found guilty by the Court of Oyer and Terminer; to be hanged
at the New Prison on Wednesday; he promised to haunt his prosecutors and ----
M'Kinley, gaoler at Kilmainham.

Londonderry.
Died: at Ramelton on the 17th, Mr. H. M'Keferty, school master.

1099 - Tues., Aug. 3, 1784

Dublin.
A letter from Waterford, July 25: the Anne, Ben Edmondson, from Cork for
Philadelphia, carried over 300 passengers, none redemptioners, all paid: 10
guineas in the cabin, 6 in the steerage, or 4 in the hold; one passenger had
been to America since the peace and returned for his family, in number 25.

Londonderry.
Married: near Rapho, John Henderson to Miss Gray of Convoy; Lt. Davis of H.M.
navy to Mrs. Porter of Bowhillan, Burt.
Died: Mrs. Magill, wife of James Magill of this city.
Cleared: the Congress, Knox, for Philadelphia; the Rebecca, West, for same.

1100 - Tues., Aug. 10, 1784

Londonderry.
Died: at Hornhead, Co. Donegal, the Lady of Charles Stewart; at Cork, Mr.
William Scot, formerly of Castlefin.
Ads: Passengers are to board the brig William on the 28th. The brig Nancy is
delayed. The ship Mary, Archibald Stevenson, 350 tons, for Newcastle and
Philadelphia Sept. 10. John Stewart jr., Cross lane, Bishop st., wants a few
tobacco spinners for America. Elizabeth Ellis has left her husband John
Ellis of Altaconny, Co. Londonderry.

1102 - Tues., Aug. 24, 1784

Londonderry.
Married: Henry Huey to Miss Tyler of Newtown Limavady.
Died: Alexander Buchanan, shoemaker in this city; at Philadelphia, Rob.
Carson, lately of Strabane.
Ads: Alexander Shannon, John Stewart, and Henry Lilly vs. Ab. Wilkinson jr.;
Abraham Wilkinson jr. will surrender himself for trial for the murder of John
Mulholland. The ship Friendship, Andrew Miller, 400 tons, for Newcastle and
Philadelphia, 20 Sept.; agents Alexander Scott, John Coningham, or Hugh
Boyle; Hugh Boyle will go with the ship. The brig Peggy, Capt. Stewart, from
Londonderry May 12, arrived at Philadelphia in eight weeks with passengers,
all well.

1103 - Tues., Aug. 31, 1784

Dublin.
Mr. O'Flinn of Ship st. had his son baptized George Washington; he has a
cellar in that street where he sells green groceries, small beer, and brick
dust. Thomas Craddock, a letter-founder who worked with Mr. Parker of
Grafton st., was shot by the soldiers guarding Dignam and is not expected to
recover; others also were killed.

Londonderry.
At the Omagh assizes: James Brown alias M'Nabb, for horse and cow stealing,
is to be executed Nov. 18.
Ads: Mary Ho___ or Dihan and William Dihan, Gortskrehan, are separating.

1104 - Tues., Sept. 7, 1784

Londonderry.
Sunday, the brig William, Capt. Kirkpatrick, sailed for Philadelphia with
cloth and 150 passengers.

1105 - Tues., Sept. 14, 1784

Dublin.
A thirteen year old son of Mr. Cunningham, Pill lane, starch and blue
manufacturer, was caught in one of the business's large wheels and killed.

Londonderry.
Ads: Notice by George Hargan: James Hargan has advertised the sale of his
interest in a tenement in Bog side where Neal O'Boyle, staymaker, dwells, but
James is only a tenant for life; the premises were the estate of James's late
wife, Catherine Hargan otherwise Peoples, deceased, mother of George Hargan,
and whose only child and heir-at-law George is; he is also heir-at-law of
Eleanor Peoples, his grandmother, who obtained the original lease.

1106 - Tues., Sept. 21, 1784

Londonderry.
Died: at Ferryquay gate, Alexander Wilson; David Fairly.
Ads: The brigantine Coningham, 300 tons, ten months old, for Baltimore and
Richmond by Oct. 4; James Moor jr. will go on her to care for the passengers.

1107 - Tues., Sept. 28, 1784

Dublin.
Died: in Dorset st., Mrs. Catherine, wife of Rev. Tristram Patterson of
Rathmelton, Co. Donegal, daughter of Frederick Cunningham, late surveyor at
Skerries; at his father's house near Fintona, Sept. 4, Rev. John Christie,
curate of Arboe.

1108 - Tues., Oct. 5, 1784

Londonderry.
Died: Tuesday last, James Buchanan, many years a butcher in our market, in
Butcher st.; at Ballyartin near Cumber, Mrs. M'Cullogh; at Rapho, William
Knox.

1109 - Tues., Oct. 12, 1784

Dublin.
Died: of a malignant fever, Counsellor Richard Barnard, eldest son of the
Bishop of Killaloe; at Garryhinch, King's Co., Rev. Peter Warburton, his
estate devolving upon John Warburton of Queen's Co.; in Cook st., Rev. Mr.
Austan, an ex-Jesuit.

Londonderry.
The St. Patrick, the Faithful Steward, the Buckskin, and the Jenny all
arrived safely in America.
Ads: The brig Mary, Jo. Curry, for New York on Oct. 18; Sam Curry, agent.

1110 - Tues., Oct. 19, 1784

Londonderry.
Cleared: the Coningham, Stevenson, for New York and the Mary, Stevenson, for
Philadelphia.

1111 - Tues., Oct. 26, 1784

Dublin, Oct. 21.
Died: last week at Newcastle near Belfast, Mrs. Elizabeth Allcock.

Londonderry.
Died: Mrs. Wilson; Mrs. Inns; at Dublin, aged 16, Miss Major; at Liverpool,
Mrs. Couts.
Cleared: the Mary, Curry, for New York.
Ads: Dorothea Babington, widow and administratrix of Rev. W. Babington, late
of Glebe House, Co. Londonderry, vs. Thomas Richard; defendant's interest in
the house in Maghera occupied by John M'Culla, innkeeper, to be sold.

1112 - Tues., Nov. 2, 1784

Londonderry.
The brig <u>Hibernia</u> (formerly the <u>Grace</u>), Capt. George, arrived safely at
Baltimore in 13 weeks.
Married: Jo. Cochran of Fahan to Miss Macky, Gallagh.
Died: Mr. Cun. Balfour of the Custom-house.
Ads: James Scott, Gortanegan, parish of Cappagh, Co. Tyrone, was murdered on
Oct. 21; reward for discovery of the murderers is offered by Robert, Edward,
John, and Robert Scott, Gortanegan.

1114 - Tues., Nov. 16, 1784

Londonderry.
Died: near St. Johnston, Mr. Alexander Cochran sr.

1115 - Tues., Nov. 23, 1784

Londonderry.
Married: John Willington to Miss Garraway.
Died: Saturday last, Miss Harrison; at Maghrecallaghan near Strabane, Miss
Ellz. Brown; at Letterkenny, Mr. William Grove.

1116 - Tues., Nov. 30, 1784

Londonderry.
Married: John Alexander to Miss King at Newtown Limavady.

1117 - Tues., Dec. 7, 1784

Londonderry.
Married: George M'Connell of this city, merchant, to Miss Mary Reynolds,
second daughter of John Reynolds of Coolbeg, Co. Donegal.

1118 - Tues., Dec. 14, 1784

Dublin.
The <u>Congress</u>, Knox, from Londonderry, the <u>Three Brothers</u>, Giles, from
Belfast, and the <u>Favourite John</u>, Hughes, from Dublin, arrived at Philadelphia
Sept. 13 with over 1,000 emigrants.

Londonderry.
Married: Mr. Brown, apothecary, to Miss Campbell.
Died: James Smith of Enoch, Co. Derry; Mrs. Porter, wife of Mr. M. Porter,
Elochmore, Co. Donegal.

1120 - Tues., Dec. 28, 1784

Londonderry.
The brig <u>William</u>, Capt. Kirkpatrick, arrived at Philadelphia after six weeks.
Married: F. Moore to Miss Jane Alexander.
Died: Thomas Ledlie, for many years a land-carriage officer in this city;
Capt. James King, son of the Dean of Rapho, companion of Capt. Cooke, at
Nice, Italy.

INDEX

133

Beasley, Edmund 402
Beasley, Thomas 376
Beatty, John 689
Beaty, John 484
Beaty, William 176
Beaufort, William 440
Bective, Earl 343
Beesley, Ed. 472
Begley, Patrick 477
Beirne, William 89
Beishane, R. 1043
Bell, --- Sgt. 900
Bell, George 229
Bell, Jeremiah 1019
Bell, Jo. 818
Bell, John 434
Bell, Joseph 815
Bell, Sarah 1019
Bellamont, Earl 232,319
Bellamont, Earl 666
Bellew, --- Mrs. 428
Bellew, Jane 618
Bellew, M. 1020
Bellew, Mark 225,236
Bellingham, Allan 232
Belsingham, --- Miss 520
Belvedere, Earl 384
Belvedere, Earl 54,338
Bennet, Mary 926
Bennet, Stephen 269
Bennet, Stephen sr. 926
Bennett, --- Widow 398
Bennett, Fortune 3
Bennett, Thomas 46
Benson, --- Miss 360
Benson, Hill Rev. 302
Benson, James 376
Benson, John B. 425
Benson, L. 621
Benson, Paul 376,733
Benson, Peter 137,142
Benson, Peter sr. 853
Benson, Richard 17
Benson, Thomas 503
Benton, --- Miss 474
Beresford, John 309,1049
Beresford, John 44,210
Berford, George 131
Bermingham, --- Miss 222
Bermingham, Edward 223
Bernard, Francis 323
Bernard, Susannah 147
Berrit, Patrick 275
Berwick, Eleanor 396
Besborough, Earl 640
Betagh, Thomas 992
Bever, --- Cornet 498
Bibby, Joseph 301
Biggar, --- 499
Bigot, Walter Rev. 386
Bindon, Elizabeth 44
Bingham, James 253
Binning, --- Miss 493
Birch, John 289,291
Bird, James 474
Birmingham, Margaret 538
Bishop, --- Miss 32
Black, Hugh 1056
Black, James 1056,1059
Black, James 706
Black, John 1,348,706
Black, Margaret 1087
Black, Robert Rev. 1087
Black, Samuel 136
Blackall, --- Miss 1024
Blackall, Roger 910

Blackall, Roger Rev 1057
Blacker, Alicia 38
Blacker, Letitia 1043
Blacker, Sam. 1002
Blacker, Stewart 257
Blacker, William 1043
Blacker, William 643,714
Blackwell, Jonathan 294
Blackwood, John 498
Blackwood, Robert 261
Blain, Susannah 329
Blair, --- Miss 1091
Blair, Arthur 392
Blair, Hu. 209
Blair, James 392,500
Blair, John 357
Blair, John jr. 33
Blake, Pat. 1002
Blake, Richard B. 384
Blake, Robert 1002
Blakeney, Charles 449
Bland, John 329
Blaquire, John 375
Blashford, --- Rev. 103
Blayney, Lady 311
Blayney, Lord 361
Bleakly, Guy 8
Blenerhasset, Rich'd 900
Blenham, Michael 876
Blessing, John 563
Bligh, --- Gen. 338
Bligh, --- Rev. 615
Blood, William jr. 44
Bloomfield, John 338
Bloss, Henry L. 281
Blow, --- Miss 289
Blundell, --- 284
Bodde, Bartholomew 255
Boggen, Patrick 473
Boggs, --- Miss 893,1035
Bogs, --- Mrs. 962
Bohilly, Catherine 797
Bohilly, James 797
Bolingbroke, Mary 8
Bolton, Cornelius 345
Bolton, William 396
Bomt---, John 386
Bond, Andrew 527
Bond, Mary 527
Bond, Thomas 1019,1020
Bond, Thomas 130,914
Bonynge, John 164,428
Booth, --- Adjt 1033
Booth, Richard 386
Borbag, Philip 381
Bourke, James 644
Bourne, Mary 277
Bourns, --- 601
Bowden, John Rev. 382
Bowe, Richard 255
Bowen, --- Miss 472
Bowson, --- Capt. 207
Boyce, Roger Rev. 122
Boyd, --- Miss 456
Boyd, Elisia 1094
Boyd, George 425
Boyd, Hugh 400
Boyd, Jane 957
Boyd, Margaret 178
Boyd, Robert 404
Boyle, --- 818
Boyle, --- Miss 219,474
Boyle, Daniel 541
Boyle, Hugh 1102
Boyle, James 1067
Boyle, James 395,532

Boyle, John 599
Boyle, Mary Ann 395
Boyne, --- Capt. 1040
Boyne, Lord 57,323
Boyne, Richard Lord 90
Bozier, --- 491
Brabazon, Edward 53
Brabazon, Philip 2
Brabazon, William 142
Bradburn, Alexander 659
Braddel, William 162
Braddell, George 5
Braddle, --- Miss 491
Bradford, J. 333
Bradley, --- 509
Bradley, --- 865
Bradley, --- Mrs. 509
Bradley, Hulton 601
Bradley, Mary 503,910
Bradley, Patrick 465
Bradly, Pat 77,279,309
Bradstreet, Samuel 275
Bradstreet, Simon 164
Brady, --- 1075
Brady, --- Rev. 437
Brady, P. 901
Brady, Patrick 414
Brampson, John B. 434
Bran, David 397
Branagan, Peter 333
Breeson, Michael 1060
Brenan, Darby 563
Brennan, James 252,256
Brereton, --- 331
Brereton, --- Capt. 273
Brerton, George 953
Brett, John 5
Brice, Edward 761
Brice, Prudence 761
Brien, John 137
Brien, Mary 454
Bringle, Sarah 493
Bristol, Earl 347
Bristow, Roger 375
Broderick, Samuel 187
Bromhall, Paul 624
Brooke, Arthur 222,345
Brooke, Gustavus 109
Brooks, --- Capt. 363
Broomer, Henry 292
Brown, --- 1118
Brown, --- 48
Brown, --- 535
Brown, --- Miss 458
Brown, --- Miss 8,14,345
Brown, --- Widow 19
Brown, Abram 1039
Brown, Alexander 199
Brown, Ann 73
Brown, David 17
Brown, Dominick 384
Brown, Ellz. 1115
Brown, George 1031,1070
Brown, James 201,1103
Brown, James jr. 553
Brown, Jenny 943
Brown, John 164,329,574
Brown, John 943
Brown, Joseph 98,368
Brown, Mary 275
Brown, Morris G. 289
Brown, Samuel 182
Brown, William 368
Browne, --- Rev. 292
Browne, Arthur 747
Browne, Edward 38

Chapman, Martha 818
Charleton, --- Miss 40
Charleton, Geo. 186,303
Charleton, Richard 360
Charlton, Thomas 637,706
Cheevers, William 1036
Chenevia, --- Col. 396
Chenevix, Richard 761
Cherry, --- 1030
Chesevix, --- Mrs. 46
Chevers, --- 241
Chevers, Norman 7,21
Chevers, William 1031
Chichester, --- Miss 412
Chichester, William 295
Chilick, George 1024
Chinnery, Geo. Rev. 858
Christian, --- Miss 470
Christie, John 297,1107
Christy, --- Rev. 1048
Church, George 527
Church, John 927
Church, Robert 676
Church, S. 527
Civil, --- Mrs. 1087
Clancy, Michael 403
Clandennan, Jane 298,344
Clanrickard, Earl 981
Clanwilliam, Lord 520
Clare, Lord 350
Clark, --- Rev. 48
Clark, Alexander 213,314
Clark, Charles 845
Clark, Henry Rev. 491
Clark, James 787
Clark, Jane 587
Clark, John 286,334,348
Clark, Michael 230
Clark, Robert 587
Clark, Thomas 481
Clarke, --- Col. 377
Clarke, --- Miss 442
Clarke, Charles 269
Clarke, Cornelius 153
Clarke, John 1056
Clarke, Matthew 292
Clarke, Michael 253,449
Clayton, --- 325
Cleary, --- 35
Cleghorn, William 1033
Cleland, --- Capt. 543
Clement, William 967
Clements, --- 240
Clements, --- 618
Clements, --- Miss 520
Clements, John Rev. 393
Clements, Nat. 520,521
Clements, Nathaniel 147
Clements, Theophilus 563
Clenachan, C. M. 1004
Clenachan, M. Miss 1004
Clendennen, --- 47
Clerk, Alexander 174
Cliboorn, --- 386
Clifford, Will. 251
Clogher, Bishop 973
Clonmore, Baron 932
Clutterbuck, Law. 472
Coates, Thomas 353
Cochran, --- Miss 1017
Cochran, Alex jr. 535
Cochran, Alex. jr 98,166
Cochran, Alex. sr. 1114
Cochran, Andrew 1017
Cochran, James 111
Cochran, Jane 294

Cochran, John Rev. 761
Cochran, Margaret 166
Cochran, Rob. 1056
Cochran, Robert 109
Cochran, Sam 987
Cockburn, George 306
Cockran, John 2
Cod, W. 486
Codd, --- Miss 393
Coddington, Dix. 449
Coffy, Thomas 333
Coghlan, --- Miss 719
Coghlan, Mary 277
Colclough, Caesar 364
Colclough, Mary 512
Cole, Alexander 382
Cole, Arthur 969
Cole, Patrick 481
Coleman, John Rev. 229
Coleman, Lawrence 277
Coleman, Lawrence 311
Coleman, Robert 592
Coleman, William 133
Colgan, James 39
Colgan, Patrick 195
Colgan, Peter 416
Colhon, Charles 53
Colhoun, Alexander 7,9
Colhoun, Ambrose 173
Colhoun, James 719
Colhoun, Jane 497
Colhoun, John 9
Colhoun, Margaret 9
Colhoun, Sarah 1019
Colhoun, William 7,9,497
Colhoun, William 940
Coll, Isabel 62
Coll, Roger 286
Coll, Rose 286
Collier, William 563
Collins, --- Miss 992
Collins, John 948
Collins, Margaret 948
Cololly, --- 530
Colthurst, John C. 345
Colvil, Robert 27
Colvill, Alexander 512
Colville, --- Capt. 808
Coman, John 793
Con, Sarah 220
Conaughan, John 793
Coningham, Catherine 317
Coningham, Charles 298
Coningham, Elizabeth 303
Coningham, Jane 614
Coningham, John 1081
Coningham, John 1102
Coningham, John 303,448
Coningham, John 947,978
Coningham, Michael 223
Coningham, Redmond 317
Coningham, Rich. 992
Coningham, Thomas 1035
Coningham, William 1081
Coningham, William 614
Coningham, William 947
Connell, --- 335
Connell, --- Miss 458
Connelly, Bryan 551
Connor, --- Miss 305
Connor, Conell 793
Connor, Edward 24
Connor, John 8,15
Connor, Michael 155,292
Connor, Thomas 448
Conolly, Thomas 901

Conrahy, Michael 759
Conroy, Michael 150
Conway, Daniel 793
Conway, Patrick 793
Conyngham, Dickson 1079
Conyngham, John 488
Conyngham, Red. 1071
Conyngham, Sylvan 713
Conyngham, William 1083
Conyngham, William 339
Conyngham, William 713
Cook, James Capt. 343
Cook, John 556
Cook, Martha 71
Cook, Stephen Lt. 210
Cooke, --- 8
Cooke, --- Capt. 874
Cooke, John 9
Cooke, Peter 472
Cooke, Thomas 8
Cooper, --- Miss 472
Cooper, --- Widow 397
Cooper, Joanna 32
Coote, --- Mrs. 666
Coots, Will 637
Cope, --- Counsellor 363
Cope, --- Mrs. 470
Cope, Anthony Rev. 498
Coppinger, --- Miss 437
Coppinger, William 574
Corbally, James 432
Corbet, Francis Rev. 338
Corcoran, Edward 18
Corkan, --- 533
Corker, --- Lt. 292
Cormick, --- 355
Corrigan, Constantine 40
Corrigan, Judith 34
Corrigan, Patrick 827
Corrigan, Terence 137
Corry, --- 152
Corry, Armar L. 386,643
Corry, Armar L. 812
Corry, Catherine 333
Corry, James 729
Corry, Mary Mrs. 386
Costigan, John 277
Cottingham, --- Rev. 725
Cottinham, George 211
Coughlan, John 142
Coulter, --- Miss 265
Councel, --- Miss 336
Count, John 1074
Courrey, Archibald 436
Courtney, Maur. 768
Courtney, Owen 14
Couts, --- Mrs. 1111
Cowan, --- 192
Cowan, John 630
Cowan, Richard 392,799
Cowdon, James 513
Cowdon, Martha 513
Cox, --- Lt. 558
Cox, George 339
Cox, Michael 17
Cox, Richard 393
Coyle, Bryan 600,639
Coyle, Charity 806
Coyle, Frederick 161
Coyle, James 906
Coyle, Margaret 906
Coyle, William 1079
Craddock, John 592
Craddock, Thomas 1103
Craddock, William 488
Cradock, John Rev. 681

Craghead, Ann 8
Craig, --- 323
Craig, Alexander 481
Craig, Elizabeth 408
Craig, Thomas 408
Craig, William 393
Cramshy, Donald 599
Cramshy, James 599
Crawford, --- 172
Crawford, --- Cnsllr 640
Crawford, --- Dr. 1066
Crawford, --- Miss 585
Crawford, Ann 252
Crawford, James 284,504
Crawford, James 89,252
Crawford, John 592
Creighton, Abraham 3
Creighton, John 384
Creighton, William 81
Creighton, William 971
Crigan, --- Mrs. 584
Crigan, James 315,316
Crigan, Margaret 316
Crilly, Patrick 2
Crimble, Charles 372
Crinnion, George 88
Croaisdale, --- Miss 12
Crofton, Lady 532
Crofton, Malby 13
Crofts, Sarah 727
Cromby, James Rev. 229
Crompton, Heape 972
Crompton, Isabella 972
Crookshank, - Aldrmn 144
Crookshank, Alex. 924
Crookshank, Eliz'th 144
Crookshank, William 553
Crookshanks, George 376
Crosdaile, Richard 343
Crosdale, Eliza 636
Cross, Ezekiel D. 974
Crosse, Hawks 14
Crotty, Bart. Rev. 26
Crow, James 292
Crowe, --- 488
Crowe, James 259
Crowe, Robert sr. 393
Cruise, --- Mrs. 314
Cruise, Val. 38
Cruthers, Adam 494
Cudbert, William 1070
Cuffe, --- Miss 442
Cuffe, --- Miss 8
Cuffe, Francis Rev. 339
Culbert, --- Miss992
Culbertson, Samuel 654
Culbertson, Thomas 270
Cullen, --- Miss 437
Cullidon, --- Miss 458
Culter, --- Miss 440
Cumberland, --- Rev. 320
Cumberland, Dennison 259
Cuming, Anne 442
Cummin, --- Capt. 558
Cummin, Alexander 939
Cummin, Alexander 968
Cummin, Rebecca 968
Cumming, John 1056
Cuningham, Archibald 300
Cuningham, Dixon 9
Cuningham, John Col. 598
Cuningham, Thomas 339
Cunningham, --- 1105
Cunningham, --- Srgn 363
Cunningham, Barbara 2
Cunningham, David 2

Cunningham, Fredk 1107
Cuppage, --- Miss 1039
Cuppage, Alexander 33
Curley, Patrick 521
Curren, Edward 408
Currin, --- Miss 399
Curry, --- Capt. 1095
Curry, Arch. 442
Curry, Elizabeth 256
Curry, Jo. 1109
Curry, Joseph 1041,1077
Curry, Joseph 207,221
Curry, Joseph 293,981
Curry, Sam. 207,209,221
Curry, Sam. 235,256,290
Curry, Sam. 768,863,1041
Curry, Samuel 1072,1087
Curry, Samuel 1095
Curtis, Charles 459
Cusack, --- 349
Cushaglen, Patrick 927
Cust, Henry 672
Custis, Samuel 2
D'Arcy, --- Rev. 333
Dainty, Joseph 1056
Dalton, --- 335
Dalton, John 244
Daly, --- Miss 285
Daly, Daniel 759
Daly, Dennis 384
Daly, Edmond 333
Daly, Joseph 116
Dancier, --- Mrs. 829
Daniel, --- 489
Daniel, --- Lt. 543
Daniel, --- Rev. 719
Daniel, Alexander 672
Daniel, Thomas Rev. 232
Darby, --- Counsel'r 396
Darby, William 222
Darcus, Henry 376,555
Darcus, John 317,724
Darcy, --- Mrs. 429
Darcy, Andrew 10
Dardis, William 312
Darley, --- 147
Darley, --- 325
Darley, --- Mrs. 829
Darquier, William 601
Darragh, --- Aldmn 323
Dartry, Lord 601
Daunt, --- Surgeon 1020
Davenport, Edward 233
Davenport, Joseph 41
Davies, Daniel 375
Davis, --- Capt. 600
Davis, --- Lt. 1099
Davis, Ann 613
Davis, Anne 700
Davis, Archibald 396
Davis, Jane 957
Davis, John 952,957
Davis, Mark 250
Davis, Thomas sr. 700
Davitt, Patrick 532
Davy, Mary 26
Davy, Samuel 402
Davys, Richard 89
Dawley, Charles 940
Dawly, Mary 62
Dawson, --- 583
Dawson, --- Miss 708
Dawson, --- Mrs. 708
Dawson, --- Rev. 601
Dawson, Arthur 304,314
Dawson, Charles 336

Dawson, James 1056
Dea, Henry 521
Deale, --- Miss 3
Dean, Robert T. 309,315
Deane, Daniel 382
Deane, Philip 150
Deane, William 275
de Arcy, James 26
Debrisay, --- Lt. Col. 7
DeCourcy, --- Miss 236
de Courcy, Baron 396
Deering, William 753,810
Deey, Christopher 244
Deey, Robert 971
Delahide, John 333
de Lamote, James B. 541
de la Mothe, James 544
Delap, Andrew 71
Delap, J. S. 1042
Delap, Robert 395,995
Delap, Samuel 387,426
Delap, Samuel 889
Delap, William 1089
Delawar, William H. 400
De Montalt, Lord 520
Dening, Isabella 128
Dening, Joseph 128
Dening, Mary 128
Denning, John 392
Denning, Monro 66
Dennis, --- Miss 333
Denny, --- Mrs. 729
Denny, David 998
Derham, Thomas 36
Dermond, Hannah 201
Dermot, Catherine 768
Dermot, Catherine 773
Dermot, Elizabeth 974
Dermot, Michael 550,637
Deroche, Stephen 376
Desart, Lord 8
Desart, Sarah 17
Desbrisay, Theophilus 13
Despard, --- Capt. 12
Despard, --- Surgeon 459
Despard, George 384
Despard, Maria 384
Devatt, Valentine 18
Develin, Mary 195
Devereu, Peter 1045
Devlin, Neal 915
Devlin, Owen 57
Devoy, Andrew 666
Deyermort, Mary 491
Diamond, --- Rev. 259
Dick, --- 488
Dick, --- 592
Dick, Samuel 230
Dickenson, --- Miss 391
Dickenson, Daniel 338
Dickenson, Patrick 974
Dickey, Patrick 974
Dickson, Bar. 1056
Dickson, Joseph 1056
Dickson, Thomas 13
Dies Monte, Antonio 760
Dignam, --- 1103
Dignam, --- Rev. 484
Dihan, Mary 1103
Dihan, William 1103
Dilkes, Michael O. 338
Dillon, --- 491
Dillon, --- Miss 535
Dillon, Edward 193
Dillon, Henry 11
Dillon, John 1002

Dillon, Luke 153
Dillon, Peter 1039
Dillon, Robert 384
Dillon, William 193
Dinsmore, Patrick 199
Dinsmore, William 191
Divin, --- Widow 914
Divin, Bridget 1027
Divin, Cha. 1027
Divin, John 914,1027
Divin, Pat. 1027
Divin, Patrick 914
Divin, Sara Mrs. 1027
Divin, William 914
Divlaghan, Owen 607
Dixon, --- Lt. 719
Doak, Frederick 953
Dobbin, --- Miss 35
Dobbin, Mary Mrs. 596
Dobbin, Sam. 1056
Dobbs, --- Lt. 630
Dobbs, --- Rev. 153
Dobbyn, Robert 382
Dobson, Elinor 375
Dobson, Richard 973
Dobson, Robert 375
Dodd, Tody 333
Doggart, Edward 104
Doggart, Jenny 104
Doggart, Mary 104
Dogharty, Catherine 191
Dogherty, Bernard 927
Dogherty, George 687
Dogherty, Hugh 124
Doherty, Edward 968
Doherty, Henry 900
Doherty, John 186
Dolan, James 144
Dombille, --- Rev. 249
Donaghy, --- Rev. 396
Donaghy, Arthur 357
Donaghy, Henry 914
Donaghy, Honor 357
Donaghy, Mary 474
Donaldson, --- Miss 574
Donaldson, James 99
Donegall, Countess 303
Donellan, --- Capt. 959
Donellan, David N. 437
Doneraile, Lady 601
Donichy, Margaret 523
Donichy, Will. 523
Donnel, Mary 416
Donnelan, Edward 17
Donnellan, --- Rev. 618
Donnelly, Dudley 234,298
Donnelly, Martha 67
Donohoe, Elizabeth 303
Donohy, Mary 510
Donovan, Daniel 160
Donovan, Edward 97
Doogan, Pat 1057
Doolan, Margaret 223
Doran, Thomas 366
Dorney, --- 232
Doude, Luke Rev. 162
Dougherty, --- 1032
Dougherty, --- 773
Dougherty, Ann 402
Dougherty, Anne 442
Dougherty, Anthony 818
Dougherty, Arthur 73,93
Dougherty, Bernard 974
Dougherty, Edward 182
Dougherty, Francis 234
Dougherty, Francis 654

Dougherty, James 353,543
Dougherty, James 562
Dougherty, John 277,607
Dougherty, John 887
Dougherty, Martha 1017
Dougherty, Mary 353
Dougherty, Michael 1085
Dougherty, Neal 36
Dougherty, Pat 1057
Dougherty, William 818
Douglas, George 233
Douglas, Hugh 33
Douglas, John 1056
Dowdall, --- Miss 9
Dowdall, James Rev. 197
Dowde, James 289
Dowker, --- Mrs. 498
Dowling, --- 1018
Dowling, James jr. 296
Dowling, John 254
Down, Patrick 873
Downes, Alexander 440
Downey, William 376,379
Downey, William 381
Downing, --- Miss 429
Downing, John 386
Downing, Wm. see Downey
Downs, --- Mrs. 257
Downs, Rose 286
Doyle, Benjamin B. 262
Doyle, Frederick 953
Doyle, James 733
Doyle, John 289,973
Doyle, Thomas 262
Doyle, William 1077
Drake, Darius 275
Draper, Henry 973
Drennon, William 481
Drew, Richard R. 27
Drought, --- Capt. 219
Drue, John 557
Drumgool, --- 585
Drumgoole, Charles 391
Dryer, Felix 192
Ducart, Davis 298
Dudgeon, John 18
Dudley, --- Widow 5
Dudy, Catherine 606
Dudy, John 477,479
Dudy, Martha 477
Duffe, Pat 10
Duffy, --- 537
Duffy, Pat 745
Dugan, Elizabeth 252
Duglass, James 200
Duglass, John 200
Duke, --- 392
Duke, John 900
Dulles, William 27
Dunbar, Charles 666
Dunbar, D. 940
Dunboyne, Lord 126
Dunkin, --- Mrs. 574
Dunkin, --- Rev. 640
Dunlap, --- Miss 286
Dunlap, William 1056
Dunlope, George 320
Dunlope, Samuel 320
Dunluce, Lord 351
Dunn, --- 22
Dunn, --- 333
Dunn, James 91
Dunn, James Rev. 621
Dunn, John 15,18,21
Dunn, Philip Rev. 878
Dunn, Polly 13

Dunn, William 899
Dunsany, Lord 339
Duprey, Joseph 878
Dutton, Sarah 520
Dwyer, --- 1018
Dwyer, --- 323
Dwyer, Edward 875
Dwyer, William 127
Dysan, William 78
Eakins, George 209
Eakins, Thomas 940
Eaton, Ed. 255
Eaton, James 878
Ebery, --- Mrs. 416
Eccles, Arthur 328
Eccles, Henry 955
Echlin, John 377
Edmiston, --- Mrs. 408
Edmonds, John 382
Edmondson, Ben 1099
Edward, Walter 257
Edwards, Edward 351,500
Edwards, Thomas Capt 615
Egan, James 588
Egan, Thomas 601
Eggar, Thomas 311
Eife, --- Miss 219
Eife, B. 219
Eife, Luke 219
Elder, John Rev. 768
Ellard, --- 131
Ellis, --- Miss 481
Ellis, Elizabeth 1100
Ellis, George 222
Ellis, Henry 375
Ellis, Humphry 41
Ellis, John 798,1100
Ellwood, S. 1095
Ely, Countess 306
Emerson, --- Aldermn 292
Emerson, John 103
Emery, John 1056
English, --- 391
English, --- Miss 474
English, John 491
Ennis, Perrot 1038
Erne, Lady 327
Erskine, John 304,322
Ersksine, Jane 304
Euant, Sarah 202
Euart, Thomas 747
Eustace, C. 409
Eustace, Christopher 234
Evans, Eyre 96
Evans, Francis 481
Evans, Pierce 103
Evary, George 229
Evelyn, William 399
Everard, R. L. 442
Evory, Geo. 261,295,317
Evory, James 295,317
Evory, Mary 295,317
Ewing, -- 98,209,320,640
Ewing, Alex 15,18,67,81
Ewing, Alex. 105,134,182
Ewing, Alex. 184,197,287
Ewing, Alex. 304,351,402
Ewing, Alex. 471,922
Ewing, Humphry 178
Ewing, John 1079
Ewing, John 566,799,1069
Ewing, Patrick 203
Ewing, Thomas 409
Eyre, Powell 162
Fagan, James 437
Fairchild, Wm. 925,930

138

Fairly, David 1106
Fairly, David Rev. 380
Fairly, John 475,1004
Fairly, Rob. 1017
Falkiner, William 457
Fall, --- Capt. 421
Fallin, Laughlin 349
Fallon, Malacky 873
Fallon, William 509
Falls, --- Miss 1093
Falls, --- Miss 610
Falls, Henry 1056
Fanning, Audley 809,1095
Fanning, Charles 188
Paris, Thomas 1056
Farley, Thomas 1056
Farnon, James 305
Farnon, Patrick 305
Farrel, --- Mrs. 355
Farrel, --- Widow 713
Farrel, Charles Rev. 706
Farrell, --- Dr. 592
Farrell, N. 1056
Farrell, Patrick 1020
Farrelly, Mary 291
Farren, Dennis 977
Farren, Jane 1037
Farren, Nola 977
Farrington, --- 498
Faucet, W. 397
Faulkner, --- Miss 640
Faulkner, George 339
Faulkner, T. T. 380
Faulkner, Thomas 68,75
Faussett, --- Miss 347
Faviere, --- Maj. 384
Fay, --- Rev. 953
Fay, P. Rev. 34
Fearnot, Captain 514
Featherstone, - Miss 403
Fehrman, Ann 457
Fehrman, Gotfred G. 457
Feloon, --- 805
Fenton, Percey 153
Ferguson, --- 336
Ferguson, --- 402
Ferguson, --- Aldrmn 355
Ferguson, --- Mrs. 509
Ferguson, Andrew 243,356
Ferguson, Andrew Rev 614
Ferguson, Catherine 394
Ferguson, D. H. 1022
Ferguson, Edward 458
Ferguson, Elizabeth 673
Ferguson, James 232
Ferguson, John 1022,1081
Ferguson, William 394
Ferris, Francis 74
Feter, Sarah 1086
Fetherson, Thomas 470
Fetherston, Francis 618
Fetherton, Francis 973
Fidder, John 4
Field, James 18
Fields, John 481
Finigan, W. 818
Finlay, --- Miss 730
Finlay, Thomas 459
Finly, John 793
Finney, Edward 565
Firebrand, Capt. 156,979
Fisher, James 1033
Fisher, James 203,541
FitzAndrew, John F. 131
FitzGerald, James 155
Fitzgerald, -- Gen. 90

Fitzgerald, -- Miss 1014
Fitzgerald, --- 1095
Fitzgerald, --- 335
Fitzgerald, --- Miss 244
Fitzgerald, Augustn 368
Fitzgerald, C. 391
Fitzgerald, Catherine 25
Fitzgerald, D. 1014
Fitzgerald, Edward 655
Fitzgerald, Emily 232
Fitzgerald, Gerald 336
Fitzgerald, P. 610
Fitzgibbon, John 393
Fitzmaurice, --- 171
Fitzmaurice, James 397
Fitzmaurice, Jn. 309,315
Fitzmorres, Thomas 583
Fitzpatrick, John 1014
Fitzpatrick, John 305
Fitzpatrick, Mary 299
Fitzpatrick, Tim. 236
Fitzsimons, Anne 28
Fitzsimons, Henry 124
Fitzsimons, James 592
Fitzsimons, Mich. 1056
Fitzsimons, Robert 155
Fitzwilliam, Viscnt 416
Fivey, W. 375
Fivir, Edmund 953
Flack, James 397
Flanagan, John 873
Flanagan, Peter 331
Fleming, --- 850
Fleming, Alexander 54
Fleming, Catherine 11
Fleming, Paul 43
Fleming, Tho. 1056
Fleming, Valentine 34
Fletcher, --- 207
Fletcher, Alexander 582
Flin, --- 8
Flood, --- 434
Flood, --- Miss 544
Flood, --- Mrs. 618
Floyd, John 471
Folliot, William 613
Foord, Timothy 137
Forbes, --- Alderman 354
Forbes, W. 359
Ford, --- Miss 345
Ford, James 249
Ford, Patrick 8
Forde, --- 331
Forrest, Charles 1040
Forster, Ann 32
Forster, Ed. 713
Forster, John 535
Forster, Robert 309
Forster, Thomas 52
Forster, William 203
Forsythe, Jacob 1024
Fortescue, --- Miss 719
Forward, Isabella 932
Forward, William 932
Foster, --- 273
Foster, --- Miss 805
Foster, C. Capt. 1027
Foster, James 799,1046
Foster, John T. 481
Foster, Nicholas 535
Fowle, Mary 148
Fownes, Elizabeth 640
Fownes, William 632,634
Fox, George 143
Fox, Henry 376
Fox, Thomas 195

Francis, John 472
Frankland, Thomas 363
Franks, John 618
Franqueford, --- 284
Franquefort, Henry 287
Frazer, --- Miss 640
Frazer, George W. 642
Freel, Philip 270
Freeman, Francis 878
Freeman, Jasper 344
Freke, John 449,504
French, --- Alderman 687
French, --- Widow 1015
French, --- Widow 386
French, Arthur 10,384
French, Arthur 601
French, Fred. 289
French, Henry 1015
French, Henry W. 396
French, James 1015
French, Jane 407
French, John 285,1015
French, Olivia 10
French, Robert 1015
French, Robert 2,697
French, Robert Lt. 35
French, Simon 407
French, William 1015
Frend, George 382
Frost, William 294
Fry, Edward 382
Fuller, Abraham 437
Fulton, --- Miss 981
Fulton, David 844
Fulton, George 897
Fulton, James 233
Fulton, Joseph 523
Fulton, Mary 831
Fulton, T. 981
Furry, --- 1017
Gaffny, --- 241
Gafney, Anne 474
Gafney, William 1091
Gage, Elizabeth 267
Gage, Hodgson 585
Gage, James 33
Gage, John 267
Gage, R. 592
Gahagan, Kedagh 563
Galan, Peter 280
Galbraith. --- Miss 525
Galbraith, Alexander 545
Galbraith, James 790(2)
Galbraith, John 386
Galbraith, Robert 130
Galbraith, Robert 914
Galbraith, Sam. 183,274
Gale, Sarah 987
Gallagher, --- 192
Gallagher, Bridget 422
Gallagher, Dan. 753
Gallagher, Denis 793,905
Gallagher, John 128,847
Gallagher, Margaret 906
Gallagher, Martha 847
Gallagher, Mary 366,422
Gallagher, Patrick 309
Gallagher, Terence 391
Gallagher, Thomas 422
Gallaugher, Francis 592
Galley, William 239
Galt, Robert 459
Galway, Viscount 54
Gamble, --- 939
Gamble, --- Miss 555
Gamble, --- Mrs. 553

Gamble, Henry 16,543
Gamble, James 981
Gamble, Mussom 1095
Gamble, Rob. 475
Gamble, Robert 16,708
Ganning, --- Miss 4
Gara, --- Miss 940
Gara, Robert 471
Gardiner, --- Mrs. 210
Gardiner, Luke 116,1062
Gardiner, Wm. Dr. 126
Garland, James 1056
Garnett, John Rev. 973
Garraway, --- Miss 1115
Garstin, --- Miss 236
Garstin, --- Miss 336
Gates, Gard., M.D. 969
Gates, George 969
Gay, Hugh 1030
Gay, Mary 992
Gaynor, David 1020
Geale, Fred. 901
Gear, --- Miss 366
Geoghegan, Owen 795
George, --- 152,209,1085
George, --- Capt. 1112
George, Rob. 1069,1077
George, Robert 1069
George, Robert 177,273
George, Robert 29,92,104
Gerran, --- 878
Gibbeny, John 334
Gibbony, John 472
Gibbs, John 801
Gibson, Robert 83
Gibson, William 977
Gibton, John 35
Gifford, G. Rev. 1076
Gilbert, F. 1033
Gilbert, Susannah 5
Gilboarn, William 24
Gilden, James sr. 29
Giles, --- 1118
Gilgan, Martin 793
Gill, Patrick 953
Gillespy, --- Surg'n 743
Gillespy, William 1035
Gillesy, Bridget 196
Gilligan, Bartholomew 35
Gillis, James 1045
Gilmour, Thomas 818
Gisborne, --- Gen. 601
Given, Catherine 513
Given, James 1027
Given, Robert 513
Given, Robert jr. 426
Gladstone, Thomas 643
Glandore, Earl 583
Glascock, --- Miss 438
Glascock, William 323
Glass, Loftus 93
Glaughan, William 481
Gledstane, --- Gen. 1070
Gledstane, George 1002
Glen, --- Miss 582
Glen, Elizabeth 211
Glen, Pat 813
Glen, William 1025
Glen, William 177,211
Glen, William 273,538
Glendowe, William 42
Glenholme, John 99
Gobbon, Charles 649
Godfrey, --- 1049
Godfrey, --- Widow 404
Goldsborough, Mary 303

Gonne, John 428,475
Gonne, Thomas 1042,1059
Good, Thomas 1057
Goodyeare, --- Miss 453
Goold, --- Miss 3
Gordon, --- Miss 577
Gordon, Alexander 327
Gordon, Gardner 80
Gordon, George 71,80,833
Gordon, James 147
Gordon, John 442,873
Gordon, Pat. 1031
Gordon, Patrick 232
Gordon, Stephen 1031
Gore, --- Alderman 459
Gore, --- Col. 366
Gore, Annesly 959
Gore, Arthur 96
Gore, Francis 88
Gore, John 1083
Gore, Manly Rev. 275
Gore, Ralph 601
Gorman, Stafford 238
Gormley, Charles 914
Gormley, Jane 436,442
Gormly, John 422
Gosford, Lord 437
Gough, George 275
Goulding, Barthol. 509
Gourney, Alice 49
Gourney, James 724
Gourney, Joseph 49
Gourney, Margaret 724
Gower, Earl 583
Gower, Louisa L. 583
Grace, John 153
Grady, Ed. 510
Grady, Standish 29
Grady, Thomas 396
Graham, --- 39
Graham, --- Col. 416
Graham, --- Miss 232
Graham, --- Miss 523
Graham, Alexander 277
Graham, Alexander 574
Graham, John 562
Graham, Thomas 232
Granard, Countess 613
Granard, Countess 901
Grange, R. C. Rev. 861
Grant, Charles 99
Grant, John 400
Grant, Samuel 459
Grattan, Henry 1014
Graves, --- Widow 391
Graves, Henry 26,32
Gray, --- Miss 1099
Gray, --- Mrs. 520
Gray, Charles 698,1071
Gray, Francis Rev. 351
Gray, Hugh 736
Gray, James 30,32
Gray, Margaret 624,1071
Gray, Richard 124
Gray, Robert 392
Graydon, --- Capt. 225
Graydon, Henry 451
Grayson, --- Miss 719
Greason, Tho. 1056
Greaves, --- Miss 592
Green, Nuttall 336
Green, Wedgeworth 28
Greene, Letitia 384
Greenfield, --- Mrs. 725
Greenhow, Joseph 103
Greenshields, William 35

Greer, --- Miss 481
Greer, A. jr. 1056
Greevaughan, Daniel 334
Gregg, --- 392
Gregg, A. 1028
Gregg, Andrew 21,193,287
Gregg, John 135
Gregg, Richard 392
Gregg, Samuel 137
Gregg, Thomas Capt. 344
Gregg, Will. 190
Gregg, William 284
Gregory, --- Dr. 1028
Gregory, John 1028
Grier, Hugh 962
Grier, Jane 8
Grier, Mildred 962
Grierson, Mary Anne 4
Griffin, Henry 220
Griffin, Michael 59
Griffith, William 301
Gronin, Charles 252
Groom, Charles 255
Grove, Blennerhasset 153
Grove, William 1115
Groves, --- Miss 743
Grumley, --- Capt. 265
Grumly, --- Capt. 966
Gudgeon, --- Lt. 236
Guerney, James 724
Guerney, Joseph 724
Guerney, Margaret 724
Gunston, John 366
Guthrie, Geo. 1056
Guy, --- Miss 147
Gwin, Henry 998
Gwyn, Mary 1033
Gwynn, George 178
Gwynn, John 422
H---, Edward 153
Hacket, James Rev. 392
Hacket, Philip 329
Hacket, Thomas 153
Hagan, --- 336
Hagan, John 191
Hagarty, Charles 1084
Hagen, Edward 116
Hall, Rebecca 323
Hall, William 393
Hallinon, Dom. Rev. 382
Halpin, John 504
Hamill, James 275
Hamilton, --- 816
Hamilton, --- Cnsllr 719
Hamilton, --- Miss 437
Hamilton, --- Miss 592
Hamilton, --- Mrs. 339
Hamilton, --- Mrs. 432
Hamilton, --- Rev. 22
Hamilton, Alexander 193
Hamilton, Alexander 422
Hamilton, Ann 41
Hamilton, Arch. 538
Hamilton, Archibald 391
Hamilton, Arthur C. 969
Hamilton, Charles 77
Hamilton, Cl. 568
Hamilton, Claudius 41
Hamilton, Claudius 968
Hamilton, Claudius 969
Hamilton, Elizabeth 397
Hamilton, Elizabeth 565
Hamilton, Flora 184
Hamilton, Francis 371
Hamilton, Fred. 1071
Hamilton, Frederic W 568

Hamilton, Frederick 503
Hamilton, Geo. 1004
Hamilton, George C. 1053
Hamilton, George C. 285
Hamilton, Gust. 58,90
Hamilton, Henry 853,991
Hamilton, Isabella 193
Hamilton, J. 363
Hamilton, James 107,183
Hamilton, James 230,339
Hamilton, John 57,273
Hamilton, John 614,818
Hamilton, John 855
Hamilton, John S. 285
Hamilton, Joseph 323
Hamilton, Patrick 183
Hamilton, Patrick 729
Hamilton, Patrick 861
Hamilton, Rebecca 521
Hamilton, Robert 8,585
Hamilton, W. 384
Hamilton, Will. 1004
Hamilton, William 184
Hamilton, William 215
Hamilton, William 914
Hamilton, William 992
Hamon, Elizabeth J. 275
Hampton, Eleanor 470
Hanagan, John 918
Hancock, --- 377
Hand, James 289
Handcock, --- Rev. 11
Handcock, Gustavus 325
Handcock, Mary 11
Handy, Samuel jr. 11
Hanger, Gabriel 72
Hanley, Oliver Rev. 7
Hanly, --- Dr. 355
Hannagan, Andrew 633
Hansard, --- Capt. 13
Hansard, Anne 13
Hard, Edward Rev. 376
Harding, --- Mrs. 192
Harding, Charles 642
Harding, Elizabeth 14
Harding, Farrel 601
Hardman, Robert 303
Hardy, John 147,366
Harford, --- Miss 333
Hargan, Catherine 1105
Hargan, George 1105
Hargan, James 1105
Hargon, Margaret 295
Hargon, Will. 295
Harkin, Charles 434
Harkin, John 548
Harkin, Sally 548
Harly, John 793
Harper, --- 145
Harper, --- 753
Harper, Samuel 164
Harper, William 202
Harpur, George 454
Harrick, John 339
Harrington, Timothy 362
Harrison, --- Miss 1115
Harrison, --- Miss 493
Harrison, Isabel 914,919
Harrison, James 331
Harrison, John 84
Harrison, Roger 1094
Harrold, Barth. 18
Hart, --- Mrs. 1021
Hart, Ed. Rev. 295,303
Hart, Edw. Rev. 475,824
Hart, Elizabeth 478,514

Hart, Fanny 303
Hart, George 478,514
Hart, George 589,1066
Hart, Henry 697
Hart, Jeremiah Rev. 270
Hart, John 475,697,1060
Hart, Nicholas 99
Hart, Robert 659
Hart, Simon 147
Hart, Winnefred 589
Hartley, --- 729
Hartpole, Robert 400
Harvey, --- 334
Harvey, --- Miss 1039
Harvey, David 1036
Harvey, George 83
Harvey, James 9,496
Harvey, John 186
Harvey, Philip 113
Harvey, Rose 496,508
Harvey, Whitfield 434
Harwood, John 142
Haslet, --- Miss 1024
Hastie, --- 152
Hastings, John 244
Hatch, Catherine 281
Hatch, Henry 281
Hauffort, Mary 26
Haven, Stephen 43,301
Hawes, Alexander 957
Hawes, Jane 957
Hawke, --- Admiral 142
Hawke, --- Lt. Col. 142
Hawkins, Christopher 393
Hay, --- Miss 555
Hay, David 63
Hayes, John 381
Hayes, Samuel 1039
Hayes, William 379
Haynes, Joseph 1080,1084
Hays, --- Miss 905
Hays, John 470
Haze, Thomas 396
Hazlet, --- Mrs. 454
Hazlet, Elizabeth 199
Healy, Daniel 173
Healy, Elms 323
Healy, John 90
Heaphy, --- 244
Hearn, Charles 37
Hearn, Philip 1056
Heathers, James 714
Hehir, Francis 332
Hehir, Spelecy 332
Hemphill, --- Adj. 585
Hemsworth, John 37
Henderson, --- Miss 396
Henderson, --- Widow 819
Henderson, James 1019
Henderson, Jane 23
Henderson, John 23,1099
Henderson, Samuel 705
Henery, Roger 291
Hennesy, John 818
Henrey, James 1056
Henry, James 350
Henzell, John 434
Heron, --- Mrs. 585
Heron, Rich. 634
Hervey, --- Miss 481
Hervey, --- Mrs. 489
Hervey, Elizabeth 385
Hervey, James 16
Hervey, John 385,408
Hervey, Mary 384
Hetterick, Sam 1072,1093

Hewet, --- Lt. 164
Hewet, James Rev. 434
Hewey, Alexander 654
Hewit, --- Rev. 618
Hezlet, James 408
Hezley, James 408
Hickey, Henry 4
Hicks, Francis 923
Hickson, --- Lt. 953
Higgenbotham, John 459
Higgins, --- Miss 384
Higgins, --- Mrs. 618
Higgins, Bridget 610
Higgins, Bryan 601,1056
Higgins, Charles 550
Higgins, Edward 1031
Higgins, Lamby 104
Higginson, Roger 396
Hill, Hugh 187,257,475
Hill, Hugh 478,514
Hill, Lancelot 11
Hill, Robert 13
Hind, --- Miss 363
Hind, --- Rev. 95
Hinds, Sarah 339
Hird, John 820
Ho---, Mary 1103
Hobart, Harriot 812
Hobbs, John 153
Hodder, William 294
Hodgings, Mary 164
Hodginson, --- Miss 391
Hodgson, --- Miss 440
Hoey, James 311
Hoey, Peter 277
Hogan, John 368
Hogarty, John 618
Hogg, --- Alderman 391
Hogg, --- Alderman 55
Hogg, Elizabeth 391
Hogg, George 701
Hogg, Will. 187,478,514
Holland, R. 1092
Holland, Robert 956
Holmes, --- Dr. 1086
Holmes, Ann 336
Holmes, Bell 306
Holmes, Benjamin 306
Holmes, Hugh 256
Holmes, James 402,974
Holmes, John 101,102,500
Holmes, John 714,1031
Holmes, Martha 257
Homan, --- 488
Homan, Brant 78
Homan, Brent 257
Homan, Richard 78,219
Homan, Richard G. 257
Homan, William 257
Honywood, D. Capt. 481
Hood, --- Miss 640
Hood, John 1067
Hood, John Rev. 214
Hoop, John 610
Hoop, John Rev. 217
Hope, --- Miss 538
Hope, Elizabeth 379
Hope, William 1025
Hope, William 177,207
Hope, William 221,273
Hope, William 379,546
Hopkins, Francis 618
Hopkins, Prudence 608
Horan, --- Alderman 386
Horan, James 359
Horan, Tobias 20

Horner, Dennis 297,304
Horner, Dennis 306
Horner, James 238
Horner, John 304,306
Horner, John jr. 297
Horner, John sr. 297
Hornidge, --- Miss 651
Horseman, Robert 636
Houston, --- 336
Houston, Francis 520
Houston, Robert 190,269
Houston, Robert 284,1058
Houston, William 507
Howard, --- Widow 382
Howard, Alfred 428
Howel, --- 448
Howison, Thomas 26
Howth, Earl 164,538
Hoyne, John Rev. 302
Hudson, --- Miss 434
Hudson, Christopher 196
Hudson, James 196
Huey, Henry 1102
Huey, James 376
Huey, Robert Rev. 186
Huggins, --- Miss 520
Hughes, --- 1118
Hughes, --- Mrs.
Hughes, Annesley 333
Hughes, James 298
Hughes, Tho. 509
Hughes, William 3
Hulbertson, William 553
Hull, --- Miss 396
Humble, --- Rev. 11
Humble, --- Rev. 612
Hume, Dinnison 333
Hume, Rt. 481
Humphrys, --- Miss 520
Humphrys, Ann 589
Hunt, --- Alderman 461
Hunt, Elmer 188
Hunt, Percival 459
Hunt, Thomas 275
Hunter, -- 7,152,203
Hunter, --- 211
Hunter, Elizabeth 299
Hunter, Elizabeth 408
Hunter, Francis 93
Hunter, James 251,314
Hunter, James 314
Hunter, James 82,103,174
Hunter, Jane 427
Hunter, John 402,743
Hunter, Margaret 402
Hunter, Nat. 427,926
Hunter, Nathaniel 207
Hunter, Rich. 1023
Hunter, Richard 299,404
Hunter, Richard 81,127
Hunter, Richard Capt 475
Hunter, Sam 1092
Hurlay, John 514
Hurry, S. Capt. 633
Hurst, Alexander Rev 973
Husband, John 292
Hussey, Dudly 323
Hussey, Nicholas 454
Huston, James 535
Huston, Margaret 535
Hutchinson, --- 399
Hutchinson, --- 520
Hutchinson, --- Dr. 1014
Hutchinson, --- Rev. 8
Hutchinson, Sam. Rev 877
Hutton, Joshua 261

Hyland, Michael 223
Hyndman, Thomas 191
Inchiquin, Earl 538,583
Ingham, Sarah 254
Ingliss, Thomas Rev. 399
Ingram, --- Mrs. 86
Ingram, Jas. Rev 250,261
Ingram, Jocelyn Rev. 28
Inns, --- Mrs. 584,1111
Irvin, Rebecca 48
Irvine, Andrew Rev. 640
Irvine, Christopher 396
Irvine, Robert 531
Irwin, --- Miss 17
Irwin, Acheson 17
Irwin, Andrew 410
Irwin, James 957
Irwin, John 143,396,456
Izod, Kevin 376
Jack, Robert 927
Jack, William 914
Jackson, --- Miss 225
Jackson, Charles 498
Jackson, Daniel Rev. 53
Jackson, George 401
Jackson, Isaac 5
Jackson, James 449
Jackson, Richard 944
Jackson, Thomas 859
Jackson, Tommy 202
Jacob, Leonard 333
Jacob, William 481
Jaffray, Robert 142
James, Martha 816
James, William 116,126
James, William 389
Jameson, --- Rev. 481
Jameson, Skeffington 290
Jamison, Elizabeth 1081
Jefferys, James S. 865
Jenkins, S. 621
Jennet, --- Miss 147
Jennings, Theobald 89
Jessop, --- Miss 440
Jessop, William 298
Jocelyn, --- Lady 2
Jocelyn, Lord 281
Johnson, --- 971
Johnson, --- Capt. 799
Johnson, Francis 152
Johnson, James 714
Johnson, John 714
Johnson, Mary 442,459
Johnson, Pat. 753
Johnson, Richard 44
Johnson, Robert 145,241
Johnson, Robert 251,509
Johnson, Robert 97,109
Johnston, --- Lt. 893
Johnston, --- Mrs. 1021
Johnston, Andrew 1001
Johnston, Gabriel 425
Johnston, Hugh 1056
Johnston, Isabella 991
Johnston, James 855
Johnston, John 349,438
Johnston, John 555,1086
Johnston, R. M. 702
Johnston, Rob. 1056
Johnston, Samuel 855
Johnston, Samuel sr. 339
Johnston, William 1056
Jones, --- 145
Jones, --- 152
Jones, --- Miss 178
Jones, --- Miss 470

Jones, Henry 9
Jones, John 143,376
Jones, Mary 144
Jones, Richard 402
Jones, Theophilus 384
Jordan, --- Capt. 363
Jordan, --- Miss 5
Jordan, Margaret 147
Joy, H. 1086
Joy, Henry 484
Judge, James 793
Judge, John 920
Kane, --- Miss 1017
Kane, --- Miss 403
Kane, Bernard 363
Kane, Denis 713
Kane, Henry 969
Kane, Honor 357
Kane, Mary 239
Kane, Pat. 1035,1057
Kane, Redmond 142,632
Karr, John 115
Kean, --- Miss 585
Kearnes, Sam. 464
Kearney, --- Rev. 592
Kearns, --- Rev. 520
Keating, James 18,99
Keating, Leo 304
Keatten, William 1017
Keeff, --- 244
Keenan, --- 1098
Keightly, Ann 679
Keightly, George 679
Keightly, William 521
Keightly, William 679
Keily, Richard 24
Keith, --- 241
Kellet, James 277
Kellet, Mary 277
Kelly, --- 015,133,137
Kelly, --- 148,977
Kelly, --- Capt. 966
Kelly, --- Major 275
Kelly, --- Miss 309
Kelly, Bryan 491
Kelly, Charles 654
Kelly, Daniel 13,18,574
Kelly, Edward 642
Kelly, Edward Rev. 1091
Kelly, Elizabeth 13
Kelly, James 1056
Kelly, James 384,1035
Kelly, Jane 23
Kelly, John 813,927
Kelly, Margaret 404,405
Kelly, Mathias Rev. 275
Kelly, Meave 164
Kelly, P. 391
Kelly, Pat. 510
Kelly, Patrick 462,876
Kelly, Sally 548
Kelly, Thomas 19,234,505
Kelso, John 989
Kenmare, Lord 535
Kenmon, Abraham 210
Kennedy, --- 131
Kennedy, --- Aldermn 558
Kennedy, --- Aldrmn 609
Kennedy, --- Aldrmn 878
Kennedy, --- Miss 491
Kennedy, --- Mrs. 180
Kennedy, Alexander 261
Kennedy, Andrew 370
Kennedy, Ann 876
Kennedy, Catherine 876
Kennedy, Catherine 953

Kennedy, George 500,957
Kennedy, George Rev. 714
Kennedy, Gilbert 101
Kennedy, James 1020,1056
Kennedy, James 400,532
Kennedy, Laurence 300
Kennedy, Maxwell Rev 983
Kennedy, Morgan 312
Kennedy, Richard 977
Kennedy, William 1024
Kennedy, William 2,160
Kennedy, William 295,317
Kennedy, William 609,878
Kenny, John 195
Keogh, --- Miss 481
Keogh, Bryan Dr. 400
Kerceval, Kene Rev. 192
Kerr, --- 192
Kerr, Charles 615
Kerr, George 186
Keys, George 392,427
Keys, John 905
Ki-kes, --- 396
Kiernan, --- Miss 470
Kiernan, Charles 135
Kildare, Lady of Bp. 329
Killaloe, Bishop 1109
Killburn, --- Rev. 464
Kilpatrick, --- Miss 580
Kilpatrick, John 481
Kimmens, John 333
Kimster, Joshua 491
King, --- 333
King, --- Miss 1002,1116
King, --- Miss 522,592
King, --- Mrs. 1060
King, --- Rev. 522
King, Ann 178
King, Anthony 363
King, Beather 1060
King, Dolly 266
King, Harriet 384
King, James 543
King, James Capt. 1120
King, Jane 8
King, John 1060
King, John 176,178,384
King, Robert 103,593
King, Thomas 582,733
King, William 690,974
Kingston, Earl 4
Kinnear, Anne 734
Kinnear, John 734,905
Kinnier, Robert 470
Kinsale, Lord 236
Kinselagh, Peter 13
Kirk, --- Miss 339
Kirk, George 834
Kirk, Hugh 238
Kirk, Robert 676
Kirk, W. M. 1070
Kirkland, --- Miss 363
Kirkland, Robert 676
Kirkpatrick, -- Miss 597
Kirkpatrick, --- 1104
Kirkpatrick, --- 1120
Kirkpatrick, Isaac 103
Kirkpatrick, Isaac 113
Kirkpatrick, Isaac 152
Kirkpatrick, Isaac 88
Kirkwood, Robert 676
Kirwan, Matt. 767
Kirwan, R. Rev. 402
Kirwin, Matt. 648
Kirwin, Matthew 547
Kirwin, Teresa 333

Knapton, Lord 391
Knight, John 376
Knight, Mary 297
Knightly, Eliza 278
Knightly, Francis 278
Knipe, --- Miss 1030
Knott, Harlow 396
Knowles, --- 209
Knox, --- 279,1099,1118
Knox, --- Col. 477,478
Knox, --- Miss 1085
Knox, --- Rev. 1028
Knox, Andrew 118,174,615
Knox, Francis 1086
Knox, George 1023
Knox, George 111,257
Knox, James 319,325
Knox, James Mrs. 132
Knox, John 29,185,240
Knox, John 333,1010
Knox, Mary 240
Knox, Samuel 768
Knox, William 410,462
Knox, William 655,1108
Kyle, Craghead 22
Kyle, Henry 451
Kyte, Thomas 879
L---, Oliver 972
Lafferty, Neal 940
Lagrayiere, Thomas 4
Laird, M. 1041
Lamb, --- 370
Lamb, Neal 252
Lamb, Neale 255
Lambert, Charles 339
Lambert, Ford 37
Lambert, Gustavus 339
Lamrock, John 125
Lamrock, Martha 125
Lamy, John 475
Lane, --- Widow 386
Lane, Robert 376
Lane, William 592
Larkin, --- 470
Laswon, --- Capt. 940
Latouche, T. Digges 345
Laughlin, --- Rev. 277
Laughlin, C. 510
Laun, Bryan 135
Laverty, William 1056
Law, --- Mrs. 4
Law, --- Mrs. 825
Law, --- Widow 1023
Law, Anne 393
Law, John Rev. 580
Law, Michael 183
Law, Samuel Rev. 393
Law, William 1056
Lawder, James 691
Lawler, Laughlin 43
Lawler, Patrick Rev. 69
Lawless, --- Miss 737
Lawless, Nicholas 94
Lawless, Peter 275
Lawlor, John 375
Lawrence, --- 497
Lawrence, --- Widow 343
Lawrence, Samuel 142
Lawrence, Thomas 3
Lawrenson, John 451
Lawson, Samuel 11
Leadly, James 193
Leahy, D. 474
Lecky, --- 241
Lecky, Alexander 725
Lecky, Catherine 190

Lecky, Hugh 515
Lecky, John 637
Lecky, Mary 74,1072
Lecky, Thomas 74,317
Lecky, Will. 17,187,478
Lecky, Will. 514
Ledlie, Thomas 117,1120
Ledwich, Edward 109
Ledwich, Edward Rev. 990
Ledwich, Thomas 434
Lee, --- 497
Lee, --- Miss 333
Lee, Benjamin 19
Lee, Mary 144
Lee, Robert 144
Lee, Thomas 479
Lee, William 275
Leech, Elizabeth 278,279
Leech, Walter 278
Leeson, Brice Mrs. 19
Leeson, Joseph 1059
Legg, Alexander 553
Leggat, John 386
Lehan, Dennis Rev. 8
Lehunte, Thomas 285
Leigh, George 19
Leinster, Duchess 95
Leinster, Duke 358
Lemmon, William 1087
Lenargan, --- Mrs. 959
Lendram, Francis 1015
Lendrum, --- 95
Lendrum, James 397
Lenergan, Edward 960
Lenergan, Thomas 960
Lennox, --- Miss 27
Lenox, Clotworthy 376
Lenox, Clotworthy 525
Lenox, George 719
Lenox, William 974
Lepper, --- 81
Leslie, --- Miss 737
Leslie, Edmund Rev. 236
Leslie, Robert 592
Letablere, Daniel 336
Lewich, Peter 48
Lewis, John 257
Lewney, --- Capt. 325
Ley, Ann 297
Ley, George 297
Ley, Mary 297
Liddy, Edward 196
Lidford, William 1001
Lightburne, --- Mrs. 142
Lighton, James 914
Lighton, Samuel 914
Lill, Godfrey 1056
Lill, William Rev. 347
Lilly, Henry 1102
Limerick, Mary 724
Linahan, Mary 271
Lindsay, Benjamin 855
Lindsay, James 397
Lindsay, Jeremiah 855
Lindsay, Robert 325
Ling, --- 15
Linn, William 369,371
Lisle, Lord 294
Lithgo, Martha 214
Little, John 1056
Little, Samuel Rev. 901
Lloyd, --- Dr. 727
Lloyd, Owen jr. 486
Lloyd, Richard Rev. 301
Lloyd, Thomas 727
Lockart, James 71

Lockart, Martha 71
Lockhart, Mary 507
Lockhart, William 1056
Lodge, Francis 8
Lodge, Mary 28
Loftus, Edward 673
Logan, Thomas D. 370
Londonderry, Countess 2
Long, Archibald 18
Long, Patrick 222
Lonnergan, Thomas 958
Lord, --- 563
Lord, --- Miss 618
Lord, Francis 261
Lord, John 306
Loughman, Stephen 865
Louther, John 391
Love, --- Rev. 1042
Low, Eusabius 401
Lowe, --- Widow 257
Lowrie, --- 270
Lowry, --- 269
Lowry, --- Miss 30
Lowry, Ann 32
Lowry, James 500
Lowry, James Rev. 585
Lowry, John 1043
Lowry, William 32
Lucas, Charles 339
Lucas, Edward 339
Lucky, John 706
Luffingham, --- Miss 23
Luffingham, William 19
Luttrell, Henry L. 425
Lyle, Hugh 621
Lynch, --- 910
Lynch, --- Miss 219
Lynch, Cicily 521
Lynch, Henry 521
Lynch, Hugh 458
Lynch, John 99,195
Lynch, Mary 884
Lynch, Nicholas 729
Lynch, Patrick 445,1018
Lynch, Thomas 101
Lynchaghan, Edward 477
Lyndon, George 343
Lyne, Thomas 304
Lyons, Ann 329
Lyons, David 12
Lyons, Thomas 636
Lysaght, --- Miss 294
Lyster, Elizabeth 97
Lyster, John 97
M'Alester, John 230
M'Alester, Sheelah 225
M'Alin, Bryan 827
M'Alley, T. 1015
M'Aneverton, Ann 183
M'Anulty, Cornelius 940
M'Attigert, Shane 182
M'Aulister, John 481
M'Award, William 62
M'Bride, Pat. 977
M'Bride, Patrick 298,309
M'Bryan, Alice 943
M'Bryan, Hugh 943
M'Cabe, James 1056
M'Cabe, James 386,827
M'Callem, Margaret 203
M'Cann, --- Miss 396
M'Cann, James 180
M'Cann, Patrick 208
M'Canna, Eugene 19
M'Carren, Pat 541
M'Carrol, Michael 977

M'Carrol, Owen 977
M'Carter, John 434
M'Carthy, Charles 457
M'Carthy, Cornelius 201
M'Carthy, Daniel 201,900
M'Carthy, Darby 9
M'Carthy, Dennis 171,201
M'Carthy, Justin 11
M'Cartin, --- Rev. 687
M'Cartney, Owen 343
M'Carty, Ann 392
M'Cauly, Thomas 637
M'Causland, --- 1092
M'Causland, --- Capt 483
M'Causland, --- Capt 948
M'Causland, Ab. 273,1093
M'Causland, Abraham 1091
M'Causland, Abraham 177
M'Causland, Abraham 184
M'Causland, Abraham 607
M'Causland, Alex. 215
M'Causland, Anne J. 458
M'Causland, Claud. 535
M'Causland, Con. 1093
M'Causland, Conolly 103
M'Causland, Conolly 7,47
M'Causland, Conolly 81
M'Causland, Conolly 88
M'Causland, Dominick 353
M'Causland, Fred. 805
M'Causland, John 535
M'Causland, Mar. 1022
M'Causland, Marcus 1091
M'Causland, Marcus 948
M'Causland, Rob. 1093
M'Causland, Sarah 500
M'Cavill, Peter 940
M'Cawell, --- Rev. 600
M'Cay, --- 296
M'Cay, James 284
M'Cay, John 927
M'Cay, Rob. 788
M'Cay, Samuel 553
M'Clane, --- Rev. 32
M'Cleary, James 752
M'Cleery, John 375
M'Clellan, --- 457
M'Clellan, George 472
M'Clellan, George 475
M'Clelland, --- Miss 27
M'Clelland, Robert 636
M'Clenachan, --- Mrs 743
M'Clenaghan, Blair 1091
M'Clenaghan, J. 1052
M'Clenaghan, James 1091
M'Clenaghan, Robert 191
M'Clintock, Alex. 312
M'Clintock, James 1056
M'Clintock, James 472
M'Clintock, John 1000
M'Clintock, Lydia 356
M'Clintock, Rob. 475
M'Clintock, Robert 356
M'Clintock, Robert 844
M'Closkey, Meave 164,171
M'Closkey, Mich. 164,171
M'Closkey, Sarah 286
M'Closky, Ann 147
M'Closky, Catherine 606
M'Closky, Henry 147
M'Closky, James 402
M'Closky, John 606
M'Closky, Marg't 404,405
M'Closky, Michael 405
M'Closky, Thomas 390
M'Clousky, Roger 481

M'Clughan, James 304
M'Clune, George 1056
M'Clure, John Capt. 585
M'Clure, Samuel 348
M'Clusky, Philimy 859
M'Colgan, Grizey 1090
M'Colgan, Michael 317
M'Colgan, Neal 1090
M'Colgan, William 940
M'Colghan, Michael 462
M'Collum, Francis 541
M'Comb, --- Miss 618
M'Combe, Arch. Capt 1056
M'Conegal, Elizabeth 74
M'Conewell, Pat 137
M'Congall, Patrick 316
M'Conkey, George 940
M'Conne, John 1056
M'Connell, --- 1046
M'Connell, --- Capt. 500
M'Connell, --- Miss 455
M'Connell, Anne 399
M'Connell, George 1117
M'Connell, James 528,553
M'Connell, Jane 528,553
M'Connell, Willm 528,553
M'Conway, Hugh 996
M'Cormick, Arthur 637
M'Cormick, Elizabeth 303
M'Cormick, James 515
M'Cormick, Robert 541
M'Coy, Margaret 756,759
M'Crab, John 844
M'Crackin, William 524
M'Crea, --- Mrs. 1009
M'Crea, James 1030
M'Crea, Samuel 531
M'Creary, Robert 62
M'Crone, James 319
M'Cue, Francis 816,817
M'Cue, Francis 818,827
M'Cue, Francis 836
M'Culla, John 1111
M'Culloch, --- 196
M'Culloch, --- 86
M'Culloch, Billy 202
M'Culloch, Eve 202
M'Culloch, James 202
M'Culloch, Jammy 202
M'Culloch, Sammy 202
M'Culloch, Samuel 202
M'Cullogh, --- 12
M'Cullogh, --- 344
M'Cullogh, --- Mrs. 1108
M'Cullogh, --- Mrs. 729
M'Culloh, --- 302
M'Cun, Frederick 191
M'Cuorkan, --- 533
M'Curdy, Archibald 180
M'Daniel, --- Widow 255
M'Daniel, Edmund 137
M'Daniel, John 393
M'Daniel, Patrick 239
M'Dead, Cath. 816,818
M'Dead, Richard 816,818
M'Dermot, Charles 437
M'Dermot, Elizabeth 974
M'Dermot, Michael 706
M'Dermotroe, Mary 884
M'Dermotroe, Michael 884
M'Dermotroe, Michael 888
M'Dermott, Francis 277
M'Dermott, Thomas 481
M'Donagh, --- Capt. 339
M'Donagh, Hen. 1027
M'Donagh, Peter 304

M'Donagh, Peter 610
M'Donagh, Peter Mrs. 137
M'Donagh, Peter Mrs. 486
M'Donald --- 89
M'Donald, Archibald 583
M'Donald, Elizabeth 550
M'Donald, James 137
M'Donald, John 654
M'Donald, Peter 46
M'Donnel, Jane 243
M'Donnel, Rachel 544
M'Donnell, Alex. 1056
M'Donnell, Alexander 351
M'Donnell, Charles 287
M'Donnell, Charles 97
M'Donnell, Charlotte 624
M'Donnell, Edward 471
M'Donnell, Margaret 308
M'Donnell, Tho. Rev. 512
M'Donnell, Thomas 137
M'Donnell, William 351
M'Elwaine, --- Capt. 91
M'Elwaine, Alexander 368
M'Elwaine, John 368
M'Elwaine, William 368
M'Elwee, James 605
M'Elwee, John 369,371
M'Elwee, Mary 605
M'Evoy, --- Miss 905
M'Fadden, --- 999
M'Fadian, --- 818
M'Fall, John 706
M'Farland, James 622
M'Farland, Robert 622
M'Farland, S. 714
M'Farland, Walter 654
M'Farlane, Andrew 7
M'Farlane, Will. 475
M'Feeley, Darby 171
M'Feeley, Jeffrey 171
M'Gaheron, John 1056
M'Gaoghy, John Rev. 1037
M'Gaurain, James 815
M'Gauran, John Capt. 57
M'Gauran, Thomas 252
M'Geagh, --- 9
M'Ghee, James 922
M'Ghee, Robert 273
M'Ghee, William 662
M'Gill, Henry 654
M'Gillicuddy, Flornc 900
M'Gilligan, O. 402
M'Ginnis, Hugh 639
M'Ginnis, John 200
M'Glown, Catherine 137
M'Glyne, --- 294
M'Golrick, Hugh 234
M'Gonagle, John 1060
M'Gonegal, Ann 348
M'Gowan, --- 500
M'Gowan, Charles 137
M'Gown, John 89
M'Grah, Hugh 299
M'Grah, John 299
M'Groary, Edward 600
M'Grorty, William 523
M'Grory, Miles 615
M'Guigan, Henry 481
M'Guigan, Thomas 477
M'Guire, --- 992
M'Guire, Charles 940
M'Guire, John 309
M'Gurnaghan, Pat. 1031
M'Gurnahan, Stephen 1031
M'Hendry, James 1049
M'Ilheney, George 649

M'Ilhone, Sara 557
M'Illether, Catherine 34
M'Illwaine, Arch. 75
M'Ilmurray, Giles 344
M'Ilpatrick, Hugh 1
M'Ilvenna, Hugh 137
M'Ilwaine, --- 1092
M'Ilwaine, --- 97
M'Ilwaine, --- Capt 1087
M'Ilwaine, Arch. 1079
M'Ilwaine, Archibald 127
M'Ilwaine, Catherine 469
M'Ilwaine, James 656
M'Ilwaine, James jr. 173
M'Ilwaine, William 81
M'Intire, --- Capt. 493
M'Intire, Ann 708
M'Intire, Robert 1035
M'Kane, --- 334
M'Kay, --- Capt. 53
M'Kay, Alex. 1056
M'Kay, Will. 440
M'Kean, John 343
M'Kean, Moses 550
M'Kean, William 643
M'Keferty, H. 1098
M'Kenzie, --- 203,241
M'Keon, Robert 222
M'Kerachan, Robert 397
M'Kiernan, James 442
M'Kiernan, John 277
M'Kim, John 348
M'Kim, Robert 543,562
M'Kinla, Elizabeth 963
M'Kinley, --- 1098
M'Laughlin, --- Mrs. 646
M'Laughlin, Charles 1084
M'Laughlin, Charles 343
M'Laughlin, Corn's 270
M'Laughlin, Daniel 299
M'Laughlin, Daniel 99
M'Laughlin, James 270
M'Laughlin, John 270,372
M'Laughlin, John 900
M'Laughlin, M. 402
M'Laughlin, Oliver 371
M'Lean, Robert 600
M'Mahon, --- 971
M'Mahon, --- Miss 574
M'Mahon, Giles 344
M'Mahon, James 269,270
M'Mahon, James Rev. 503
M'Mahon, Michael 344
M'Mahon, Patrick 502
M'Mahon, William 1031
M'Manus, Chas. 409,478
M'Manus, Chas. 514
M'Manus, Elizabeth 514
M'Manus, Jane 514
M'Manus, Mary 514
M'Minamen, --- 344
M'Mollan, John 1069
M'Morice, Joseph 1017
M'Morice, Martha 1017
M'Morran, Fran. 1056
M'Morris, Catherine 394
M'Mullan, --- 399
M'Mullen, Patrick 974
M'Murry, Jer. 1056
M'Nabb, James 481,1103
M'Naghten, --- 1085
M'Naghten, Barth. 1059
M'Nally, Leonard 26
M'Namee, Martha 477
M'Namee, Patrick 462
M'Neal, --- Miss 484

M'Neil, Archibald 492
M'Neil, Daniel 265
M'Neil, Elizabeth 265
M'Neil, Henry 265
M'Neil, Isabella 391
M'Neill, --- Laird 512
M'Neill, Daniel 265,267
M'Neill, Elizabeth 187
M'Neill, Henry 187
M'Nirlan, Manus 199
M'Nogher, Bryan 927
M'Nutt, --- 598
M'Nutt, Mary Ann 322
M'Partlan, Edward 1056
M'Paul, Neal 348
M'Pherson, Isabella 991
M'Pherson, James 991
M'Pherson, Mich. 1057
M'Pole, Dennis 350
M'Powell, Dennis 402
M'Quoid, John 1056
M'Shane, --- 41
M'Swine, Hugh 910
M'Tier, --- Capt. 1053
M'Whinnery, Tho. 1056
M'Williams, Alice 943
Macbride, David 687
Mackay, --- Capt. 1087
Mackelwain, Andrew 789
Mackenzie, --- Capt. 624
Mackey, --- 89
Mackey, James 987
Mackey, W. 381
Mackey, William 147,366
Macklin, Elizabeth 458
Macklin, J. 806
Macklin, James 458
Macky, --- 232,1091
Macky, --- Miss 1112
Macky, David 416
Macky, Jane 277
Macky, John 277,322
Macky, Moses 416
Macky, Robert 193,209
Macky, Robert 266
Maclean, Ham. 1056
Maclean, Matt. 1056
Maclean, Prussia 1056
Madcap Setfire 400
Madden, Samuel 987
Maffert, Hugh 344
Maffet, --- Cnslr 420
Magan, Art 553
Magarry, Mary 222
Magawly, --- Miss 660
Magawly, Anthony 103
Magee, --- 509
Magee, James Rev. 1024
Magee, John 124,156
Magennis, --- Miss 36
Magennis, Margaret 5
Magennis, Pat'k Rev. 402
Maghan, Thomas 152
Magill, Elizabeth 644
Magill, James 1099
Magill, John 309
Magill, William 644
Magrath, Mark 275
Magrath, Thomas 28
Magraw, John 974
Maguigan, Pat 58
Maguire, --- Col. 191
Maguire, --- Widow 845
Maguire, James 618
Maguire, John 99
Maguire, Mary 34

145

Maguire, Thomas 442
Mahon, James 803
Mahon, M. 1023
Mahon, Winnefred 589
Maine, Edward S. 437
Mains, George 1075
Mains, Matthew 608
Mains, Prucence 608
Maire, --- 593
Maitland, Adam 1060
Major, --- Miss 1111
Major, Alexander 1031
Major, Anne 399
Major, Fanny 398
Major, James 1046
Major, James 398,919
Major, Jane 1046
Major, John Rev. 325
Major, Thomas 228,646
Malcolm, --- Capt. 7
Mallay, --- Capt. 354
Mallay, --- Capt. 355
Maloghry, Bridget 286
Maloghry, James 286
Malone, --- Mrs. 96
Malone, Anthony 412
Malone, Edmund 197,229
Malone, Edward 1084
Malone, James 1007
Malone, Joseph, 1007
Malone, Patrick 297,304
Maneely, John 979
Mankin, Francis 820
Mankin, George 820
Mankin, John 820
Mann, --- Miss 329
Mannin, Catherine 18
Mannin, John 99
Mannin, Patrick 18
Mansergh, Ed. 481
Manville, Edward 396
Mar---, --- Miss 971
Marlay, --- Mrs. 451
Marsden, --- 333
Marshal, --- Capt. 54
Marshall, --- 320
Marshall, --- Mrs. 478
Marshall, Allen 574
Marshall, Elizabeth 395
Marshall, George 190,259
Marshall, George 284
Marshall, George 8,108
Marshall, Jane 528,553
Marshall, Jo. Rev. 1008
Marshall, John 1056
Marshall, Josiah 910
Marshall, Martha 574
Marshall, Thomas 269,395
Marshall, Walter 269
Marst, --- Lt. 373
Martha (?), Jane 553
Martin, --- 43,396
Martin, --- Miss 464
Martin, Alexander 974
Martin, Catherine 762
Martin, J. 610
Martin, Jane 762
Martin, John 1033
Martin, John 996,999
Martin, John Rev. 7
Martin, Mary 442,459
Martin, Owen 915
Martin, Peter 920
Martin, Rachael 996
Martin, Richard 493
Martin, Robert 525

Maskimmen, James 927
Mason, --- Lt. Col. 255
Mason, John M. 386
Mason, Richard 186
Massy, William 481
Mathews, --- Widow 147
Mathews, Edward 271
Mathews, James 500
Matruine, --- Rev. 416
Matthewes, Hill 203
Matthews, --- 336
Maude, Cornwallis 632
Maudesley, John C. 164
Mauleverer, --- 183
Mauleverer, John 376,487
Mauleverer, Thomas 325
Maunsel, Thomas 618
Maunsell, Richard 977
Maxwel, James sr. 53
Maxwell, --- 1056
Maxwell, --- Miss 38
Maxwell, --- Miss 535
Maxwell, --- Surgeon 573
Maxwell, --- Surgn 1089
Maxwell, Boyd 624
Maxwell, Catherine 109
Maxwell, James 38,578
Maxwell, Jane 23
Maxwell, John 18
Maxwell, William 306,578
Mayfield, Samuel 122
Mayne, Charles 618
Mayne, Robert 277,459
Mayne, Robert 574
Mayns, Patrick 208
Mazych, Paul 275
Mead, Thomas 409
Meade, --- Mrs. 520
Meade, Richard 236
Meadows, --- 363
Meadows, William 366
Meagher, Dennis 14
Meagher, Edmund 19
Meagher, Thomas 14
Meare-, Charles 387
Meares, Bleaket Capt 940
Meares, William 150
Mears, Charles Rev. 249
Mears, George 618
Mease, William 1039
Medlicot, C. D. 442
Meehan, Margaret 160
Megly, Mary 479
Melt, Paddy 239
Meredith, --- Miss 20
Meredith, --- Miss 442
Mervin, Art 403
Mervyn, Richard R. 384
Metham, Thomas 818
Middleton, Is. 563
Middleton, Isaac 521
Mihan, William 14
Miles, Thomas 107,399
Miles, William 289
Miligan, William 1056
Millar, --- Miss 165
Millar, Elizabeth 612
Millar, Frances 475
Millar, H. 275
Millar, James 475
Millar, James Capt. 612
Millar, Joseph 375
Miller, --- 127,817
Miller, --- Miss 636,947
Miller, --- Mrs. 284
Miller, Andrew 1102

Miller, Andrew Capt. 730
Miller, Ann 654
Miller, Catharine 375
Miller, David 818,822
Miller, H. Mrs. 1080
Miller, James 1071
Miller, James 209,235
Miller, James 290,657
Miller, James Capt. 698
Miller, Jane 285
Miller, Jo. 986
Miller, John 500
Miller, Patrick 108,213
Miller, Patrick Capt 596
Millian, Arthur 795
Millian, James 795
Milltown, Earl 1059
Minchin, --- 275
Minchin, H. 486
Minckleroy, Anne 34
Minett, John 14
Minigan, M. 818
Minnan, John 161
Mitchel, --- 103,209,249
Mitchel, --- Capt. 53
Mitchel, --- Miss 255
Mitchel, --- Miss 53
Mitchel, --- Surgeon 695
Mitchel, Blaney 32
Mitchel, Hugh H. 614
Mitchel, James Capt. 387
Mitchel, Jane 78
Mitchel, John 453
Mitchel, Mary 54,331,387
Mitchel, Rebecca 141
Mitchel, William 141
Mitchell, --- 219,241
Mitchell, H. 1072
Mitchell, Hannah 296
Mitchell, James 1090
Mitchell, James 243,287
Mitchell, James 296,1072
Mitchell, James 80,182
Mitchell, John 305
Mitchell, Rob. 1056
Mocks, Edward 31
Moffat, R. 1017
Molesworth, Robert 403
Mollan, Jane 470
Molloy, --- Miss 481
Molloy, Catherine 449
Molloy, John 257
Molony, Lucius 293
Molyneaux, Charlotte 11
Molyneus, Capel 486
Monachan, --- 816
Monaghan, --- 554,556
Monaghan, Ann 68
Monaghan, Edward 940
Monck, --- Miss 314
Monck, Geo. Paul 314
Monck, Isabella 632
Monck, Thomas 38
Monckton, --- Gen. 54
Moncrieff, Richard 380
Monkham, Richard 827
Monsell, William 442
Montgomery, --- 939
Montgomery, --- Miss 11
Montgomery, --- Miss 470
Montgomery, Anne 103,458
Montgomery, Jean 751
Montgomery, John 1079
Montgomery, Richard 43
Montgomery, Robert 640
Montgomery, Sam. 1024

Montgomery, Samuel 183
Montgomery, Samuel 751
Montgomery, Will. 116
Montgomery, William 103
Montgomery, William 210
Montgomery, William 375
Montgomery, William 527
Moody, --- 256
Moody, --- Rev. 252
Moody, Elizabeth 343
Moody, James Rev. 730
Moody, Marcus 343
Moody, Thomas 784
Mooney, John 455
Moor, Ann 1056
Moor, James jr. 1106
Moore, --- 171,183,474
Moore, --- 640
Moore, --- Miss 3,550
Moore, --- Miss 587,765
Moore, --- Rev. 162,719
Moore, --- widow 546
Moore, Acheson 259
Moore, Andrew T. S. 199
Moore, Anne 180
Moore, Archibald 199
Moore, Bryan 303
Moore, Elizabeth 199
Moore, Emanuel Rev. 187
Moore, Ezekiel 199
Moore, F. 1120
Moore, George 607
Moore, James 1024,1056
Moore, James Capt. 1077
Moore, Jane 297
Moore, John 325,951,1056
Moore, Mary 303
Moore, Ponsonby 532
Moore, Richard 275
Moore, Richard 28,30,257
Moore, Robert 355
Moore, Samuel 622
Moore, Thomas 36,39,81
Moore, Thomas 83
Moore, William 201,297
Moore, William 563,1056
Moore, William Dr. 199
Moore, William Rev. 199
Moorhead, Wallace 372
Moran, Edward 18
Moran, Hugh 99
Moran, Mary 132
Morgan, --- 11
Morgan, --- Capt. 79
Morgan, --- Rev. 550
Morgan, Chidly 222
Morgan, Daniel 254
Morgan, Elizabeth 289
Morgan, John 239,697
Morgan, Michael 706
Morgan, Olivia 222
Morgan, Patrick 254
Morony, John 127
Morrell, --- Rev. 44
Morris, Ed. 470
Morrison, --- 27,176,320
Morrison, Alexander 89
Morrison, John 1078
Morrison, Samuel 382
Morrison, Thomas 11,21
Morrison, Thomas 159
Morrison, Thomas 56,103
Morrow, Briship 1056
Morrow, James 1005
Morrow, Martha 382
Morrow, Mary 422

Mortimer, Mary S. 949
Mortimer, William 1005
Mortimer, William 949
Morton, --- Miss 488
Mosse, --- Miss 255
Mossom, Eland 200
Mossop, Henry 271
Motherel, Sam. 1030
Mothriel, John 1068
Mothriel, Samuel 1068
Mountcashel, Lord 333
Mountflorence, Lady 303
Mountgarret, Visct. 702
Montgarret, Vscntss 130
Mountgarret, W. 940
Mountgarrett, Viscts 615
Mousley, --- 865
Moutray, James 520
Moutray, John 729
Muckerlane, Ann 708
Muckerlane, Hugh 708
Mulally, --- 335
Mulaoney, Charles 331
Mulgrave, Lord 347
Mulhall, Thomas 147
Mulhern, William 601
Mulholland, John 1102
Mulhollen, Robert 9
Mullally, Thomas 144
Mullan, Edward 830
Mullan, James 1084
Mullan, John 601
Mullconry, Patrick 910
Mullen, Charles 506
Mullin, Alex. 1056
Mullouny, Daniel 303
Mullowney, --- 512
Mullowney, John 876
Mulowny, Mary 32
Mungan, --- Dr. 660
Munroe, --- Miss 306
Murphy, --- 277
Murphy, Ann 491
Murphy, Constantine 40
Murphy, Daniel 2,344
Murphy, Ed. 553
Murphy, John 289,381
Murphy, Owen 2
Murphy, Rosanna 133
Murray, --- 22,119,276
Murray, --- Dr. 834
Murray, --- Miss 393
Murray, --- Mrs. 662
Murray, Aeneas 514
Murray, Andrew 420
Murray, Cath. 841,1002
Murray, Dennis 18
Murray, Euphemia 344
Murray, John 364,952,974
Murray, Robert 126
Murray, Roger 1057
Murray, Susan 952
Murray, Thomas 372
Murray, William 319,1002
Murren, George 131
Murren, Patrick 974
Murrin, George Capt. 475
Musgrave, --- Capt. 24
Nagle, --- Rev. 271
Nagle, Athenasius 768
Nagle, James 90
Nally, James 344
Nat--, Patrick 396
Naughton, Thomas 384
Nealy, William 187
Neely, William 182

Neeson, John Rev. 151
Neil, Arthur 239
Neilson, John 1056
Nelson, Joseph 946
Nelson, Robert 179
Nenoe, John 401
Nesbit, --- 292
Nesbit, Albert 401
Nesbit, Alexander 568
Nesbit, Charles 655
Nesbit, Elinor 48
Nesbit, Elizabeth 655
Nesbit, Matthew 384
Nesbit, Richard 659
Nesbit, Susanna 859
Nethry, Robert 556
Netterville, E. 459
Nevil, William 378
New, George 290
Newburgh, --- Miss 488
Newburgh, Brockhill 133
Newburgh, Elizabeth 133
Newburgh, William 285
Newburgh, William 532
Newcoman, Thomas 116
Newcomen, Charles 42
Newell, Robert 199,334
Newenham, Edward 219,303
Newton, Henry 174,213
Newton, Henry 314
Newton, Joseph 1056
Newtown, --- Dr. 719
Neynoe, John 28
Neynoe, Will. 311
Nichol, Martha 372
Nicholson, Chr 336,338
Nicholson, William 474
Nicolls, Alice 8
Nicolls, Jonathan 597
Nicolls, Jonathan 84,348
Nicolson, Catherine 434
Nicolson, William 819
Nix, E. 425
Nixon, --- Capt. 126
Nixon, --- Miss 249
Nixon, Frances 126
Nixon, Humphrey 391
Nixon, J. Rev. 640
Noonan, D. Rev. 640
Norcliff, William 474
Norris, --- Miss 384
Norton, --- Capt. 355
Noseda, --- 729
Nowlan, --- 435
Nowlan, --- Dr. 355
Nugent, --- Miss 391
Nugent, --- Mrs. 615
Nugent, Arthur 39
Nugent, Catherine 281
Nugent, Charles 292
Nugent, Edward 504
Nugent, John 459
Nugent, Louisa 350
O'Boyle, Neal 1105
O'Brien, Charles 273
O'Brien, David Rev. 437
O'Brien, Francis 203
O'Brien, Lucius 95
O'Brien, Mary 583
O'Brien, Michael 349
O'Brien, Patrick W. 225
O'Brien, William 17
O'Cain, Bartholomew 456
O'Callaghan, Corn's 265
O'Callaghan, Denis 26
O'Callahan, --- Mrs. 789

Powel, Isaac 520
Powell, Bridget 354
Powell, Catherine 354
Powell, Samuel 363
Powell, T. H. 687
Power, --- 93
Power, Ambrose 366,368
Power, Ambrose 376,379
Power, Ambrose 592
Power, James 252
Power, John 160
Power, Thomas 131
Powerscourt, Lady 20
Pratt, --- Miss 319
Prentice, --- Miss 936
Prerin, James 998
Preston, James 455
Preston, Mary 455
Price, --- Miss 512,660
Price, James 454
Price, Robert 440
Priest, Patrick 294
Priestly, Michael 553
Prince, Thomas L. 451
Pue, --- 1074
Punch, Daniel 6
Purcel, John Dr. 244
Purcell, --- Rev. 2
Purcell, James 263
Purcell, John 319
Pye, --- Mrs. 725
Pym, --- 88
Pyne, John 396
Pynsent, Robert 676
Quigley, John 81
Quignan, Richard 30
Quin, Ann 286
Quin, Bryan 1056
Quin, Darby 286
Quin, Edward 940
Quin, James 481
Quin, John 254
Quin, Neal Rev. 296
Quin, Patrick 18,21
Quin, Thomas 654
Quinlan, Ann 910
Quinlan, John 910
Quinlean, Thomas Rev. 24
Quinlon, Catherine 299
Quinn, Patrick 15
Quorkan, Hugh 551
Quorkan, Michael 551
Raby, Richard 10,954
Radcliffe, Thomas 382
Rainy, James 254
Ralston, --- Mrs. 568
Ramage, --- 113
Ramage, Hannah 654
Ramage, James 348
Ramage, James 94,287,296
Ramage, James Capt. 654
Ramage, James jr. 1077
Ramsay, Alexander 298
Ramsay, Alexander 344
Ramsay, Alexander 346
Ramsay, Anne 791
Ramsay, Charles 462,914
Ramsay, Ed. 49
Ramsay, James 791
Ramsay, John 543
Ramsay, Robert 493,543
Rankin, --- Capt. 876
Rankin, --- Miss 905
Rankin, John Rev. 678
Rapho, Bishop 809
Ravenhill, --- 512

Rea, Thomas 818
Read, --- Miss 4
Read, David 713
Read, Isaac 478,514
Read, John 4,382,494,724
Read, John 729
Read, Mary 478,514
Read, Mathias 275
Read, Robert 520
Reavy, Jane 198
Reddy, Richard 407
Redford, Anne 458
Reed, --- 22
Reed, David 715
Reed, Sarah 244
Regan, James 131
Regan, Margaret 341
Reid, John 49
Reilly, James 500
Reilly, Margaret 877
Reilly, Patrick 459
Reily, --- Mrs. 615
Reily, James 44
Reily, Michael 150
Reney, Daniel 1033
Rentoul, --- Rev. 162
Reynell, Edward 488
Reynolds, -- Lt. 302,303
Reynolds, --- 708
Reynolds, --- Miss 486
Reynolds, Alexander 268
Reynolds, Alexander 27
Reynolds, Anne 354
Reynolds, Catherine 292
Reynolds, Elizabeth 386
Reynolds, John 1117
Reynolds, Mary 1117
Reynolds, Richard 956
Reynolds, Will. 983
Reynolds, William 354
Ribton, David 93
Richard, Thomas 1111
Richardson, --- 981
Richardson, --- Capt 553
Richardson, --- Rev 1092
Richardson, Ann 981
Richardson, David 981
Richardson, Galbr'th 297
Richardson, James 592
Richardson, M. Miss 981
Richardson, William 306
Richey, Thomas 172
Richy, David 220
Richy, Sarah 220
Rider, Abraham 493
Ridge, John 397
Rielly, Michael 940
Rife, Ann 52
Ringland, --- 14
Ringland, --- Mrs. 14
Ringrose, Jacob 818
Ringrose, Margaret 818
Rise, Ann 52
Risher, Robt. 1017
Rispan, James 11
Rispan, Judy 11
Riverston, Lord 10
Robbins, Richard 244
Roberts, --- Col. 598
Robeson, --- 41
Robinson, --- Capt. 382
Robinson, --- Capt. 90
Robinson, --- Miss 397
Robinson, --- Rev. 320
Robinson, James 706
Robinson, John 18

Robinson, Lettice 287
Robinson, Mary 344
Robinson, Victor 507
Robison, John 331
Roch, --- Lt. 1004
Roche, Hannah 141
Roche, Ulick 107
Rochfort, --- Miss 481
Rochfort, Robert 256,391
Rochfort, William 54
Roden, --- Miss 535
Rodery, William 334
Rodger, --- 464
Roe, John 162
Roe, Peter Rev. 716
Roe, William 18
Rogers, --- 464
Rogers, --- Miss 142
Rogers, --- Rev. 481
Rogers, Elizabeth 458
Rogers, James 654
Rogers, Mathew 957
Rogers, Samuel 654
Rogers, Sarah 458
Rol, William 500
Rolleston, Francis 729
Rolls, Ann Mrs. 375
Ronayne, Maurice 3
Rooney, Owen 191
Rorke, Mich. 815
Rorke, Michael 829
Rosborough, Lord 1059
Roscommon, Earl 1002
Ross, --- 1088
Ross, --- Aldermn 448
Ross, --- Capt. 1048
Ross, --- Capt. 1054
Ross, --- Capt. 1072
Ross, --- Rev. 1028
Ross, Catherine 471
Ross, Charles 815
Ross, D. 514
Ross, David 187,270,317
Ross, David 437,471,1023
Ross, Earl 147
Ross, Edward 940
Ross, Elizabeth 513,1028
Ross, James 948
Ross, John 1017
Ross, John 1044
Ross, John 375,387,815
Ross, Lydia 1079
Ross, Martha 990
Ross, Mary 1010
Ross, Michael 974
Ross, Will. 240,270,391
Ross, Will. 478,514,558
Ross, Will. 577,990,1000
Rourke, Francis 27
Rouse, --- Mrs. 39
Rowland, G. 497
Rowley, --- Mrs. 708
Rowley, Clot. 486
Russell, --- Corp. 335
Rutherford, Matt. 317
Rutherford, Matthew 486
Rutherford, Matthew 724
Rutty, --- Dr. 304
Ruxton, --- Lt. 303
Ryan, --- 116
Ryan, --- Miss 474
Ryan, --- Rev. 143,636
Ryan, Edmond 772
Ryan, Peter 977
Ryder, --- Rev. 498
Ryder, John Dr. 285

151

Wolsely, James Lt. 117
Wolverton, John 185
Wood, --- 437
Wood, Bernard 1056
Wood, Hans 22
Woodhouse, Samuel 830
Woodroffe, -- Surg'n 339
Woods, --- Miss 277
Woods, --- Widow 905
Woods, Andrew 130
Woods, Arthur 551
Woods, George 986
Woods, James 989,1056
Woods, Robert 914
Woodward, --- 574

Woodworth, John 876
Woolsey, William 520
Work, Alexander 530
Work, Frederick 73
Work, Sarah 73
Workman, Jane 514
Workman, Meredyth 514
Worthington, --- 658
Wray, --- 1071
Wray, Letitia 289
Wray, William 118,289
Wren, --- Mr. 7
Wright, --- Dr. 563
Wright, Alexander 827
Wright, Henry Rev. 93

Wright, Hin. 1056
Wright, John 1031
Wright, Mary 248
Wyne, --- Col. 592
Wynne, Cornelius 729
Yeats, Benjamin 131
Yeats, Thomas 99
Young, --- Rev. 28
Young, Alexander 1016
Young, David Rev. 577
Young, Elizabeth 210
Young, Hugh Rev. 210
Young, John 28,137
Young, Martha 755
Young, Thomas 52,1042

Appendix

Many notices of persons in the <u>Londonderry</u> <u>Journal</u> contain no information of a genealogical nature, but, given the scarcity of Irish records in the Eighteenth Century, any clue to a person's whereabouts in Ireland might be useful to the researcher. For this reason, all notices of persons which included (1) a full name (with a few exceptions where a first initial was accepted) and (2) a location defined at least to the parish level have been gathered into this appendix and are listed alphabetically. By referring from the number of the issue of the newspaper to the abstracts, where the associated dates are supplied, the three research keys of name, time, and place are all known for these persons. Names which appear more than once, such as in merchants' advertising, are only repeated if additional information is provided in a later appearance. The names in this appendix do not appear in the index of abstracts.

The following abbreviations and symbols have been used:

aka	also known as, alias	mfr	manufacturer
appr	apprentice	mkr	maker
bar	barony of	mkt	market
betw	between	mn or mnr	manor of
co	county	nr	near
Dln	Dublin	occ	occupies, occupied
fmly	formerly, formerly of	outsd	outside
fmr	former	p/o or pt	part of
hrs	heirs	pr	parish of
hse	house	res	resides, resided, residence
ipo	in possession of	st	street
J.P.	Justice of the Peace	ten	tenement
Ld	Londonderry	w/	with
ln	lane	ws	west side
m	mile(s)	@	age
mcht	merchant		

A note of caution regarding the place names and locations is in order. In some news articles, the exact location of an event was specified by the name of a townland but no other information was given. In these cases, the name of the city given in the dateline of the article was taken to give the general area of Ireland referred to and the location is given as "near" that city. It remains for the researcher to determine how "near" the location actually was to the larger city. (When no exact location was given and no nearby city was indicated, the case was excluded from the list.) Where no other information is supplied, it would be fair to assume that the location was either a larger town, well-known throughout the country, or else was a townland near Londonderry.

Name	Issue	Location
Abernathy, John	151	Coleraine
Abraham, Thomas	35	Ld
Acheson, John	953	p/o Leckragh, pr Langfield, co Tyrone
Achison, James	777	Ld
Achison, John	777	Ld
Adair, Henry	814	criminal, Downpatrick
Adair, Mary	238	criminal, Lady Hull nr Antrim
Adams, John & Wm.	511	shoemakers, Artillery lane, Ld
Adams, John & Wm.	805	shoemakers, Ferryquay st, Ld
Adamson, Alexander	25	nr Cumber, co Down (fmly army sergeant)
Adems, Dunlap	327	soap, Coleraine
Agnew, Hugh	528	distiller & tobacconist, Carrickmacross
Ahern, Maurice	251	Rathnasligeen nr Clonmel
Aickin, David	1109	Blue Ball inn, Newtown Limavady
Alcorn, James	951	Ballynelly
Alcorn, Mich.	777	Ld
Aldon, John	1119	fmr tythe farmer, nr Fertagh
Alexander, Andrew	351,358	Newtown Lemavady
Alexander, James	628	fmr tenement in Butcher st, Ld
Alexander, John	386	pr Ardstraw
Alexander, John	671	cabinet mkr, Bishop st, Ld
Alexander, Peter	361,420	mcht, Ld
Alexander, Robert	252	mcht, Ld
Alexander, Robert	810	Moneydig, pr Desertoghill, co Ld
Allen, John	387	Letterkenny
Allen, John	600	Crackadoos
Allen, Richard	269	Kevin's port
Alleyn, John	287	Coolprivane, co Tipperary
Allison, Joseph	341	Presbyterian, pr Ballykelly
Allison, Robert	341	Presbyterian, pr Ballykelly
Allison, Widow	216	farm at Moneygreggan
Allison, Will.	341	Presbyterian, pr Ballykelly
Alsop, James	737	Freeschool lane, Ld
Anderson, Alex.	777	Ld
Anderson, David	341	Presbyterian, pr Ballykelly
Anderson, George	794	importer, Newry
Anderson, James	777	Ld
Anderson, Thomas	900	staymaker, Ld
Anderson, William	1078&1104	fraud; of pr Ballinderry, co Antrim
Andrews, John	1046	lottery winner, Comber, co Down
Andrews, Michael	533	Cumber
Armstrong, Isaac	456	innkeeper, Lifford
Armstrong, James	191	formerly occ a tenement in Omagh
Armstrong, James	276	Omagh
Armstrong, John	186	Lifford
Armstrong, Robert	40	Ballendrate
Armstrong, William	602	woollen draper, Butcher st, Ld
Ash, George	55	Dungannon
Ash, George	777	Mayor of Ld
Askin, Samuel	989	tailor, fmly London, Bishop st, Ld
Atchison, John	148	Ld
Auchinleck, Hugh	183	attorney, Strabane
Aull, John	341	Presbyterian, pr Ballykelly
Babington, George	309	Ld
Babington, Mathew	309	innkeeper, Sligo
Babington, Richard	263	lottery winner, Ld
Babington, Wil.	391	Marblehill
Baker, Rich.	1024	Dristernan or Dristrien, pr Culdaff
Baldrick, Robert	1045	shoemaker outside Ferryquay gate, Ld
Balfour, Jer.	1081	flaxseed, Ld
Balfour, Jeremiah	430	Lower Kildrum
Balfour, John	1018	brewery, Ld

Name	Issue	Location
Balfour, John Dr.	811	res Cross lane, Ld
Balfour, Lettice Mrs.	430	Ld
Balfour, Thos.	777	Ld
Balfour, Wm. Dr.	909	res Rosemary lane, Ld
Ball, Benj.	1104	Luggelaw, co Wicklow
Ball, John	806	stage coach line, Cavan, co Cavan
Bar, Mary Mrs.	456	Loughtylobe, pr Banagher, co Ld
Barboot, Richard	247	dance teacher, Strabane
Barclay, George	22	Drumboe
Barclay, John	320	Stranorlar
Barclay, Joseph	44	Ballybofey
Barclay, William	315	inn in Omagh
Barnwell, Thomas	139	robber, gaoled at Dublin
Barr, George	127	Buncranagh area
Barr, James	127	Buncranagh area
Barr, John	66	ipo a farm in the Liberties of Ld
Barr, Owen Roe	127	Buncranagh area
Barr, Owen jr.	127	Buncranagh area
Barr, Patrick	127	Buncranagh area
Barr, Walter	336	clock mkr, Cross lane, Ld
Barret, Patrick	278	post chaise, Drogheda
Barrett, Eliz'th Miss	270	stables, Nunnery Yard, Mullinihack
Barton, Christopher	562	nr Newtown Stewart
Bateman, John	1025	Lensfort nr Ld
Bateman, John	126	Ardaravin, Ennishowen
Bateman, John	160	salt, Buncrana
Bateman, John	777	Ld
Bateson, Thomas	777	Ld
Batsford, William	375	Raphoe
Baxter, James	387	Letterkenny
Baxter, Joseph	276	Omagh
Bayles, John	540	fmr res Ferryquay st, Ld
Beard, Henry	93	Strabane
Beasley, Robert	53	corp of Sheermen & Dyers, Dublin
Beath, William	1011	Newry
Beats, David	1065	Killygordon nr Ld
Beaty, Arch.	127	Buncranagh area
Beaty, Mary	125	Buncranagh
Beaty, William	1057	Glenmecain, pr Cumber
Beesley, Thomas	242	mcht, Ld
Bell, Francis	454	former hse in Ferryquay st, Ld
Bell, James	794	importer, Newry
Bell, John	151	Coleraine
Bell, Rob.	888	Guild of Trades, Ld
Bennet, Stephen	74	mcht, Ld
Bennett, Francis	987	Coleraine
Benson, Eliz. Mrs.	184	par Fahan, bar Ennishowen, co Donegal
Benson, Fred.	565	Shantalion, liberties of Ld
Benson, Frederick	243	Broomfield
Benson, Hamilton	1105	fmly res the Diamond, Ld
Benson, Hamilton	32	mcht, Ld
Benson, Peter	118	former farm in Elagh Beg
Benson, Peter	588	ipo hse at head of Rosemary lane, Ld
Berry, James	69	mcht, the Diamond, Ld
Berry, Nat.	1001	fmr shop, Ferryquay st, Ld
Betagh, Thomas	294	watchmaker, Ld
Bible, Thomas	233	of the Corporation of Weavers, Dublin
Billingsly, James	722	Sallowbrook
Black, Henry	387	Letterkenny
Black, John	348	ipo land in Liberties of Ld
Black, Thomas	195	rope maker, Ld
Blackall, John	1030	Englishtown nr Armagh

Name	Issue	Location
Blackhall, Honor	756	criminal, Limerick
Blackwood, John	25	nr Comber, co Down
Blair, Arthur	256	the Royal George Inn, Strabane
Blair, James	392	Carnone
Blair, James	500	apothecary, Rapho, fmly of Dublin
Blair, William	954	Powderly nr Castlefin
Blake, Patrick	333	Drum, in a duel at Galway
Blake, Patrick	865	magistrate, Galway
Blyth, James	242	bookseller, Ld
Blythe, James	9	bookseller, Ld
Boggs, Gardiner	828	Ld
Boggs, James	77	Raphoe
Boggs, Ninian	15	mcht, Ld
Boggs, Rob.	608	Ld
Bolton, Chichester	277	assaulted in Dublin
Bond, Andrew	233;320	mcht, Ld
Bond, John	128	Hill head
Bond, Oliver	1111	woollens, 13 Bridge st, Dublin
Borland, Archibald	293	new saddler, Omagh
Bourne, Mary	277	gaoled in Dublin for theft
Bowes, James	294	tenant of Fr. Flood, co Kilkenny
Boyce, Daniel	891	dealer in spirits, Ld
Boyd, Archibald	812	woollen draper, Ferryquay st, Ld
Boyd, John	641	Ballymoney, co Antrim
Boyd, Mathew	583	Munreagh nr Church of Taughboyne
Boyd, Mossom	777	Ld
Boyd, Ponsonby	304	jockey, Belfast races
Boyd, Robert	404	Recorder of Ld
Boyle, Alexander	358	Newtown Lemavady
Boyle, Charles	870	staymaker, Shipquay st, Ld
Boyle, Charles	891	dealer in spirits, Ld
Boyle, Con	164	Ballyshannon
Boyle, Henry	1005	Dungiven
Boyle, Henry	1013	cotton works, Tura nr Ld
Boyle, Hugh	1078	attorney, Dungiven
Boyle, James	183	pr Kilroot, bar Belfast, co Antrim
Boyle, James	341	Presbyterian, pr Ballykelly
Boyle, James	358	Newtown Lemavady
Boyle, James	792	bleach green, Dungiven
Boyle, John	126	mcht, Ballishannon
Boyle, John	772	Killygordon nr Lifford
Boyle, Neal	1102	res Bogside nr Butcher's gate, Ld
Boyle, Thomas	1078	Drumcovit nr Dungiven
Boyle, Thomas jr.	608	Drumscovitt
Brackin, James	103	Ld
Braddock, Mary	333	Newry
Bradley, John	127	Buncranagh area
Bradley, Mary (wid)	646	now of Artillery lane, Ld
Bradley, Mary widow	503	innkeeper, Ld
Bradley, Mich.	127	Buncranagh area
Bradley, Pat	190	innkeeper, Ld
Bradley, William	127	Buncranagh area
Brady, Cornelius	78	school master, William st., Dublin
Brandon, Gerard	722	Cash, co Fermanagh
Braston, William	215	Ld
Bray, Mary	1119	maid of Mary Spear, Temple st, Dublin
Breden, Thomas	386	pr Ardstraw
Bredin, Alexander	387	Letterkenny
Breslin, Mich.	127	Buncranagh area
Brew, John	1099	res Ray Charter School, co Donegal
Brice, Ezekiel	272	Ballybofey
Brien, Roger	794	White Boy captured nr Kilkenny

Name	Issue	Location
Broderick, Samuel	17	Mountgarret
Brodie, Francis	956	acquitted of murder, Dublin
Brodley, Cornelius	420	Lisboney, pr Cumber, co Ld
Brown, Ab.	151	Coleraine
Brown, Alexander	420	oak bark, Ld
Brown, Ann	201	millinery, Ld
Brown, David	777	Ld
Brown, George	519	publican, (in or nr) Ld
Brown, Hugh	341	Presbyterian, pr Ballykelly
Brown, Hugh	70	Maghrecallaghan
Brown, James	1027	Cloughglass nr Ld
Brown, James	426	Cogglass
Brown, James	519	publican, (in or nr) Ld
Brown, James	597	ipo tenement in Ballybofey
Brown, James	983	Manor Cuningham
Brown, James jr.	304	Manor Cunningham
Brown, Jane	25	nr Cumber, co Down
Brown, John	295	Magherafelt
Brown, John	471	ipo p/o Knockfair, Manor of Stranorlar
Brown, John	814	school, Cross lane in Bishop st, Ld
Brown, Samuel	70	Maghrecallaghan
Brown, Thomas	519	publican, (in or nr) Ld
Brown, William	447	chandler nr Butcher's gate, Bogside, Ld
Brown, William	903	overseer of Bishop's Demense, Ld
Browster, James	151	Coleraine
Bryan, Samuel	99	Coleraine
Buchanan, Alexander	703	cordwainer, Ld
Buchanan, Archibald	791	watch maker, Dublin; fmly of London
Buchanan, James	968	Donegal town
Buchanan, Margaret	818	acquitted of murder, Ld
Buchanan, William	717	Shipquay st, Ld
Buchanan, William	818	acquitted of murder, Ld
Buchanan, William	891	dealer in spirits, Ld
Bunton, Robert	829	criminal, Sligo
Burnside, James	688	mcht, Ld
Burnside, John	497	Waterside, Ld
Burnside, Micah	992	Slaughmanus nr Ld
Burnside, William	277	hse to let, Ld
Burton, William	232	Lifford
Butler, Thomas	899	stucco, Ld
Byrn, Anthony	25	nr Cumber, co Down
Byrne, Charles	277	slater, gaoled in Dublin
Byrne, Edmund	310	Ballyagget nr Kilkenny
Byrne, Jacob	837	Spawhill nr Borris, co Carlow
Byrne, James	226	Palmerstown
Byrne, Robert	138	Cabinteely nr Dublin
Cain, Alexander	334	outside Ferryquay gate, Ld
Cairns, John	182	pr Carnmoney, bar Belfast, co Antrim
Cairns, John	519	publican, (in or nr) Ld
Caldwell, James	249	Ld
Caldwell, John	170	Port Rush
Caldwell, John	341	Presbyterian, pr Ballykelly
Caldwell, John	386	pr Ardstraw
Caldwell, Noble	777	Ld
Caldwell, Richard	21	mcht, Ld
Caldwell, Richard	518	fmr hse, upper end of Rosemary lane, Ld
Caldwell, Samuel	386	pr Ardstraw
Caldwell, Samuel	76	Killeter
Caldwell, William	7	mcht, Ld
Calhoun, Alex.	619	Omagh
Calhoun, Cha.	630	Letterkenny
Calhoun, James	977	clock mkr, Ferryquay st, Ld; fmly Dln

Name	Issue	Location
Calhoun, Owens	1071	Carnamoyle nr Birdstown
Callaghan, James	244	arrested, Dublin
Camble, John	181	mcht, Omagh
Campbell, Allen	93	Strabane
Campbell, Charles	134	house, Ld
Campbell, David	279	Omagh
Campbell, Ephraim	348	ipo land in Liberties of Ld
Campbell, Ephraim	437	innkeeper, Bishop's gate, Ld
Campbell, Geo.	891	dealer in spirits, Ld
Campbell, George	277	slater, gaoled in Dublin
Campbell, James	116	shipbuilder, Rathmullan
Campbell, James	229	surveyor, Erginagh, formerly of Omagh
Campbell, James	320	Omagh
Campbell, James	869	teacher, Ld, fmly of Dublin and Eaton
Campbell, John	227	mcht, Omagh
Campbell, John	25	nr Cumber, co Down
Campbell, John	940	Ferryquay st opposite the Blue Ball, Ld
Campbell, Mark	1035	Ballymagowan nr Ld
Campbell, Mathew	183	pr All Saints, bar Rapho, co Donegal
Campbell, Patrick	750	ipo p/o Cloghfin
Campbell, Rob.	568	Omagh
Campbell, Robert	1005	Newtown Limavady
Campbell, William	14	Strabane
Cannon, Andrew	445	gaoled for bank fraud, Dublin
Carey, Michael	889	gaoled, Clonmel
Carlihon, John	295	weaver nr Ld
Carlon, Elizabeth	819	Rosemary ln, Ld
Carlon, Neal	475	wigmaker, Ld
Carmichael, Andrew	99	Bride st., Dublin
Carpenter, Dan.	53	Newry
Carr, Joseph	105	Aughasessey
Carrothers, John	25	nr Cumber, co Down
Carson, James	1118	chamberlain, Belfast White Linen Hall
Carson, Robert	521	druggist, Belfast
Carson, Will.	341	Presbyterian, pr Ballykelly
Carton, William	819	apprentice seaman, from Drogheda @ 16
Cary, Chas.	777	Ld
Cary, John	393	Coxtown
Cary, Robert	88	house painter, Ld
Cary, William	290	saddler, Omagh
Casey, Maurice	27	Clonmel
Caskey, John	853	Coleraine
Cassidy, John	420	tailor, Ld
Cather, Frances	205	Carricue, pr Fochanvale, co Ld
Cather, Francis	341	Presbyterian, pr Ballykelly
Cather, Francis	891	dealer in spirits, Ld
Caulfield, Henry	338	independent freeman of Ld
Chamberlin, Arthur	127	Buncranagh area
Chamberlin, Will.	127	Buncranagh area
Chambers, And.	387	Letterkenny
Chambers, Andrew	471	nr Pennyburn Mill
Chambers, Da.	387	Letterkenny
Chambers, Dan.	235	Rockhill, co Donegal
Chambers, James	445	Letterkenny
Chambers, John	1041	Lifford
Chambers, John	320	Ld
Chambers, John	387	Letterkenny
Chambers, John	962	Ballykelly
Chambers, Thomas	43	Butcher st., Ld
Chambers, Thomas	524	mcht, now in Shipquay st, Ld
Charleton, George	176	Roxton near Ld
Charleton, Richard	839	Birdstown nr Ld

Name	Issue	Location
Charlton, Richard	572	Birdtown, J.P. for cos Donegal & Ld
Christian, Ben.	777	Ld
Christy, Andrew	200	Dungiven
Church, Paul	983	pr Aughinlow, co Ld
Clark, Alexander	213	Maghera
Clark, Andrew	309	Grange betw Ld & Strabane
Clark, James	889	gaoled, Clonmel
Clark, John	1041	innkeeper, Bishop's gate, Ld
Clark, John	176	buckskins, Ld
Clark, John	348	ipo land in Liberties of Ld
Clark, John	839	Bishop st, Ld
Clark, Sam.	341	Presbyterian, pr Ballykelly
Clark, Will.	168	Ld
Clark, Wm. Living	187	school master, Ld
Clarke, Thomas	603	Lifford
Clingans, James	29	formerly ipo p/o Sleadron, near Ld
Clingans, John	29	formerly ipo p/o Sleadron, near Ld
Clingans, Thomas	29	formerly ipo p/o Sleadron, near Ld
Clinton, Richard	1052	Marnaclia nr Carrickmacross co Monaghan
Close, Max.	808	lessee, Ballycastle nr Newtown Lemavady
Cochran, Alexander	308	Creevagh
Cochran, Alexander	742	Clashegowan nr St. Johnston, co Donegal
Cochran, Alexander jr.	182	pr Taughboyne, bar Rapho, co Donegal
Cochran, Alexander jr.	237;282	mcht, Ld
Cochran, Alexander jr.	591	nr St. Johnston
Cochran, Geo & Richard	150	occ house in Ld
Cochran, George	156	former house, Ld
Cochran, John	190	pr Taughboyne, bar Rapho, co Donegal
Cochran, John	303	high constable, bar Raphoe
Cochran, Joseph	6	arrested for robbery, Dublin
Cochran, Rob.	812	Strabane
Cochran, Robert	220;420	grocer, Strabane
Cochran, Robert	23;183	Glashgowan, pr Taughboyne
Cochran, Robert	246	tobacco mfr, Ld
Cochran, Zacheus	1065	Edenmore nr Ld
Cockran, Joseph	6	arrested, Dublin
Cockran, Thomas	55	mcht, Sligo
Coghlan, Mary	277	assaulted in Dublin
Colclough, Adam & Pat.	959	colliery, Garrindinny, co Kilkenny
Colebrook, George	14	banker, Carlow (?)
Coleman, Lawrence	277	gaoled in Dublin
Coleman, Patrick Dr.	503	Dundald (papist)
Colgan, Ber.	891	dealer in spirits, Ld
Colgan, Michael	295	Magherafelt
Colhoun, Al.	568	Omagh
Colhoun, Cha.	387	Letterkenny
Colhoun, John	731	Labadish
Colhoun, Owens	1058	Carnamoyle nr Ld
Colhoun, Thomas	866	Manor Cuningham
Colhoun, William	159;375	Raphoe
Colhoun, Wm.	387	Letterkenny
Collier, W.	650	master coach mkr, Kevan st, Dln
Con, Gabriel	341	Presbyterian, pr Ballykelly
Con, George	341	Presbyterian, pr Ballykelly
Conaghan, Hugh	460	Lifford (poor man, large family)
Coningham, Dickson	10	mcht, Ld
Coningham, John	882	fmr hse next to Butcher's gate, Ld
Coningham, L. Mrs.	387	Letterkenny
Coningham, Red.	1036	Letterkenny
Coningham, Tho.	1073	spirits, Butcher st, Ld
Coningham, Wm.	777	Ld
Connell, Morgan	748	gaoled, Corke

Name	Issue	Location
Connelly, Bryan	551	criminal, Monaghan
Connor, Dennis	534	Sharon
Connor, John	393	gaoled; of nr Rathdrum, co Wicklow
Connor, Thomas	438	peruke mkr, Pump st., Ld
Conry, John	29	Ballyshannon, co Donegal
Conway, Andrew	284	in co Kilkenny gaol as a White Boy
Conway, James	284	in co Kilkenny gaol as a White Boy
Conyngham, Richard	445	Letterkenny
Cooke, William	127	Buncranagh area
Cookley, Charles	149	maimed, Dublin
Cooper, James	169	King's Arms Inn, Belfast
Corbet, Archibald	546	proprietor, Corn Mill of Ruskey
Cordner, James	190	Coleraine
Cornwall, Esther Miss	148	Ld
Corr, Michael	25	nr Cumber, co Down
Corran, William	505	earthen ware, Ferry quay, Ld
Costello, J.	650	master coach mkr, Henry st, Dln
Costello, P.	650	master coach mkr, Jervis st, Dln
Cottingham, George	1112	nursery nr six-mile stone, Grand Canal
Cousland, Robert	452	Lismacarroll, pr Glendermot, co Ld
Cowan, Richard	240;392	Lifford
Cowan, Thomas	239	attorney, Lifford
Cowden, James	617	mcht, Castlefin
Cox, George	339	escaped from Newgate prison, Dublin
Coyle, Dennis	1120	hatter, Ferryquay st, Ld
Coyle, Neil	615	criminal, Ld
Coyle, William	1018	ipo p/o Upper Tullydish nr Ld
Coyle, William	127	Buncranagh area
Cracket, William	184	pr All Saints, bar Rapho, co Donegal
Craig, Alex.	1091	school, outside Butcher's gate, Ld
Craig, Sam.	183	pr Antrim, bar Antrim, co Antrim
Craige, Alex.	1107	school, Shipquay st, Ld
Crampsey, Jas. & Darby	566	fmly ipo pt Upper Carran nr Ballybofey
Cramsey, Andrew	907	Cow bog, Ld
Crawford, Andrew	254	Portglenone
Crawford, Isa.	387	Letterkenny
Crawford, James	953	ipo Mineclay, pr Langfield, co Tyrone
Crawford, John & Sam.	709	Ballynehatty, pr Drumra, bar Omagh
Crawford, Thomas	375	Raphoe
Crawford, Thomas jr.	236	Donegal town
Crawford, William	327	shop in Castlefin
Crawford, William	386	pr Ardstraw
Crawford, William	853	Strabane
Creighton, Abraham	296	Killybegs
Crigan, Charles	315	Omagh
Crilly, George	794	Garvagh nr Ld
Criswell, John	341	Presbyterian, pr Ballykelly
Criswell, Michael	341	Presbyterian, pr Ballykelly
Criswell, Will.	341	Presbyterian, pr Ballykelly
Crocker, John	814	Cross ln betw Bishop st & Widows row Ld
Crocket, Anthony	627	innkeeper, Ld
Crocket, William	1081	pr All-Saints, co Donegal
Crockit, Ant.	1008	Bishop st, Ld
Cromie, John	151	Ballylease, pr Ballyachron
Cromie, John	151	Coleraine
Cromie, John	383	J.P., Ballymoney, co Antrim
Crompton, Heape	174	sail maker, Ld
Crone, Thomas	309	Passage nr Waterford
Crookshank, Alexander	171	seneschal for Lord Donegal
Crookshank, Eliz. Miss	434	former hse in Butcher st., Ld
Crookshank, Eliz. Mrs.	145	former house, Ld
Crosby, Ann	25	nr Cumber, co Down

Name	Issue	Location
Cross, Hugh	341	Presbyterian, pr Ballykelly
Crozier, Samuel	25	nr Cumber, co Down
Cudbert, William	1102	mcht, Waterside, Ld
Culbert, Matthew	845	Rye
Culbertson, Thomas	270	butcher, escaped from gaol, Ld
Cullen, Francis & Wm.	849	Enniscrone, co Sligo
Cullen, Patrick	849	gaoled, Sligo
Cumerford, And.	1019	stay maker, opposite the Gaol Wall, Ld
Cummin, Alexander	58	cabinet maker, Rosemary lane, Ld
Cuningham, Edw.	676	whitesmith, Ld
Cuningham, Henry	143	jockey, Ld Races
Cuningham, Nat.	891	dealer in spirits, Ld
Cuningham, Thomas	339	escaped from Newgate prison, Dublin
Cuningham, Thomas	446	residence in Butcher st., Ld
Cuningham, Waddel	946	Hercules lane, Belfast
Cuppage, Adam	987	Lurgan
Curry, Joseph	1029	groceries, Ld
Curry, Samuel	209	mcht, Ld
Curry, Tristram	222	Rushfield, nr Ld
Cust, John	399	Whey House inn, Magilligan
Cuttle, John	533	saddler, Stabane, fmly of Dublin
D'Evelyn, Daniel	25	nr Cumber, co Down
Dalton, Michael	291	pickpocket, Dublin, age 13
Daly, Dennis	333	Dunsandle, in a duel at Galway
Darrogane, Thomas	163	Clonmel
Daugherty, Francis	421	Ld
Davis, James	987	Newry
Davis, John	1070	watch maker, Strabane
Davis, John	364	Manor Cuningham
Davis, John & Thomas	472	Manor Cuningham
Davis, Mark	250	shoemaker, Ld, newly from London
Davis, Richard	78	occ p/o Tuban near Ld
Davis, Robert	670	fmly occ p/o Tuban, pr Fahan, Inishowen
Davis, Thomas	21	baker, Ferryquay st., Ld
Davis, Thomas	722	Manor Cuningham
Davis, Will.	341	Presbyterian, pr Ballykelly
Davis, Will. jr.	341	Presbyterian, pr Ballykelly
Davis, William	956	trial witness, Dublin
Davison, Mary	25	nr Cumber, co Down
Day, Leighton	1007	painter, Ld
Deechan, Hugh	127	Buncranagh area
Deechan, Neal	127	Buncranagh area
Deechan, Neil	1018	ipo p/o Upper Tullydish nr Ld
Delap, Samuel	307	Rathmelton
Denning, Joseph	420	occ farm nr Letterkenny
Denning, Monro	66	watchmaker from London, now of Strabane
Denniston, Noble	75	cabinet mkr, nr the Barrack Gate, Ld
Denniston, Samuel	191	Tavenaclare, Donaghedy, co Tyrone
Denny, Daniel	529	saddler, Omagh, fmly of Dublin
Denny, David	710	saddler, Omagh
Denny, Samuel	432	sadler, Strabane
Dermot, Henry	127	Buncranagh area
Dermot, John	891	fmly ipo farm in the Colins, 2m from Ld
Desart, James	839	res Bogside, Ld
Devatt, Valentine	18	pick pocket, Dublin
Devlin, Henry	254	tenant in Ballynease Downing
Dezart, Saml.	1107	shopkeeper, the Diamond, Ld
Dick, James	386	pr Ardstraw
Dick, Samuel	641	Dublin
Dickey, Charles	478	Randalstown, co Antrim
Diermont, Arch.	341	Presbyterian, pr Ballykelly
Dignam, Patrick	1103	a lad, criminal, Dublin

Name	Issue	Location
Dimond, Henry	254	tenant in Ballynease Downing
Dimond, John	254	tenant in Ballynease Downing
Dinning, Will.	341	Presbyterian, pr Ballykelly
Dixon, Sam.	341	Presbyterian, pr Ballykelly
Doak, James	777	Ld
Doak, James jr.	777	Ld
Dobbin, Archibald	1107	innkeeper, Monaghan (for 20 years)
Dobbin, Richard	257	nr Clonmel
Dobson, Thomas	125;387	Letterkenny
Docharty, Owen	127	Buncranagh area
Dodd, James	650	master coach mkr, Earl st, Dln
Doherty, Ant.	454	hse in Ferryquay st, Ld
Donaghey, Henry	151	former farm in pr Glendermot
Donaghey, Hugh	1114	Ballymagorey, co Tyrone
Donagho, Owen	245	Dublin
Donaghy, Ar.	1080	Strad, pr Banagher, co Ld
Donaghy, Bryan	127	Buncranagh area
Donaghy, Henry	127	Buncranagh area
Donnelly, Pat.	568	Omagh
Donohoe, J.	650	master coach mkr, Strand st, Dln
Doran, James	539	dealer, Thomas st, Dublin
Dougan, David	127	Buncranagh area
Dougherty, Ant.	127	Buncranagh area
Dougherty, Bryan	127	Buncranagh area
Dougherty, Corn.	1018	ipo p/o Upper Tullydish nr Ld
Dougherty, Dan.	127	Buncranagh area
Dougherty, Dennis	66	ipo a farm in the Liberties of Ld
Dougherty, Edward	364	Carmaquigley
Dougherty, F. Mr.	896	Waterside, Ld
Dougherty, Francis	234	criminal, Omagh
Dougherty, Francis	489	Waterside, Ld
Dougherty, Hu.	127	Buncranagh area
Dougherty, Hugh	6	arrested for robbery, Dublin
Dougherty, John	1071	fmly ipo p/o Glashogh nr Ld
Dougherty, John	127	Buncranagh area
Dougherty, John	277	gaoled in Dublin
Dougherty, Mich.	127	Buncranagh area
Dougherty, Pat.	127	Buncranagh area
Dowd, Mathew	701	Bigsurs (?), nr Dunboyne, co Meath
Dowdall, William	954	robbed, Drogheda
Dowling, Edward	1029	Dame st, Dublin
Dowling, Pat.	940	pirate, cruising off the west coast
Downing, John	296	Rowesgift, co Ld
Downing, John	951	Ld
Doyle, Con.	391	gaoled, Ld
Doyle, Dennis	22	arrested, Dublin
Doyle, Judith	588	servant, Waterford (lottery winner)
Doyle, Matthew	293	thief, Dublin
Doyle, Nicholas	470	fishmonger, Dublin
Draper, George	722	silk mkr, 45 Bridge st, Dublin
Drysdale, William	12	writing school, Strabane
Dudgeon, John	1012	Old White Cross Inn, Dln; fmly of Omagh
Dudgeon, John	568	Omagh
Duff, Michael	239	criminal, Dublin
Duffy, Patrick	136	tried at Armagh
Dugall, Thomas	1081	pr All-Saints, co Donegal
Dugall, Thomas	118;151	Ballyhasky
Dugall, Thomas	8	nr Castle Cuningham
Dugall, William	1081	pr All-Saints, co Donegal
Dugall, William sr.	1000	Portlough nr Ld
Dugan, Elizabeth	252	criminal, Dublin
Duke, Robert	103	Branchfield nr Boyle, co Sligo

Name	Issue	Location
Dunbar, David	1017	Butcher st, Ld
Dunbar, David	181	contractor, Ld
Dunbar, David jr.	1080	new commission mcht, Ld
Dunbar, Rob.	777	Ld
Dunbar, William	1030	carpenter, Cross lane, Ld
Dunbar, William	931	attorney, Ferryquay st, Ld
Dunkin, John	193	mcht, Ld
Dunlap, Alexander	87	Wallworth
Dunlap, Henry	777	Ld
Dunlap, James	338	independent freeman of Ld
Dunn, Bryan	310	near Ballyagget nr Kilkenny
Dunn, Christopher	92	fish dealer, Dublin
Dunn, George	245	Dublin
Dunn, William	289	surgeon & apothecary, Ld
Dunn, William Dr.	913	Church lane, Ld
Duquerny, Henry	251	Dublin
Dutton, Ralph	375	Raphoe
Dwyer, Thomas	137	White Boy taken near Kilkenny
Dyzart, Arch.	1006	Portglenone, co Antrim
Eccles, Arthur	363	Ld
Eccles, Dan.	568	Omagh
Ecles, George	387	Letterkenny
Edgar, James	1105	shoe maker, the Diamond, Ld
Edgar, James	434	shoemaker, Butcher st., Ld
Edie, Nathaniel	76	Newtown Stewart
Edmiston, James	1101	occ p/o Garshewy, pr Taughboyne
Edmiston, Robert	274	Garshewey, co Donegal
Egan, James	588	shoemaker, Armagh (wf & 7 children)
Egan, Peter	569	cooper, Morrison's Island nr Corke
Elkin, Edward	933	Binian (on the sea coast)
Elliot, Charles	445	Letterkenny
Elliot, George	445	Letterkenny
Elliot, Mat.	387	Letterkenny
Ellis, John	429	fmly coachman for Robt. Pensent, now Ld
Ennis, John	91	Keenaghan nr Dungannon, co Tyrone
Espey, David	165	Ballygruby
Ewing, Alexander	166	Bogside, Ld
Ewing, Charles	777	Ld
Ewing, James	841	Freeschool lane, Ld
Ewing, James	891	dealer in spirits, Ld
Ewing, John	127	Buncranagh area
Ewing, John	505	mcht, Butcher st, Ld
Ewing, Robert	387	Letterkenny
Ewing, Samuel	184	pr Templemore, bar Terkerin, co Ld
Ewing, Samuel	338	independent freeman of Ld
Exshaw, John	488	bookseller, Dublin
Fairey(?), Will.	341	Presbyterian, pr Ballykelly
Fairly, David	84	occ hse in St. Columb's court, Ld
Fairly, John	113	poor house treasurer, Ld
Fairly, Rob.	777	Ld
Faloon, Daniel	819	boarding house, Rapho
Fanning, Audley	593	Matsmount nr Dungiven
Faron, John	700	gaoled, Ld
Farrel, Henry	476	mcht, Aran quay, Dublin
Farrell, Bridget	1035	from co Wicklow, criminal in Dublin
Farren, Bryan	1076	ipo tenement in Bogside, Ld
Feath, Edward	811	Bushmills, co Antrim
Feeney, John	1060	fmly ipo p/o Gransaghard, pr Fahan
Fenton, Benjamin	174;280	apothecary, Strabane
Fenton, John	892	hearthmoney collector, Sligo
Ferguson, And.	188	par Templemore, bar Ennishowen, Donegal
Ferguson, Andrew	290;354	mcht, Ld

Name	Issue	Location
Ferguson, Doctor	20	Scotch Ale House, Ld, to let
Ferguson, James	209	Donegal town
Ferguson, John	324	Ld
Ferguson, John	381	Letterkenny, hse destroyed by fire
Finlay, John	327	former hse, Ld
Finlay, John	611	bakery, Pump st, Ld
Finlay, Patrick	439	fmly butler of Geo Young, Culdaff
Finn, Peter	44	ipo house in Knockfair, mn Stranorlar
Fisher, James	50	New Inn, Ld
Fisher, T.	686	a poor weaver, Meath st, Dublin
Fitzgerald, Catherine	145	near Athy, alledgedly raped
Fitzpatrick, John	760	Belfast (master of the Industry)
Fitzsimons, James	512	Strahulter nr Newtown Stewart
Flanagan, Francis	121	patient, Co. Galway Infirmary
Flanigan, Edmund	541	dancing master, Ld
Flattery, Neal	1100-1101	publican, Ormond quay, Dublin
Fleming, James	387	Letterkenny
Fleming, John	109	bookseller, Drogheda
Fleming, Joseph	341	Presbyterian, pr Ballykelly
Fleming, Pat.	1044	Strabane
Fleming, Sam.	341	Presbyterian, pr Ballykelly
Fleming, William	990	brush maker, Dublin
Fletcher, John	519	publican, (in or nr) Ld
Fletcher, Joseph	931	linen mcht, Dublin
Foord, Timothy	137	tried for riot at Leitrim
Foot, Nicholas	139	alias of Thomas Fox, q.v.
Ford, James	1102	Green hills, co Dublin
Ford, Pat	314	nr Abbotstown nr Dublin
Forrester, William	919	Mullan, co Ld
Forster, Arthur	386	pr Ardstraw
Forster, William	203	Ballydogan, co Down, a Steel Boy
Forsythe, Jacob	983	pr Aughinlow, co Ld
Forsythe, Jacob jr.	983	pr Aughinlow, co Ld
Forsythe, John	44	ipo house in Knockfair, mn Stranorlar
Forsythe, John	983	pr Aughinlow, co Ld
Forsythe, Will.	341	Presbyterian, pr Ballykelly
Forsythe, William	983	pr Aughinlow, co Ld
Foster, James	1046	Bogside, Ld
Foster, James	891	dealer in spirits, Ld
Foweler, James	167	Carlow
Fox, Thomas	139	of Kevin st., Dln; gaoled at Wexford
Foy, John	427	Butcher's gate, Ld
Franks, John	649	jeweller, 33 Skinner row, Dublin
Franks, John	785	fmly Dublin; jeweler, Ferryquay st, Ld
Freel, John	1009	Ld
Freel, Neal	1071	fmly ipo p/o Glashogh nr Ld
French, Savage	744	Corke
French, Thomas	109	Cookstown, co Tyrone
Fuller, George	233	of the Corporation of Weavers, Dublin
Fullerton, Seth	360	Strabane
Fulton, Henry	288	mcht, Ld
Fulton, Henry	690	Newtown Lemavady
Fulton, James	1;345	mcht Bishop st., Ld
Fulton, John	1081	pr All-Saints, co Donegal
Fulton, Wm.	445	Letterkenny
Funston, John	64	Derg bridge
Gage, Robert	879	Longhill nr Coleraine
Galbraith, James	1	mathematician, Ld
Galbraith, Samuel	270	nr Omagh
Galbraith, Samuel	291	Greenmount
Gallagher, Ant.	839	ipo land in Garshewy, co Donegal nr Ld
Gallagher, Bridget	818	criminal, Ld

Name	Issue	Location
Gallagher, Ch.	387	Letterkenny
Gallagher, Cha.	499	Castle Cuningham
Gallagher, Charles	535	across the river from Prehen
Gallagher, John	3	Inniskilling, co Fermanagh
Gallagher, John	310	Rathmelton
Gallagher, Thomas	777	Ld
Galt, Jn. and Ch.	151	Coleraine
Galt, Rob.	151	Coleraine
Galvan, Roger	432	gardener, Sharon nr Castle Cuningham
Gamble, Andrew	303	stamp agent, Strabane
Gamble, Daniel	524	iron monger, Ld
Gamble, Henry	445	Letterkenny
Gamble, James	899	glazier and painter, Ld
Gamble, James jr.	777	Ld
Gamble, John	430	former farm at Lower Kildrum
Gamble, John	777	Ld
Gamble, William	349	apothecary, the Diamond, Ld
Gamble, William	37	mcht, Strabane
Garmully, Thady	29	in Galway gaol
Garraway, Widow	575	ipo hse in Bishop st, Ld
Gault, John	38	Ld
Gaussan, David	1052	Newry
Gaven, Luke	228	jockey, Ld Races
Geale, Eben, Fred, Dan	402	flax seed, Ld vicinity
Gelling, John	53	guild clerk, Dublin
Geoghegan, John	873	Galway
George, Daniel	341	Presbyterian, pr Ballykelly
Gernon, James	49	Cookstown, co Meath
Gerrell, Will	519	publican, (in or nr) Ld
Getty, Richard	1111	fmly at Meeting House gate, Maghera
Getty, Robert	900	new mcht, Bridge st, Belfast
Gibbeny, John	334	bricklayer, Ld, late from London & Dln
Gibson, Alexander	950	expelled from Kilkenny Rangers
Gibson, John & Thomas	810	ipo p/o Termon lands of Clooney, co Ld
Giffen, John	341	Presbyterian, pr Ballykelly
Giffen, John jr.	341	Presbyterian, pr Ballykelly
Giffen, Joseph	341	Presbyterian, pr Ballykelly
Gillan, Daniel & Neal	1	ipo Ballynelly, pr Moville
Gillard, Rob.	777	Ld
Gillespie, William	25	Comber, co Down
Gillespy, Edw.	127	Buncranagh area
Gilmour, James	1066	carpets, the Diamond, Ld
Gilmour, John	341	Presbyterian, pr Ballykelly
Ginn, James	722	Strabane
Girvin, James	190	pr Aghalow, bar Dungannon, co Tyrone
Given, James	953	ipo Dromeen, pr Langfield, co Tyrone
Given, Rt.	151	Coleraine
Given, Rt. jr.	151	Coleraine
Glasco, James	568	Omagh
Glass, John	231	attorney, Roscommon
Glen, James	923	Bogside, Ld
Glen, John	8	ipo house in Ld
Glen, William	20;363	woollen draper, the Diamond, Ld
Glenn, Wm.	891	dealer in spirits, Ld
Glenny, William	1011	Newry
Goff, Patrick	869	Oakfield nr Rapho
Going, Robert	512	Tullamoylan, co Tipperary
Gomie, Martha Mrs.	696	Ld
Gond, Thomas	766	ipo p/o Ferrydermont
Gonne, Martha Mrs.	140	shoe shop, Ferryquay st., Ld
Gonne, Thomas	812	Ld
Goold, George	14	Cork

A-13

Name	Issue	Location
Gordon, Gardner	777	Ld
Gordon, John	1011	Newry
Gordon, John	442	tried, Ld
Gordon, John	808	lessee, Ballycastle nr Newtown Lemavady
Gordon, Wm.	777	Ld
Gorman, Henry	136	tried at Armagh
Gorman, Morris	228	jockey, Ld Races
Gormly, Arthur	957	tailor, Ld; son-in-law of Mrs. Hamilton
Gormly, James	568	Omagh
Gorrell, William	891	dealer in spirits, Ld
Gould, John	1028	linin printer, Bogside, Ld; fmly Augher
Gouldsbury, Francis	780	Ld
Gourney, Jas, Jos, Mgt	724	tenement, Waterside, Ld
Graham, Ann	891	dealer in spirits, Ld
Grannon, Pat.	139	robber, gaoled at Dublin
Grant, Archibald	546	drawing teacher, Ld
Gray, Charles	1060	Ferry quay, Ld
Gray, David	338	independent freeman of Ld
Gray, Hugh	341	Presbyterian, pr Ballykelly
Gray, James	341	Presbyterian, pr Ballykelly
Gray, Matthew	521	saddler, Rapho
Gray, Robert	392	Gortin
Grayburn, Thomas	9	gaoled for robbery, Dublin
Grayson, Anthony	815	Linenhall st, Dublin
Greaves, Arch.	891	dealer in spirits, Ld
Green, Christ.	341	Presbyterian, pr Ballykelly
Green, George	288	St. Thomas parish, Dublin
Green, Roger	921	deputy mayor of Youghal
Greer, James	568	Omagh
Greffon, William	765	mcht, King st, Dublin
Gregg, Cuningham	1015	rum, Ann st, Belfast
Gregg, Tho.	151	Coleraine
Gregg, Thomas	168;420	mcht, Ld
Gregg, Thomas	430	former hse in Ferryquay st., Ld
Gregg, Thomas	987	Belfast
Gregg, Wm.	151	Coleraine
Gregory, William	543	Ballybofey
Grey, David	348	Thornhill
Griffith, Anthony	64	inn keeper, Strabane
Griffith, Henry	379	Ballytivenan, co Sligo
Grogan, Cornelius	20	hse in College Green, Dublin
Grove, C. Miss	387	Letterkenny
Grove, Humphrey	198	surgeon, Co. Donegal Infirmary
Grove, Thomas	172	Lifford
Grovenor, John	545	hatter from London, now of Ld
Groves, James	1029	outside Bishop's gate, Ld
Guben, Lau.	127	Buncranagh area
Gullion, Patrick	91	tried at Carrickfergus (robbed a ship)
Gwin, Richard	229	rope maker, ws of Diamond, Ld
Gwin, Richard	891	dealer in spirits, Ld
Gwyn, John	430	grocer, Ferryquay st., Ld
Gwyn, John	642	grocer, now Butcher st, Ld
Gwyn, Moore	25	nr Cumber, co Down
Hadfield, Sam	195	Ld
Hadskis, Stewart	345	iron foundry, Ld
Haffan, Edward	396	ipo Tullagowan, pr Banagher, co Ld
Hagan, Charles	113	inn, Strahmore, betw Dungiven-Cookstown
Haggarty, John	149	whipped, Dublin
Hagon, Edward	127	Buncranagh area
Halloran, John	147	glue, Kilkenny
Haly, Thomas	51	attorney, Mermount
Hamill, Hugh jr.	931	linen mcht, Dublin

Name	Issue	Location
Hamill, James	325	Coleraine
Hamilton, Alexander	808	lessee, Ballycastle nr Newtown Lemavady
Hamilton, Catherine	865	criminal, Omagh
Hamilton, Geoffrey	721	White Castle nr Ld
Hamilton, George	191	pr Donaghedy, co Tyrone
Hamilton, Hen.	151	Coleraine
Hamilton, Hugh	488	linen factory, Ld
Hamilton, James	1059	carpenter, Ld
Hamilton, James	303	English school master, Ld
Hamilton, James	568	Omagh
Hamilton, John Capt.	442	salt to sell, Ld
Hamilton, Margaret	611	Ballindret
Hamilton, Mathew	1081	pr All-Saints, co Donegal
Hamilton, Myrton	989	theatre, Ld
Hamilton, Rebecca Mrs.	521	widow, Ballindrate
Hamilton, Robert	1108	tobacconist, Bishop st lane, Ld
Hamilton, Samuel	25	nr Comber, co Down
Hamilton, Thomas	1019	opposite the Gaol Wall, Ld
Hamilton, Thomas	147	Strabane
Hamilton, William	375	Raphoe
Hamilton, William	772	Omagh
Hamilton, William	983	surgeon, Ferryquay st, Ld
Hammel, James	186	Coleraine
Hanlon, Lawrence	973	illegal voter, gaoled, Dublin
Hanna, John	309	Antrim town
Hannagan, Bryan	955	Rathmullon, co Donegal
Hannagan, Dennis	3	pr Cumber, co Ld
Happer, Duncan	887	fmly res of Tullyrusk, 3 m from Omagh
Hardy, Henry	136	bleach green, Clare, co Armagh
Hargan, James	907	Cow bog, Ld
Hargreaves, Abraham	280	fmly Strabane, now of Heir's court
Harkin, Alexander	375	Raphoe
Harkin, Mich.	478	Ld
Harkin, Pat.	870	peruke maker, Shipquay st, Ld
Harkin, Patrick	323	peruke maker, Butcher st., Ld
Harkins, John	445	Letterkenny
Harold, George	614	Strabane
Harper, James	69	outside Butcher's gate, Ld
Harpur, George	956	trial witness, Dublin
Harragon, Corn.	127	Buncranagh area
Harragon, James	127	Buncranagh area
Harricks, D.	650	master coach mkr, Marlbro st, Dln
Harris, Eliz.	190	pr Conwall & Tullyachnish, co Donegal
Harris, William	507	criminal, Dublin
Harton, Dan.	127	Buncranagh area
Harton, Hugh	127	Buncranagh area
Harton, James	127	Buncranagh area
Harton, Neal	127	Buncranagh area
Harton, Walter	376	cooper, Ferryquay st., Ld
Harvey, Jer.	1119	silk mcht, Ld
Harvey, John	777	Ld
Harvey, Rose Mrs.	285	ashes to sell, Ld
Harvey, William	762	Millenan nr Ld
Haslet, James	391	mcht, Ld
Haslet, John	696	res Ferryquay st, Ld
Haslet, William	983	pr Aughinlow, co Ld
Haslet, Wm.	777	Ld
Haslett, James	79	mcht, Ld
Hasties, Thomas heirs	136	farm in Ga_key
Haston, Walter	296	former residence, Ld
Haughy, Cha.	387	Letterkenny
Haughy, James	310	Letterkenny

Name	Issue	Location
Haughy, John Rev.	1051	Catholic pastor of pr Taughboyne
Haughy, William	445	Letterkenny
Hay, James	341	Presbyterian, pr Ballykelly
Hay, Joseph	581	nr Letterkenny
Hay, Pat.	387	Letterkenny
Hay, Samuel	427	Convoy
Hayes, David	956	tythe proctor nr Dingle; age near 80
Hazlet, James	151	Coleraine
Hazlet, William	853	Newtown Lemavady
Hazlett, Moses	134	Ballylaun
Heasty, John	127	Buncranagh area
Hegarty, William	383	to open a school, Ld
Hemphill, James	341	Presbyterian, pr Ballykelly
Henderson, Kennedy	353	Castle Dawson
Henderson, Robert	182	pr Aughalow, bar Dungannon, co Tyrone
Henderson, Sam.	673	Rathmullan
Henderson, William	310	Rapho
Hennessey, Martin	4	nr Rusheen, co Kerry
Henry, David	126	appr apothecary, Cookstown, co Tyrone
Henry, Francis	480; 493	Three Tuns inn, Cookstown, co Tyrone
Herraghty, Hugh	49	Ards
Hervey, James	121	former lease of Donmore
Hetherington, John	588	Tullynegarnan
Hetrick, Finley	635	ipo p/o Middle Creggan, Liberties of Ld
Hewetson, Christopher	284	justice of the peace, co Kilkenny
Hewey, Alex.	338	independent freeman of Ld
Heyland, Dom.	151	Coleraine
Heyland, Rich.	151	Coleraine
Heyland, Rob.	151	Coleraine
Hicks, Francis	314	formerly of Ld
Hickson, John	951	Cahirbothuen (?) nr Tralee
Hill, John	15	town clerk of Enniscorthy
Hill, John	9	innkeeper, Omagh
Hird, John	820	gardener, Belfast
Hodgson, William	575	Castle Dawson
Hoey, James	488	bookseller, Parliament st, Dublin
Hogg, George	955	Sligo
Holden, Andrew	127	Buncranagh area
Holland, Rob.	777	Ld
Holmes, Da.	341	Presbyterian, pr Ballykelly
Holmes, David	341	Presbyterian, pr Ballykelly
Holmes, James	1119	nr Longwood, co Meath
Holmes, James	341	Presbyterian, pr Ballykelly
Holmes, John & James	984	Belfast
Holmes, Richard	767	Ballyart, King's co
Holmes, Sam.	341	Presbyterian, pr Ballykelly
Holmes, Samuel	40	jeweler, Dublin
Homan, Brant	256	woollen draper, Dublin
Hood, John	1060	mathematician, Moyle
Hood, Nathaniel	386	pr Ardstraw
Hood, William	675	Newtown Stewart
Hope, Mary Mrs.	554	late house, Butcher st, Ld
Hope, William	29	Ld
Hopps, William	1111	Maghera, ws of st leading to Garvagh
Hornick, George	325	parish clerk, Killanna, co Wexford
Hosty, James	865	sedan chairman, Galway
House, William	562	hse in Newtown Stewart
Houston, Francis	296	Tullydowey nr Armagh
Houston, Patrick	127	Buncranagh area
Houston, Robert	190	mcht, Ld
Houton, Wm.	127	Buncranagh area
Howes, Alex.	963	Letterkenny

Name	Issue	Location
Hudson, John	233	of the Corporation of Weavers, Dublin
Hudson, Thos.	782	Sligo
Huey, Alexander	452	Upper Gortegarty, pr Faughanvale, co Ld
Huey, James	376	linen draper, Muff
Huey, James	684	distiller, Flowerfield nr Muff
Huey, Margery widow	295	Magherafelt
Hughes, Barrington	981	Slaughterhouse lane on Ship quay, Ld
Humphress, Michael	710	hosier, Dublin
Hundleston, John	1040	town inspector of measures, Donaghadee
Hunter, Abraham	186	post chaise, Coleraine
Hunter, Alexander	78	Rathmelton
Hunter, John	341	Presbyterian, pr Ballykelly
Hunter, John	387	Letterkenny
Hunter, Nathaniel	777	Ld
Hunter, Walter	387	Letterkenny
Hussey, J.	650	master coach mkr, Henry st, Dln
Ingram, Sampson	361	inspector of brown linens, Dungannon
Innot, William	523	Rathpatrick, co Kilkenny
Inns, Charles	891	dealer in spirits, Ld
Irwin, Henry	495	Ray, pr Aughnish, co Donegal
Irwin, James	386	pr Ardstraw
Irwin, John	353	lately occupied hse in Castle Dawson
Irwin, Robert	285	Moree; sub sheriff of co Tyrone
Irwin, Thomas	1059	bookseller, Enniskillen
Irwin, Thomas	188	pr Aghalow, bar Dungannon, co Tyrone
Irwin, Thomas	535	Bishop's gate, Ld
Irwin, Widow	7	ipo tenement in Ld
Irwine, Andrew	441	Camas, co Tyrone
Irwine, Hen.	387	Letterkenny
Irwine, Will.	341	Presbyterian, pr Ballykelly
Jack, John	386	pr Ardstraw
Jackson, Richard	186	Coleraine
Jackson, Thomas	143;227	jockey, Ld Races
Jacob, Luke	257	Dublin
Jacob, Mathew jr.	163	Clonmel
Jago, Samuel	316	s/o Capt. Jago, Waterford
James, John	304	jockey, Belfast races
James, Stephen	309	Passage nr Waterford
Jamison, Robert	590	leather, Strabane
Jenkin, Caleb	946	58 Dame st, Dublin
Jenkins, William	35	former house in Raphoe
Jennings, Thomas	371	Ld
Jervis, T.	650	master coach mkr, Britain st, Dln
Johnson, Francis	641	ipo p/o Cove, 1/2 mile from Buncranna
Johnson, Richard	25	J.P., Guilford, co Down
Johnson, William	977	hair dresser, Church lane, Ld
Johnston, Catherine	182	houses to let, Ld
Johnston, Charles	184	butcher, Omagh (?)
Johnston, James	1057	Rash nr Omagh
Johnston, John	4	Warrenstown, co Meath
Johnston, Michael	294	Moneymore, co Ld
Johnston, Rob. Capt.	817	outside Ferryquay gate, Ld
Johnston, Thomas	1098	shopkeeper, Dundalk
Jolly, William	813	artist, 2 Bachelor's lane, Dublin
Jordan, James	62	school and bookkeeper, Strabane
Joyce, Edmund	137	White Boy taken near Kilkenny
Kane, Henry	969	outlaw, nr Magherafelt
Kane, Michael	806	stage coach line, Cones, co Monaghan
Kane, Patrick	222	Birdstown, co Donegal
Kane, Richard	717	Lurgan, co Antrim
Kean, William	324	Clontarf nr Dublin
Keane, John	157	hats, Ld

Name	Issue	Location
Kearns, John	245	gaoled in Dublin
Kearns, Samuel Rev.	190	school master, Cookstown
Keating, James	18	prisoner, Dublin
Keightly, George	611	mcht, Rapho
Keightly, William	375	Raphoe
Kelly, Bernard	597	cares for the Wood of Kincraghy
Kelly, Ed.	967	ipo Kilfeak & Clanbracken (w/M'Elhenny)
Kelly, John	127	Buncranagh area
Kelly, John	239	criminal, Dublin
Kelly, John	270	accused of robbery, Dublin
Kelly, John	436	peruke maker, Ferryquay st., Ld
Kelly, John	598	shoemaker, Ballinasloe
Kelly, Pat.	510	criminal, Clonmel
Kelly, Pat.	865	criminal, Omagh
Kelly, Peter	953	at Church of Taughboyne
Kelly, Rich.	139	robber, gaoled at Dublin
Kelly, Thomas	139	robber, gaoled at Dublin
Kelly, Thomas	234	criminal, Omagh
Kelly, Thomas	465	Rich hill, co Armagh
Kelly, William	127	Buncranagh area
Kelso, Hugh	107	cancer cures, Newtown Hamilton
Kelso, Hugh	386	pr Ardstraw
Kennedy, George	245	farm at Ture
Kennedy, George	314	Ld
Kennedy, James	400	aka Capt. Madcap Setfire, Queen's co
Kennedy, John	387	Letterkenny
Kennedy, John	532	seneschal, Manor of Lismonaghan
Kennedy, Mary Miss	383	abducted, Corke
Kennedy, Maxwell	338	independent freeman of Ld
Kennedy, Richard	970	eacaped from Carrickfergus gaol; @ §40
Kennedy, Sam.	341	Presbyterian, pr Ballykelly
Kennedy, William	25	nr Comber, co Down
Kennedy, William	430	former farm at Lower Kildrum
Kennedy, William	871	innkeeper, Bishop st, Ld
Kenny, Charles	240	arrested, Dublin
Ker, Robert	437	Strabane
Kerr, Alexander	184	houses in Omagh
Kerr, David	1045	Ballymena, co Antrim
Kerr, John	341	Presbyterian, pr Ballykelly
Kerr, Patrick	386	Killstroll, pr Ardstraw
Kerr, Robert	341	Presbyterian, pr Ballykelly
Kerr, Wm.	777	Ld
Keys, Robert	169	Ld
Keys, Will.	127	Buncranagh area
Kidner, Walter	171	robbed, Ld
Kiernan, Mary	889	Roscrea nr Clonmel
Kilpatrick, John	891	dealer in spirits, Ld
Kilpatrick, Matthew	375	Raphoe
Kilpatrick, Samuel	25	nr Cumber, co Down
Kinear, John	231	Cloon, co Donegal
King, Daniel	323	gaoled for theft, Dublin
King, Henry	234	shipwright, Dublin
King, John	178	lately of Newtown Limavaddy
King, John	644	Aughlihard nr Letterkenny
King, John	722	Bogside, Ld
King, John	722	Graky
King, Richard	8	Mulkeiragh
King, Rob.	722	Galdenagh
King, Robert	931	linen mcht, Dublin
King, Sam.	720	fmly occ shop, Ferryquay st, Ld
King, Samuel	160;327	grocer, Ld
King, Samuel	930	Ferryquay st, Ld

Name	Issue	Location
King, Samuel sen.	548	mcht, Newtown Lemavady
King, William	1036	Coleraine
King, William	40	Drumnaha, pr Lifford
King, William	8	formerly of Mulkeiragh
Kingston, Del.	387	Letterkenny
Kinkead, George	76	hse at Ardstraw Bridge
Kinkead, John	382	surgeon etc., Strabane
Kinkead, Robert	386	Carnkenny, par Ardstraw
Kinnear, Andrew	211	cloth, Ld
Kinnear, John	341	Greenfield
Kinnear, John	530	Cloon
Kinnear, Thomas	290	Carrigans
Kinnier, Robert	662	printer & bookseller, Dln
Kinnter, John	1081	pr All-Saints, co Donegal
Kirk, George	718	Cross lane, Ld
Kirk, Lodowick	227	saddler, Bishop st., Ld
Kirkpatrick, George	1109	ipo p/o Ballymagard nr Ld
Kirkpatrick, John	435	innkeeper, Bogside, Ld
Kirkpatrick, John	664	mcht, outside Butcher's gate, Ld
Kirwin, Matt.	648	jeweller, Ship quay, Ld, fmly of Dublin
Knowles, William	1027	watchmaker, Dublin
Knox, Andrew	17	Prehen
Knox, George	495	Prehen
Knox, James	102	Glenfin
Knox, James	42	Killcaddon
Knox, James	420	innkeeper, Strabane
Knox, Jas & Wm	244	farm at Killcaddon
Knox, John	196	Ballymena, book seller
Knox, John	241	inn, Strabane
Knox, Thomas jr.	772	Dungannon, co Tyrone
Knox, William	292	Kilcadden, co Donegal
Kyle, James	811	Dungiven
Kyle, Joseph	445	Letterkenny
Laban, John	1007	wool card factory, Ferryquay st, Ld
Laban, John	140	shoemaker for Mrs. Martha Gonne, q.v.
Laban, John	675	shoemaker, Ferryquay st, Ld
Lafferty, Edward	986	Waterside, Ld
Laird, James	375	Raphoe
Lamb, Neal	250	Dublin
Lamy, John	307	Rapho
Lang, James jr.	987	Newry
Langan, T.	650	master coach mkr, Capel st, Dln
Lavens, James	628	crock mkr, Brickfield nr Ld
Lavery, Hugh	143;227	jockey, Ld Races
Lawler, James	223	aka Jeminy the Shuffler, gaoled in Dln
Lawrence, Al.	151	Coleraine
Lawson, James	794	importer, Newry
Lawson, Samuel	11	Newtown Stewart
Leard, Richard	235	Bogstown, Ld
Leckey, James	386	pr Ardstraw
Leckey, Robert	219	Newgarden, co Carlow
Lecky, Alex.	338	independent freeman of Ld
Lecky, Holland	294	Ld
Lecky, Hugh	183	Agevey
Lecky, James	411	mcht, Dublin
Lecky, John	1003	inn, Monaghan town
Lecky, Robert	298	Killnock nr Corke
Lecky, Thomas	777	Ld
Lecky, William	338	independent freeman of Ld
Ledlie, Thomas	293	former hse in Ld
Lee, John	127	Buncranagh area
Lee, Jonathan	598	weaver, Ballinasloe

Name	Issue	Location
Lee, Thomas	226	Dublin
Leech, Oliver	777	Ld
Leighton, Thomas	595	tanner, Strabane
Leitch, James	473	apothecary, Augher
Leitch, John	1026	Manor Creegan nr Strabane
Leitch, John	722	Maghrecrigan
Lendrum, James	397	at Rathaniny (? Ld vicinity)
Lenox, Wm.	777	Ld
Leonard, Thomas	730	res Ross lane; Brazen Head Inn, Dln
Leper, James	916	Three trees nr Ld
Lepper, John	184	pr Carnmoney, bar Belfast, co Antrim
Leslie, James	151	Coleraine
Leslie, James	341	Presbyterian, pr Ballykelly
Levinge, Richard	338	Colvertown, co Kildare
Lewis, Joseph	388	Strabane
Liggat, John	341	Presbyterian, pr Ballykelly
Liggate, John	458	Newtown Lemavady
Lighton, John	232	Rossberry hill, pr Cumber, co Ld
Lindsay, Arthur	752	Castlebar, co Mayo
Lindsay, James	143	jockey, Ld Races
Lindsay, James	397	Rathaniny (? Ld vicinity), age 24
Lindsay, Owen	752	Castlebar, co Mayo
Linton, Frederick	341	Presbyterian, pr Ballykelly
Lithgo, David	269	Carn, pr Glendermot
Little, John	127	Buncranagh area
Lloyd, Rich.	1111	mayor of Coleraine
Lloyd, William	857	Ballincollig nr Cork
Logan, George	127	Buncranagh area
Logan, John	127	Buncranagh area
Logan, Samuel	127	Buncranagh area
Logan, Thomas	25	nr Cumber, co Down
Long, Andrew	665	Ervy, pr Cumber
Long, Henry	863	nr Gortnagaren [co Tyrone?]
Long, James	276	former hse in Omagh
Long, James	461	Omagh
Long, James	604	Green st, Dublin
Long, James	857	Paradise lane, Dublin
Long, Pat.	581	flaxseed, Dublin
Long, William jr.	445	Letterkenny
Long, William sr.	445	Letterkenny
Longwell, James	127	Buncranagh area
Lotta, John	199	St. Johnston
Loughery, John	127	Buncranagh area
Loughery, Luke	484	Ballindrate nr Ld
Love, Alex.	1012	Bishop st, Ld; fmly of Strabane
Lowrey, James	341	Presbyterian, pr Ballykelly
Lowry, James	927	nr Donaghedy Church, co Tyrone
Lowther, Georges	203	Kilbrue, co Meath
Loyd, Rich.	151	Coleraine
Lyle, Hu.	151	Coleraine
Lynch, John	386	pr Ardstraw
Lynch, John Rev.	1031	Catholic parish priest of Ld
Lynch, Patrick	171	alledged robber, Ld
Lynch, Patrick	445	Oughernone, co Kerry
Lynch, Timothy	951	Maumanorig nr Dingle
Lynchaghan, Edward	477	butler to Col. Knox, Ld
Lyon, Joseph	386	pr Ardstraw
Lyster, Thomas	69	butcher, Ormond quay, Dublin
M'Adoo, John	891	dealer in spirits, Ld
M'Aleer, John	143;227	jockey, Ld Races
M'Allister, Robert	289	letter carrier, Dublin
M'Anelly, Henry	700,714	Ld; given 7 years for crime nr Claudy

Name	Issue	Location
M'Anulty, W.	471	ipo p/o Knockfair, Manor of Stranorlar
M'Aulay, James	919	at Mullan, co Ld
M'Avee, John	556	acquitted, Ld
M'Brearty, Charles	853	the Old Billiard Table, Shipquay st, Ld
M'Brerty, Cha.	891	dealer in spirits, Ld
M'Bride, John	127	Buncranagh area
M'Cabe, Thomas	1104	Belfast
M'Caffar, John	896	carman, Ld
M'Caley, Patrick	617	Castlefin
M'Call, John	700	gaoled, Ld
M'Can, Cornelius	1009	tythe viewer, nr Randalstown, co Antrim
M'Cann, Pat.	1	woollen draper, Dublin
M'Canna, Daniel	127	Buncranagh area
M'Capher, Simon	143	jockey, Ld Races
M'Carnon, Daniel	280	Strabane
M'Carran, Neal	127	Buncranagh area
M'Carran, Pat.	127	Buncranagh area
M'Carren, Darby	891	dealer in spirits, Ld
M'Carrick, Roger	649	pr Killoren
M'Carter, Daniel	800	Mill of Aghaglassen, pr Culdaff
M'Causland, Abraham	350	mcht, Bishop st., Ld
M'Causland, Abraham	511	shop keeper, Ship quay, Ld
M'Causland, Conolly	43	Fruithill nr Newtown Limavaddy
M'Causland, John	565	Letterkenny
M'Causland, John	568	Omagh
M'Causland, Marcus	303	Daiseyhill nr Newtown Limavaddy
M'Causland, Oliver	802	Admirand, bar Rapho
M'Causland, Wm.	568	Omagh
M'Cavell, Denis	184	occ house in Omagh (?)
M'Cay, Archibald	216	nr Castle Cunningham
M'Cay, Archibald	710	Newtown Cuningham
M'Cay, James	69	dyer and stamper, Ld
M'Cay, John	387	Letterkenny
M'Cay, Mat.	891	dealer in spirits, Ld
M'Cay, Matthew	216	farm at Ardee (nr Ld)
M'Cherie, Will.	341	Presbyterian, pr Ballykelly
M'Claran, Hugh	853	dyer and clothier, Ld
M'Cleery, John	375	Raphoe
M'Clellan, John	157	Newtown Stewart
M'Clelland, Hugh	836	dyer, Ld, from London & Glasgow
M'Clelland, Robert	636	of Belfast, seaman on the Loyalty
M'Clelland, Sam.	341	Presbyterian, pr Ballykelly
M'Clenachan, John	46	Convoy
M'Clerey, James	341	Presbyterian, pr Ballykelly
M'Clerey, John	341	Presbyterian, pr Ballykelly
M'Clintock, Cath. Mrs.	156	house to let, Ld
M'Clintock, James	1017	Trinta nr Ld
M'Clintock, James	270	Castle Cuningham
M'Clintock, John	675	Ld
M'Clintock, Robert	583	Dunmore
M'Clintock, Robert	586	hse, Artillery lane, Ld
M'Clintock, William	229	former teacher of mathematics at Omagh
M'Closky, Bryan	1080	nr Strad, pr Banagher, co Ld
M'Closky, Bryan	396	ipo Tullagowan, pr Banagher, co Ld
M'Closky, Hugh Oge	396	ipo Cullomony, pr Banagher, co Ld
M'Closky, Isaac	1080	nr Strad, pr Banagher, co Ld
M'Closky, John	824	nr Muff, co Ld
M'Closky, Thomas	390	gaoled for murder, pr Banagher, co Ld
M'Closky, Will.	1080	nr Strad, pr Banagher, co Ld
M'Clughan, James	264	Ballygomartin nr Lisburn
M'Clure, Ann Mrs.	909	Shipquay st, Ld
M'Clure, John	1063	Magherafelt (tenant of Hen. Montgomery)

Name	Issue	Location
M'Clure, Joseph	987	Newry
M'Clure, Samuel	891	dealer in spirits, Ld
M'Concky, Wm.	568	Omagh
M'Conegal, David	915	auctioneer, Ld
M'Conegal, Pat	538	scythes & sickles, Ld
M'Conehey, Joseph	386	pr Ardstraw
M'Conkey, William	772	shop, Omagh
M'Connell, George	688	tobacco factory, Ld
M'Connell, James	23	Ballymacrally, co Down
M'Connell, Robert	1101	occ p/o Garshewy, pr Taughboyne
M'Connell, Stephen	25	nr Cumber, co Down
M'Connell, Thomas	166	watchmaker, Dublin
M'Connell, William	881	Omagh
M'Cool, David	338	independent freeman of Ld
M'Cool, David	61;264	surveyor, Ld
M'Corkell, Ann Mrs.	907	Bogside, Ld
M'Corkell, William	1076	ipo tenement in Bogside, Ld
M'Corkell, Wm	135	innkeeper, Ld
M'Corkill, Mrs.	145	house in Bogside, Ld
M'Corkle, David	722	nr the Linen Hall, Ld
M'Cormick, Charles R.	866	professor of French, Freeschool ln, Ld
M'Cormick, William	42	late hse in Ballybofey
M'Crackin, Willock	524	wig mkr, Ld, newly arrived from Paris
M'Crea, Coningham	608	mathematics teacher, Lifford
M'Credy, Hugh	814	criminal, Downpatrick
M'Cree, Sam	219	Ld
M'Creery, William	597	fmly ipo tenement in Ballybofey
M'Culla, John	1111	innkeeper, Maghera
M'Culloh, Thomas	142	Ballivally bet Banbridge & Gilford
M'Davett, Philip Dr.	855	Ld (Catholic Bishop)
M'Davit, Henry	127	Buncranagh area
M'Dede, Wm.	891	dealer in spirits, Ld
M'Dermot, Ann	1103	criminal, Omagh
M'Donagh, C. Mr.	947	the Cross Guns, outsd Bishop's gate, Ld
M'Donagh, Cha.	891	dealer in spirits, Ld
M'Donagh, John	338	independent freeman of Ld
M'Donagh, Peter	528	attorney, Ld
M'Donald, Hugh	341	Presbyterian, pr Ballykelly
M'Donald, Randal	956	trial witness, Dublin
M'Donall, Laughlin	504	cabinet mkr, Rosemary Lane, Ld
M'Donnel, Patrick	1098	Catholic, Volunteer ensign, Downpatrick
M'Donnel, Randal	528	tobacconist, Carrickmacross
M'Donnel, William	309	Ransford st., Dublin
M'Donnell, Edward	471	Brendrem nr Castlebar
M'Donnell, Laugh.	777	Ld
M'Dougal, Cornelius	1080	Cary's Arms, Dungiven
M'Dowel, Nat.	341	Presbyterian, pr Ballykelly
M'Dowell, Benjamin	339	Dissenting Minister, pr Ballykelly
M'Elheney, John	891	dealer in spirits, Ld
M'Elhenny, James	967	ipo Kilfeak & Clanbracken (w/Ed Kelly)
M'Elwaine, Alexander	79	Lissfanan
M'Elwaine, James	127	Buncranagh area
M'Elwee, James	227	watchmaker, Ferryquay st., Ld
M'Elwee, John	1048	glazier, Bishop st, Ld
M'Erlain, John	254	tenant in Ballynease Downing
M'Fall, Da.	341	Presbyterian, pr Ballykelly
M'Fall, David	855	Ld (Catholic)
M'Farland, Arthur	614	ipo p/o Dergal nr Strabane
M'Farland, Daniel	229	former house, ws Diamond, Ld
M'Farland, Francis	239	Omagh
M'Farland, Francis	887	Drumcololly
M'Farland, John	341	Presbyterian, pr Ballykelly

Name	Issue	Location
M'Farland, Rob.	891	dealer in spirits, Ld
M'Farland, Sam.	695	res Coningham's row, Ld
M'Feel, James	855	Ld (Catholic)
M'Feely, Mich.	891	dealer in spirits, Ld
M'Garraghy, Hugh	649	yarn mcht, Sligo
M'Ghee, Corn.	127	Buncranagh area
M'Glead, Cormick	817	Tonagh, pr Ballynaskreen, co Ld
M'Golrick, Hugh	234	criminal, Omagh
M'Gonetry, William	184	mcht, Omagh
M'Gongall, Patrick	411	coin exchange etc., Ld
M'Gothin, Owen & John	85	ipo Mullanavey, pr Lifford, co Donegal
M'Gowan, Thomas	777	Ld
M'Greggor, James	953	ipo Annalough, pr Langfield, co Tyrone
M'Groarty, Daniel	252	Cloon nr Carrigans
M'Guckian, Christopher	295	Magherafelt
M'Guigan, Thomas	338	independent freeman of Ld
M'Guigan, Thomas	477	wigmaker, Ld
M'Guigan, Thomas	69	Pump st., Ld
M'Guinnis, Arthur	25	nr Cumber, co Down
M'Guire, John	309	alledged horse thief, Sligo
M'Gwiggan, Charles	16	occ ten in Strabane
M'Ilhenny, Rob.	777	Ld
M'Ilhinny, John	91	ipo house & garden in Ld
M'Illheney, Cha.	516	Forestewart Ferry
M'Ilreway, James	891	dealer in spirits, Ld
M'Ilvaine, William	52	linen mcht, Lissfahan
M'Ilwaine, James jr.	156	crops at Lissanan to sell
M'Ilwaine, William	81	Lisfanan
M'Intyre, William	103	surveyor, nr Bishop's gate, Ld
M'Kane, John	855	Ld (Catholic)
M'Kanes, John	127	Buncranagh area
M'Kea, John	127	Buncranagh area
M'Kean, William	17;545	mcht, Ld
M'Keever, Hugh	18	porter, Belfast
M'Keever, James	102	hatter, Ferryquay st., Ld
M'Kenna, Matt.	855	Ld (Catholic)
M'Kenny, Neale	127	Buncranagh area
M'Kim, John	116	ipo hse in Ld
M'Kimm, John	127	Pennyburn Mill
M'Kinlow, John	127	Buncranagh area
M'Laughlin, Cornelius	270	mason, escaped from gaol, Ld
M'Laughlin, Cornelius	556	acquitted, Ld
M'Laughlin, Dan.	923	Ship quay, Ld
M'Laughlin, Daniel	99	sail and rope maker, Ld
M'Laughlin, Edm.	127	Buncranagh area
M'Laughlin, Edward	729	fmr hse in the Cow Bog, Ld
M'Laughlin, James	127	Buncranagh area
M'Laughlin, James	270	escaped from gaol, Ld
M'Laughlin, John	270	Glen Wood nr Ards, co Donegal
M'Laughlin, Mat.	341	Presbyterian, pr Ballykelly
M'Laughlin, Owen	136	farm in Ga_key
M'Laughlin, Pat.	127	Buncranagh area
M'Leese, John	14	ipo corn mill of Burt
M'Lenahan, George	119	tan yard, Donegal town
M'Loughlin, Hugh	516	Oldtown, Letterkenny
M'Manamon, Den.	387	Letterkenny
M'Michael, Jo.	1097	fmly ipo hse in Bogside, Ld
M'Monagle, Alexander	471	ipo p/o Knockfair, Manor of Stranorlar
M'Monegal, Nougher	982	Roughan Mill Town
M'Murdy, Robert	842	Millfield nr Cumber Claudy
M'Naughten, Ba.	151	Coleraine
M'Naughten, Ed.	151	Coleraine

Name	Issue	Location
M'Neahs, Michael	815	criminal, Sligo
M'Neil, Dan.	1086	Woodtown, Magilligan, co Ld
M'Neil, Hector	208	Carn, Enishowen
M'Neil, Henry	31	Woodtown, Magilligan
M'Nut, James	646	Trooperstown nr Birdstown pr Templemore
M'Nutt, John	995	grocery, Butcher st, Ld, fmly of Tumock
M'Nutt, Susannah Mrs.	265	half of Forsetmore to let
M'Paul, Neal	348	ipo land in Liberties of Ld
M'Phetrick, Da.	341	Presbyterian, pr Ballykelly
M'Quone, Thomas	898	tailor, Bishop st, Ld, fmly of Dublin
M'Shane, Andrew	1105	cabinets, Cow bog nr Butcher's gate, Ld
M'Shane, Manus	891	dealer in spirits, Ld
M'Swine, Catherine	1013	Tully, pr Ray nr Manor Cuningham
M'Williams, James	25	nr Comber, co Down
Macartney, Dennis	25	nr Cumber, co Down
Mackey, James	891	dealer in spirits, Ld
Mackey, William	75	Carrigans nr Ld
Macklin, Eliza	617	teacher, Freeschool lane, Ld
Macklin, James	295	Magherafelt
Macklin, James	43	writing master, Ld
Macky, David	183	pr Templemore, bar Tirkerin, co Ld
Macky, Francis	691	farm, Drumina (aka the Kiln Park)
Macky, James	777	Ld
Macky, John	1035	Eloghbeg nr Ld
Macky, Joseph	809	ipo farm in Culmore, Inishowen
Macky, William	314	dyer, Carrigans
Madden, C.	650	master coach mkr, King st, Dln
Madden, Elizabeth	338	water colors, Widow's row, Ld
Madden, Elizabeth	725	and daughters, school, Ld
Maddox, John	269	hatter, Dublin
Maffit, Richard	1100-1101	Ormond quay, Dublin
Magee, James	429	printer and bookseller, Belfast
Magenis, Arthur	276	Drogheda
Magennis, Barnaby	909	blind seaman, Dublin
Magill, James	153	carpets, Ld
Magill, Sam.	991	jury, Ld
Maginness, Ham.	692	shop, Ferryquay st, Ld
Maginness, Hamilton	150	surgeon, fmly Newtown Limavaddy, now Ld
Maginnis, Edward	505	Prehen, pr Glendermot, co Ld
Maginty, William	375	Raphoe
Maguire, Charles	293	counterfeiter, Dublin
Maguire, John	116	robber betw Drogheda & Duleek
Mahar, Edward	98	gambling hse, Crane lane, Essex st, Dln
Mahon, James	707	at Sign of Admiral Hawke, Ship Quay, Ld
Mahon, Nat.	891	dealer in spirits, Ld
Maitland, Adam	1060	warehouse, Canal quay, Newry
Major, Alexander	456	Tillybrisland
Major, Henry	456	Muff
Major, James	75	woollen draper, Ld
Major, Thomas	100	mcht, Ferryquay st., Ld
Major, Widow	644	Rossnagallagh
Malcolm, William	25	nr Comber, co Down
Malone, Arthur	60	writing master, Ld
Manly, James	632	jeweler, Dame st, Dln, moving to London
Mansfield, Fra.	965	Coleraine
Marks, John	616	seaman, George's quay, Dublin
Marly, James	141	Castle st., Dublin
Marshal, Thos.	777	Ld
Marshall, Geo.	909	outside Bishop's gate, Ld
Marshall, Walter	174	mcht, Ld
Marshall, Walter	317	Caroreagh
Marshall, William	959	Crivagh

Name	Issue	Location
Martin, And.	824	Newtown Lemavady
Martin, Daniel	1095	Ardshannon nr Bushmills
Martin, Hugh	341	Presbyterian, pr Ballykelly
Martin, James	309	Passage nr Waterford
Martin, James	763	baker, Ld
Martin, John	1048	Culmore
Martin, John	1079	Drumcork, co Tyrone, undersheriff
Martin, John	341	Presbyterian, pr Ballykelly
Martin, John	777	Ld
Martin, Rob. jr.	341	Presbyterian, pr Ballykelly
Martin, Rob. sen.	341	Presbyterian, pr Ballykelly
Martin, Robert	235	Tubermoney (nr Dublin ?)
Martin, Robert	899	mason, Ld
Martin, Solomon	1048	Culmore
Martin, Thomas	341	Presbyterian, pr Ballykelly
Martin, Widow	1094	Carrymuddle nr Newtown Limavady
Mathews, Edward	271	Johnston, co Dublin
Mathews, Pat.	1052	Carrickmacross, co Monaghan
Mathews, William	842	Millfield nr Cumber Claudy
Mathews, William	962	at the Paper Mill of Cumber
Mathewson, James	386	pr Ardstraw
Mathewson, Thomas	386	pr Ardstraw
Matthewson, Robert	441	Ardstraw
Mauleverer, John	105	mcht, Ld
Mauleverer, John	538	Cross lane nr Pump st, Ld
Mawxell, Henry	369	apothecary, Omagh
Maxwell, James	545	surgeon, Tyrone Infirmary
Maxwell, James	568	Omagh
Maxwell, James sr. hrs	184	occ house in Omagh
Maxwell, John	18	convicted of manslaughter, Dublin
Maxwell, John	549	Bonnyglin
Maxwell, John	568	Omagh
Maxwell, Marshall	568	Omagh
Maxwell, Thomas	983	pr Aughinlow, co Ld
Maxwell, William	360	provost of Strabane
Maxwell, William	931	linen bleacher, Omagh
May, Felix	23	Whitechurch, co Tipperary
Mease, Robert	183	mcht, Strabane
Mease, Will	592	Strabane
Mease, Will.	369	tobacco, Ld
Meenan, John	433	fmly postilion of Henry Irwin (Ld?)
Mercer, Nicholas	1104	cotton factory, Mill st, Newry
Millen, John	1120	outlaw, nr Desart, co Kilkenny
Miller, George	752	Castlebar, co Mayo
Miller, James	389	mcht, Ld
Miller, James	497	Ferry quay, Ld
Miller, Mathew	341	Presbyterian, pr Ballykelly
Milligan, Thomas	25	nr Cumber, co Down
Mills, Rob.	188	pr Templemore, bar Tirkerin, co Ld
Misaroon, James	777	Ld
Misaroon, Peter	338	independent freeman of Ld
Misaroon, Wm.	777	Ld
Mitchel, John	341	Presbyterian, pr Ballykelly
Mitchel, William	932	the Diamond, Ld
Mitchell, John	256	Monaghan
Mitchell, Nathaniel	163	Clonmel
Mitchell, William	1105	fmr leather cutter, the Diamond, Ld
Mitchell, William	801	Waterside, Ld
Mont, William	386	pr Ardstraw
Montgomery, Alexander	75	linen dying, Mt Charles nr Ballyshannon
Montgomery, Henry	341	Presbyterian, pr Ballykelly
Montgomery, John	145	Glenarmin, co Antrim

Name	Issue	Location
Montgomery, Patrick	382	clerk of the peace, Omagh
Montgomery, Rob.	1063	Magherafelt
Montgomery, Sam.	777	Ld
Montgomery, Thomas	617	Donegal town
Moody, John	1005	Newtown Limavady
Moody, John	875	Ferryquay st, Ld
Moody, Rob.	341	Presbyterian, pr Ballykelly
Moody, William	358	Newtown Lemavady
Mooney, Arth.	1091	secretary, Catholic meeting at Newry
Mooney, Wm.	127	Buncranagh area
Moor, Ed.	1072	hse at Castle of Buncranagh
Moor, James	794	importer, Newry
Moor, James	865	criminal, Omagh, to be tried at Armagh
Moor, John	341	Presbyterian, pr Ballykelly
Moor, Joseph	341	Presbyterian, pr Ballykelly
Moor, Mark	341	Presbyterian, pr Ballykelly
Moor, Mat.	445	Letterkenny
Moor, Newman jr.	341	Presbyterian, pr Ballykelly
Moor, Newman sen.	341	Presbyterian, pr Ballykelly
Moor, Thomas	445	Letterkenny
Moore, Ezekiel	979	Ballymagrorty, Liberties of Ld
Moore, James	320	Convoy
Moore, John	25	Portadown, co Down
Moore, John	265	Letterkenny
Moore, John	494	Lisnagad, pr Baldrashane, co Ld
Moore, John	568	Omagh
Moore, Matthew	78	Letterkenny
Moore, Robert	671	iron monger, fmly of Bishop st, Ld
Moore, Samuel	201	school teacher, Strabane
Moore, Walter	387	Letterkenny
Moore, William	237	mcht, Ld
Moore, William	631	Glentaugher
Moorhead, James	276	nr Belfast
Morcuornough, Edward	588	Lettermoney
Morison, Hugh	96	caretaker, Farm of Grange
Morren, Robert	127	Buncranagh area
Morren, Samuel	127	Buncranagh area
Morrin, Robert	1018	ipo p/o Upper Tullydish nr Ld
Morris, Rich.	293	criminal, Dublin
Morrison, Andrew	341	Presbyterian, pr Ballykelly
Morrison, Hugh	309	Grange betw Ld & Strabane
Morrison, John	341	Presbyterian, pr Ballykelly
Morrison, Thos.	777	Ld
Morton, Robert	434	Tullybogly, pr Raymoghe, co Donegal
Morton, Sam.	1082	Strabane
Morton, Thomas	1104	of nr Rapho; accused of horse stealing
Moss, Owen	184	occ house in Omagh
Mulally, Pat.	139	robber, gaoled at Dublin
Mulhallan, David	295	Magherafelt
Mulhollan, Barnard	1040	town inspector of measures, Donaghadee
Mulholland, Hugh	556	acquitted, Ld
Mulholland, Will	465	tailor, outside Butcher's gate, Ld
Mullan, Grace	249	house on road to Coleraine
Mullan, John	736	ipo p/o Kilhoyle nr Ld
Mullan, Patrick	396	ipo Templemoyle, co Ld
Mullholland, Joseph	254	tenant in Ballynease Downing
Mullholland, Richard	254	tenant in Ballynease Downing
Mullholland, Sarah	254	tenant in Ballynease Downing (widow)
Mulligan, Steuart	871	Ballynany, co Tyrone, co coroner
Mulloy, James	127	Buncranagh area
Munday, John	126	Ardfarney, pr Ennis M'Saint, co Donegal
Mundee, Robert	107	cabinet maker, Dublin

Name	Issue	Location
Murdagh, Daniel	25	Comber, co Down
Murphy, Charles	227	jockey, Ld Races
Murphy, James	13	Ballygihan, Queen's co
Murphy, James	284	in co Kilkenny gaol as a White Boy
Murray, Arch.	309	Ballyshannon
Murray, Eneas	103	Ld
Murray, Hugh	899	quarryman, Ld
Murray, John	551	acquitted, Kilkenny
Murray, Philip	551	acquitted, Kilkenny
Murray, Roger	338	independent freeman of Ld
Murray, Timothy	551	acquitted, Kilkenny
Murray, William	368	Lifford
Murren, James	140	occ house in Butcher st, Ld
Murtagh, James	710	chairman, Dublin
Naughton, Lawrence	249	proctor, nr Freshford nr Kilkenny
Neil, Henry	308	New st., Dublin
Neilson, Nathan	239	Strabane
Neilson, Nathan jr.	239	Strabane
Neilson, Rob.	1000	linen warehouse, Strabane
Neilson, Robert	239	Strabane (son of Nathan)
Neilson, Robert	386	pr Ardstraw
Nelson, Richard	763	baker, Ld
Nelson, Rob.	151	Coleraine
Nelson, Robert	127	Buncranagh area
Nelson, William	616	Strabane
Nesbit, Chas.	802	Greenhill, bar Rapho
Nesbit, Robert	668	fmr shopkeeper, Rathmelton
Nesbit, Thomas	556	Kilmacraden
Nesbitt, Charles	134	Scurmore, co Sligo
Nevill, John	842	linen mcht, Newry
Nevin, Thomas	1098	Methodist, Volunteer Lt., Downpatrick
Newton, Henry	213	mcht, Coleraine
Nichol, William	675	Deer Park
Nicholson, William	145	near Athy, accused of rape
Nicholson, William	819	apprentice seaman, from Whitehaven
Nicolls, Jon.	777	Ld
Nielson, Robert	386	Carnkenny, par Ardstraw
Noble, Joseph	878	Broadpath
Nocker, Thomas	23	ipo p/o Ballow, co Down
Norris, Charles	187	pr Aughalow, bar Dungannon, co Tyrone
Nugent, Henry	1048	acquitted of counterfeiting, Dublin
Nun, Richard	545	paper, 46 Bridge st, Dublin
O'Brien, George	127	Buncranagh area
O'Brien, John	341	Presbyterian, pr Ballykelly
O'Brien, John	989	White Cross Inn, Pill lane, Dublin
O'Cain, Bartholomew	456	? Loughtylobe, pr Banagher, co Ld
O'Callaghan, Eug.	855	Ld (Catholic)
O'Connor, Matthew	241	Carlow
O'Donnel, Con.	127	Buncranagh area
O'Donnel, Hugh Rev.	976	(Catholic) Belfast
O'Donnell, C. Rev.	855	Ld (Catholic)
O'Donnell, Dennis	855	Ld (Catholic)
O'Donnell, John	591	brewer, fmly in Letterkenney
O'Donnell, Neal	843	Erris, co Mayo
O'Donnell, Richard	408	hse at Craige (?), co Ld
O'Dun, Timothy	241	Carlow
O'Finney, Marcus	1047	ipo Polysnaught near Dearg, co Tyrone
O'Finney, Moses	1047	ipo Polysnaught near Dearg, co Tyrone
O'Flagherty, Neal	855	Ld (Catholic)
O'Hanlon, Hugh	1091	chairman, Catholic meeting at Newry
O'Hare, Roger	80	apprehended betw Guilford & Tandragee
O'Malley, Anne Mrs.	956	acquitted of murder, Dublin

Name	Issue	Location
O'Malley, George	752	Castlebar, co Mayo
O'Neil, Charles	258	servant to John Richardson, Ld
O'Neil, John	386	pr Ardstraw
O'Neil, John	855	Ld (Catholic)
O'Neil, Ma. Kerr	151	Coleraine
O'Neil, Roger	334	imported tobacco, Drumqueen
O'Nut, Bryan	254	tenant in Ballynease Downing
O'Regan, Lau.	855	Ld (Catholic)
O'Reilly, Myles	275	Dorset st., Dublin
O'Scullian, Pat.	254	tenant in Ballynease Downing
Ogilby, Alexander	1005	Newtown Limavady
Ogilby, John	1005	Newtown Limavady
Ogle, Hen.	1011	Newry
Ogle, James	1011	Newry
Ogle, William	1011	Newry
Ogleby, Alexander	358	Newtown Lemavady
Ogleby, John	358	Newtown Lemavady
Ogleby, Robert	358	Newtown Lemavady
Olphert, Wybrants	270	Ballyconnell
Olpherts, Richard	294	Armagh
Orr, James	568	Omagh
Orr, James jr.	1005	Ballybritain
Orr, John	126	Strabane
Orr, John	157	Legnathraw
Orr, John	341	Presbyterian, pr Ballykelly
Orr, John	468	Ballybrittin, co Ld
Orr, Joseph	1011	brass goods, foot of Pump st, Ld
Orr, Rob.	453	Gallony nr Strabane (?)
Orr, Robert	341	Presbyterian, pr Ballykelly
Orr, Robert	615	fmly ipo hse next to Hood's Inn, Omagh
Orr, Sam	1119	res nr Omagh
Orr, Wm.	777	Ld
Osborn, Henry	771	Dressig, pr Dromore, co Tyrone
Osborne, Henry jr.	491	brewery, Newtown Lemavady
Osborne, James	1012	fmly White Horse Inn, Bishop st, Ld
Owens, Robert	482	Custom house, Dublin
Parkinson, James	99	sail maker for Daniel M'Laughlin
Parkinson, Thomas	1015	Downpatrick
Parkinson, Thomas	447	Ld
Parks, Samuel	25	nr Cumber, co Down
Parseley, Joseph	341	Presbyterian, pr Ballykelly
Parsley, John	341	Presbyterian, pr Ballykelly
Patchelt, Edward	836	Cumber Meeting House
Paterson, James	66	Ld
Paton, Thomas	188	pr Taughboyne, bar Rapho, co Donegal
Patterson, David	777	Ld
Patterson, Henry	765	Newtown Cuningham
Patterson, James	696	outside Bishop's gate, Ld
Patterson, James	987	moved to the Diamond, Ld
Patterson, Rob.	777	Ld
Patterson, Thomas	127	Buncranagh area
Patterson, William	418	distiller, Ld
Patterson, William	592	Castlehill, pr Templemore, co Donegal
Patterson, Wm., Dr.	245	Ld
Patton, Andrew	420	Springfield nr Letterkenny
Patton, John	386	pr Ardstraw
Patton, Mat.	983	pr Aughinlow, co Ld
Patton, Thomas	341	Presbyterian, pr Ballykelly
Paul, James	351	inn, Omagh
Paul, John	341	Presbyterian, pr Ballykelly
Paul, Rich.	777	Ld
Peerey, John	341	Presbyterian, pr Ballykelly

Name	Issue	Location
Peoples, Samuel	375	Raphoe
Peppar, Elizabeth	252	criminal, Dublin
Phelan, Kiran	310	proctor, Cullow hill, Queen's co
Phenix, Thomas	259	baker, Letterkenny, alledged murderer
Pigot, Patrick	310	at the Dinan Ford nr Kilkenny
Pike, Wight	270	stables, Nunnery Yard, Mullinihack
Pilkington, Wm.	568	Omagh
Pinkerton, John	159	St. Johnston
Pinkerton, William	976	nr the Ferry quay, Ld
Plowman, James	1097	woollen draper, attacked, Dublin
Pollock, John	241	farm in Leckpatrick, co Tyrone
Pollock, John	456	Leck, co Tyrone
Pollock, John	987	Newry
Polock, John	492	Carickatain
Porter, James	40	Gavstown
Porter, James	521	Ballindrate
Porter, Richard	171	nr Ld
Porter, Robert	127	Buncranagh area
Porter, Robert	195	Strabane
Porter, Robert	390	carpenter, Ld, formerly of Dublin
Porter, William	309	Newry
Porter, William	348	Burt
Porterfield, Charles	733	Drumcrow nr Rapho
Potts, James	946	74 Dame st, Dublin
Powell, Patrick	257	gaoled for theft, Dublin
Power, Edmond	1120	Drumglane, co Kilkenny
Preston, James	958	new woollen drapery, the Diamond, Ld
Preston, Thos.	777	Ld
Proctor, Ephraim	255	printer, Athlone
Purdy, Hugh, Jas, Will	977	Redemon, pr Kilmore, co Down
Purviance, Jn.	387	Letterkenny
Quigley, Charles	338	independent freeman of Ld
Quigley, Hugh	127	Buncranagh area
Quigley, John	81	Clenally, fmly ipo land in Glentaugher
Quigly, Hugh	1018	ipo p/o Upper Tullydish nr Ld
Quigly, John	127	Buncranagh area
Quin, Peter	568	Omagh
Quinn, Hugh	254	tenant in Ballynease Downing
Raby, Rich.	429	mcht, Ld
Rafter, Thomas	101	a gaoled White Boy, Clonmel
Rainy, Andrew	23	ipo p/o Ballow, co Down
Ralison, Oliver (?)	1067	St. Johnstown
Ralston, Joseph	445	Letterkenny
Ralston, Rob.	777	Ld
Ramage, James	270	houses to let, Ld
Ramage, John	777	Ld
Ramage, Marmaduke	466	nr Ballymoney
Ramsay, Charles	239	nr Ballybofey
Ramsay, James	908	Butcher st, Ld
Ramsay, John	22	ipo house in Ballybofey
Ramsay, Robert	387	Letterkenny
Randels, William	474	cooper, Ld
Rankin, Dav.	983	pr Aughinlow, co Ld
Rea, John	14	Lifford
Rea, Widow	307	former house, Ld
Read, Samuel	149	house, Ld
Read, Thomas	1053	acquitted of arson, Dundalk
Reagh, Archibald	597	cares for the Wood of Kincraghy
Reagh, Joseph	891	dealer in spirits, Ld
Reagh, Joseph	978	res tenement on west side of Wapping
Reavy, Jane	198	Eagle hill nr Hacket's town co Carlow
Reed, Joseph	226	Dublin

Name	Issue	Location
Reed, Robert	203	earthenware, Ld
Reed, Robert	366	Letterfadd, pr Kilmacrenan, co Donegal
Reed, Robt. Capt.	664	mcht, Ld
Reed, Sam	519	publican, Ld
Reed, William	1083	carman, Ld
Reilly, John	1104	criminal, Ld
Reynolds, John	183	pr Killbaron, bar Tirehugh, co Donegal
Reynolds, John	420	Coolbeg nr Ballyshannon
Rice, Rob.	151	Coleraine
Rice, Tho.	151	Coleraine
Richardson, Benjamin	881	woollen draper, Grafton st, Dublin
Richardson, David	279	Drum
Richardson, John	1105	Somerset
Richardson, John	151	Coleraine
Richmond, John	777	Ld
Riddle, William	25	nr Comber, co Down
Ridfern, James	295	Magherafelt
Ridle, Hugh	341	Presbyterian, pr Ballykelly
Ripley, John	127	Buncranagh area
Ripley, Mathew	127	Buncranagh area
Rix, Stephen	343	former bailiff, Kilkenny
Roane, Patrick	141	accused murderer, Co. Corke
Robb, William	524	Cat and Bagpipes (pub), Long Tower, Ld
Robinson, Edw.	777	Ld
Robinson, James	952	baker, Bishop st, Ld
Robinson, John	18	convicetd of manslaughter, Dublin
Robinson, John	184	occ house in Omagh (?)
Robinson, John	331	imprisoned, Dublin
Rodd, John sen.	127	Buncranagh area
Roddy, Hugh	127	Buncranagh area
Roddy, John	127	Buncranagh area
Rodgers, John	291	Edergole nr Omagh
Roe, Jason	485	writing teacher, Bishop st, Ld
Rogan, Francis	26	Castlefin
Rogan, James	341	Presbyterian, pr Ballykelly
Rogan, James	537	fmly ipo hse in Ball Court, Ld
Rogers, Mathew	957	ipo kiln, Manor Cuningham
Rogers, Pro.	499	Castle Cuningham
Roney, Alexander	214	innkeeper, Antrim town
Rooney, Patrick	386	ale draper, Dublin
Rorke, Michael	829	criminal, Sligo
Ross, Da. jr.	387	Letterkenny
Ross, David	1005	Cumber
Ross, David	584	hse & shop, end of William st, Ld
Ross, David jr.	352	flour, Ld
Ross, Edward	766,1036	innkeeper, Newtown Lemavady
Ross, James	1005	Cumber
Ross, James	1029	inside Bishop's gate, Ld
Ross, John	186	innkeeper, Newtown Limavaddy
Ross, Mich.	1024	outside Bishop's gate, Ld
Ross, Samuel	931	now of Butcher st, Ld
Ross, Thomas	163	salt & iron, Ld
Ross, Thomas	341	Presbyterian, pr Ballykelly
Ross, William	358	Newtown Lemavady
Ross, William	84	Beauford Lodge, co Ld, new J.P.
Ross, William jr.	358	Newtown Lemavady
Rudagh, John	165	Moneymore
Russel, James	386	Carnkenny, par Ardstraw
Russell, Geo.	387	Letterkenny
Russell, James	386	pr Ardstraw
Rutledge, Robert	226	Rathfarnham
Ryan, James	228	jockey, Ld Races

Name	Issue	Location
Ryan, James	398	tenant of Thos. Newcomen nr Clonmel
Ryan, Luke	888	pirate, lurking off Inishowen
Ryder, Thomas	276	theater manager, Dublin
Sampson, Mary Mrs.	552	Porthall
Sanderford, Alexander	136	Cloverhill, co Cavan
Sands, Henry	25	nr Cumber, co Down
Savage, Richard	25	nr Cumber, co Down
Savers, Andrew	375	Raphoe
Savers, Andrew	878	Convoy
Sayers, Eliz. Mrs.	611	Rapho
Schoales, Adam	777	Ld
Schoales, Adam & Geo	229	mchts, Ld
Schofield, Joseph	1013	cotton works, Tura nr Ld
Scot, Abraham	341	Presbyterian, pr Ballykelly
Scot, Alex.	777	Ld
Scot, Alex.	983	pr Aughinlow, co Ld
Scot, Andrew	762	Millenan nr Ld
Scot, Catherine	507	criminal, Dublin
Scot, David	114	late occ a house in Muff, co Donegal
Scot, Henry	777	Ld
Scot, John	102	Castleton nr St. Johnston
Scot, Moses	777	Ld
Scott, Al., M.D.	807	Ld
Scott, Alexander	314	mcht, Ld
Scott, Andrew	127	Buncranagh area
Scott, Andrew	807	Mullenan
Scott, Bridget	163	Clonmel
Scott, James	471	ipo p/o Knockfair, Manor of Stranorlar
Scott, John	219	timber mill, Castletown, co Donegal
Scott, John	493	linen weaver, Buncranna, co Donegal
Scott, Joseph	190	pr Templemore, bar Tirkerin, co Ld
Scott, Joseph	39	Rapho, ipo part of Mullangar farm
Scott, Joseph	917	Mullenan
Scott, Mat.	387	Letterkenny
Scott, Moses	629	mcht, Ld
Scott, Moses	642	fmr hse, Butcher st, Ld
Scott, Samuel	14	Strabane
Scott, Thomas	171	lately occ house at Dunfanaghy
Scott, William	248	nr Omagh
Sealy, Geo. jr.	137	property to let, Ld
Seaton, Charles	386	pr Ardstraw
Seed, William	221	Belfast
Shannon, Hugh	105	appr of Jos. Carr, Aughasessey, age 18
Shannon, James	190	post chaise, Coleraine
Shannon, James	194	house, Ld
Shannon, John	389	violins & guitars, Ld
Shannon, John	86	organist, Ld
Shannon, Neil	1068	master of the brig Memphis at Dublin
Sharkey, John	338	independent freeman of Ld
Sharkey, John jr.	129	Ld, appr chandler wanted
Sharky, Ann	69	milliner, Ld
Sharky, John	293	chandler, Ld
Shaw, James	777	Ld
Shaw, Rob	206	former shop, Ld
Shaw, Rob.	891	dealer in spirits, Ld
Shaw, Thomas	879	Lurgan
Shaw, W.	650	master coach mkr, Stafford st, Dln
Shea, Henry	26	nr Douglas, nr Corke
Shea, John	752	Castlebar, co Mayo
Shee, John	107	woollen draper, Kilkenny
Sheehy, John	1036	dealer in spirits, Templebar
Sheerer, David	452	Ballykelly, co Ld

Name	Issue	Location
Sheils, Mich.	127	Buncranagh area
Sherard, Michael	341	Presbyterian, pr Ballykelly
Sherard, Rob.	429	Newtown Limavady
Sherard, Rob. jr.	341	Presbyterian, pr Ballykelly
Sherard, Rob. sen.	341	Presbyterian, pr Ballykelly
Sherer, John	341	Presbyterian, pr Ballykelly
Sheridan, Andrew	1104	exporter, Dublin
Sheridan, Charles F.	1090	attacked, Dublin
Sherlock, Widow	119	shop, Castle market, Dublin
Sherrard, Hugh	324	Newtown Limavady
Sherrard, William	1082	Ballynasey, bar Toome, co Antrim
Sherwood, Tobias	242	Ld
Shinks, James	814	criminal, Downpatrick
Short, Thomas	20	former hse in the Diamond, Ld
Short, Thomas	269	mcht, Ld
Sidebottom, George	996	cloth finisher, Buncrana
Sidelbottom, George	975	Buncranagh
Simpson, William	577	teacher, Strabane
Sinclair, Alexander	305	Strabane
Sinclair, George	965	Strabane
Sinclair, William	168	Strabane
Sinclair, William	611	Claudy
Siree, John	11	Saelfield nr Rathmelton
Skilling, Hans	25	nr Comber, co Down
Skipton, George	350	Croman Lodge
Slator, Thomas	279	paper mill, Rathfarnham
Sloan, Hen.	888	Guild of Trades, Ld
Sloan, Henry	58	former hse, Rosemary lane, Ld
Sloan, Henry	588	attorney, res Cross lane, Ld
Small, Oliver	341	Presbyterian, pr Ballykelly
Smiley, William	506	mcht, Strabane
Smily, Thomas	1027	St. Johnstown nr Ld
Smily, William	298	Strabane
Smith, Dan.	1110	res outside Ferryquay gate, Ld
Smith, James	720	Enogh, pr Glendermot, co Ld
Smith, John	341	Presbyterian, pr Ballykelly
Smith, John	39	Moneymore, pr Rye, co Donegal
Smith, Robert	1027	tanyard, distillery, house, Coleraine
Smith, Samuel	1047	farm at Finglass bridge nr Dublin
Smith, Samuel	268	Fingall, Dublin
Smith, William	339	escaped from Newgate prison, Dublin
Smith, William	358	Newtown Lemavady
Smith, William	800	fmly ipo p/o Back nr Ld
Smith, Wm.	151	Coleraine
Smith, Wm.	387	Letterkenny
Smyth, David	348	Claudy
Smyth, Elinor	551	criminal, Monaghan
Smyth, John	437	breeches mkr, outside Ferryquay gate Ld
Smyth, W.	650	master coach mkr, Britain st, Dln
Smyth, William jr.	506	Lisdillon
Snow, Charles	536	pr Meavough, co Donegal
Sodan, Clotworthy	49	Ld
Somerly, William	226	Dublin
Somervell, John	62	Strabane
Somerville, Pierce	25	nr Cumber, co Down
Somewell, John	411	distiller, Ld
Somewell, John	733	Strabane
Span, William	119	house in Newtown Limavaddy
Spear, Mary	1119	Temple st, Dublin
Speer, Alexander	126	appr to Mr. Oliver, atty, (Cookstown?)
Spence, Nath.	746	Rathmelton
Spence, Rob., Dr.	777	Rapho

Name	Issue	Location
Spiller, John	568	Omagh
Sproul, John	176	seeds, Strabane
Sproul, Robert	319	Claudy
St. Lawrence, Thomas	215	linen printer & dyer, Ld
Steel, Andrew	341	Presbyterian, pr Ballykelly
Steel, Christ.	341	Presbyterian, pr Ballykelly
Steel, James	375	Raphoe
Stephenson, James	425	mcht, Raphoe
Sterling, James & John	899	stone cutters, Ld
Sterrit(t), Tho.	387,733	Letterkenny
Stevenson, Catherine	304	bookseller, Ld
Stevenson, David	792	Brayhead, Liberties of Ld
Stevenson, George	1078	gaoled for fraud, Belfast
Stevenson, John	151	former farm in pr Glendermot
Stevenson, John	962	Buncranagh
Stevenson, Robert	548	Toperneal, pr Lifford
Stevenson, William	66	ipo Spawell farm in the Liberties of Ld
Stewart, Alexander	46	cross st. in Pump st., Ld
Stewart, Ann	614	boarders, nr head of Rosemary lane, Ld
Stewart, Arch.	766	ipo p/o Back
Stewart, Charles	323	peruke maker, Butcher st., Ld
Stewart, Hugh	550	Liskey nr Ld
Stewart, John	387	Letterkenny
Stewart, John	776	apothecary, the Diamond, Ld
Stewart, John jr.	1100	Cross lane, Bishop st, Ld
Stewart, Noble	13	shopkeeper, Ld
Stewart, Robert	105	Killygordon, co Donegal
Stewart, Robert	21	flax mcht, Ld
Stewart, Thomas	912	bookseller, Dublin
Stewart, Will.	480	Killymoon
Stewart, William	445	Letterkenny
Stewart, William	851	undertaker & carpenter, Ld
Stinson, William	1064	baker, Ld
Stinton, Michael	92	Colleflin nr Castlefin
Stirling, James	182	pr Templemore, bar Terkerin, co Ld
Stirling, James	341	Presbyterian, pr Ballykelly
Stirling, James	341	Wallworth
Stirling, John	1105	Farloe nr Newtown Limavady
Stirling, John	341	Presbyterian, pr Ballykelly
Stockwell, John	184	occ house in Omagh (?)
Strangeways, John	265	Sutton's rath nr Kilkenny
Strean, Samuel	254	Portglenone
Strong, C.	650	master coach mkr, Dominic st, Dln
Stuart, John	118	mcht, Ld
Stuart, John	348	ipo land in Liberties of Ld
Stuart, Rob.	190,1110	mcht, res Bishop st, Ld
Stuart, Samuel	718	fmly ipo p/o Gortegranagh
Sullevan, Peter	5	arrested, Dunamond fair, co Galway
Sullivan, James	137	tried for riot at Leitrim
Sutherland, Kenneth	497	fmly gardener to Lady Antrim; Belfast
Sweeney, Daniel	563	quitting haberdashery, Butcher st, Ld
Sweeney, Daniel	643	mcht, now outside Bishop's gate, Ld
Sweeney, John	983	butcher, Patrick st, Dublin
Sweeny, Ch.	387	Letterkenny
Sweeny, Daniel	87	ipo a house in Bogside, Ld
Swettenham, John	854	Inch
Swettenham, Joshua	50	cattle pound, Inch island
Swettenham, William	289	Ld
Swinny, Charles	23	hse & garden, Coleraine
Tagert, Samuel	859	mcht, Ld
Tallon, Nicholas	92	fish dealer, Dublin
Tate, William	228	Belfast

Name	Issue	Location
Taylor, Antisell	145	Dublin, robbed
Taylor, Arch.	1050	linen shipper, Newry
Taylor, George	1048	Newtown Limavady
Taylor, Rebecca	810	young ladies' school, Artillery ln, Ld
Templeton, Alexander	1028	linen inspector, Ld
Templeton, Thomas	108	schoolmaster, Ld
Tharp, Ann	411	woollen draper, Ld
Tharp, Charles	796	plasterer etc., N. Cumberland st, Dln
Tharp, Paul	537	shop, Butcher st, Ld
Tharp, Paul	793	fmr res Butcher st, Ld
Thompson, Acheson	1011	Newry
Thompson, Andrew	585	mcht, Newry
Thompson, Ant.	184	par Taughboyne, bar Rapho, co Donengal
Thompson, James	13	hse, Ld
Thompson, James	204	timber, Ld
Thompson, Jane Mrs.	747	widow, Summer Hill nr St. Johnston
Thompson, John	1081	pr All-Saints, co Donegal
Thompson, John	151	Coleraine
Thompson, John	235	Moyle
Thompson, John	341	Presbyterian, pr Ballykelly
Thompson, John	375	Raphoe
Thompson, John	777	Ld
Thompson, John	987	Newry
Thompson, Rob.	341	Presbyterian, pr Ballykelly
Thompson, Robert	127	Buncranagh area
Thompson, Ross	1011	Newry
Thompson, Will.	341	Presbyterian, pr Ballykelly
Thwaites, Richard	231	Coleraine Barracks
Tisdall, Thady	277	sedan chairman, gaoled in Dublin
Todd, Will.	341	Presbyterian, pr Ballykelly
Tolling, John	504	cabinet mkr, Rosemary Lane, Ld
Torrans, John	341	Presbyterian, pr Ballykelly
Torrans, Pa.	341	Presbyterian, pr Ballykelly
Torrens, Andrew	1006	Magherafelt
Tracy, James	863	innkeeper, Dungannon
Tracy, Richard	324	Slator nr Dublin
Trainor, John	387	Letterkenny
Turner, William	191	formerly occ a tenement in Omagh
Tuttle, Thomas	309	boatman nr Passage, Waterford
Tyler, George	1005	Newtown Limavady
Tyrell, John	387	Letterkenny
Usher, John	187	pr Aghagallan, bar Killultagh, Antrim
Venables, Thos.	777	Ld
Walker, Arthur	332	mill stones, Donegal
Walker, George	236	shoemaker, Ferryquay st., Ld, fmly Dln
Walker, James	960	innkeeper, Bishop st, Ld
Walker, Robert	352	mcht, Newry
Walker, Samuel	14	Sheriff's Mountain
Walker, William	1019	Plaster nr Newtown Cuningham
Wall, Daniel	855	Ld (Catholic)
Wallace, John	375	Raphoe
Wallace, John	568	Omagh
Wallace, Will.	341	Presbyterian, pr Ballykelly
Wallace, William	794	importer, Newry
Waller, John	387	Letterkenny
Walsh, John	989	kelp, Ld
Walsh, Joseph	207	Lislea, co Monaghan
Walsh, Marks	1120	Desart, co Kilkenny
Walsh, Thomas	252	distiller, Athy
Walter, Sam.	341	Presbyterian, pr Ballykelly
Warburton, Thomas	295	Magherafelt
Ward, James	855	Ld (Catholic)

Name	Issue	Location
Ward, John	610	fmly res at hotel nr mkt hse, Strabane
Ward, John	610	new pub, Ld
Wardlaw, James	933	Red Lion inn, Castlefin
Waring, Thomas	1011	Newry
Wark, David	341	Presbyterian, pr Ballykelly
Wark, Elizabeth	347	Killrea, Liberties of Ld
Wark, Joseph	341	Presbyterian, pr Ballykelly
Wark, Sam.	341	Presbyterian, pr Ballykelly
Warneck, John	819	apprentice seaman, from Whitehaven
Warren, James	108	watch & clock maker, Ld
Warring, Thomas	987	Newry
Waters, Dom.	276	Corke
Waters, Peter	815	criminal, Sligo
Watson, John	248	Freehall, pr Dunboe, co Ld
Watson, William	248	Coleraine
Watt, James	71	Rathmelton
Watt, John	341	Presbyterian, pr Ballykelly
Wauchop, William	337	Castlefin
Webber, John	524	Strabane
Wellington, John	437	leather cutter, Bishop st., Ld
Welsh, John	284	in co Kilkenny gaol as a White Boy
West, Hamilton	53	corp of Sheermen & Dyers, Dublin
West, Henry	337	King's Arms, Fintona
West, James	30	hse & tanyard, Ld
West, John	595	Fintona, fmr res Killdrum
Weston, Thomas	293	criminal, Dublin
Wetherall, Joseph	455	Letterkenny
Wetherall, Thomas	386	pr Ardstraw
White, A. Miss	387	Letterkenny
White, Ann	445	Letterkenny
White, George	25	nr Cumber, co Down
White, Luke	946	6 Crampton ct, Dublin
White, Patrick	25	nr Cumber, co Down
White, Peter	1104	innkeeper, Waterside, Ld
White, Sylvester	137	White Boy taken near Kilkenny
White, William	1102	Nicholas st, Dublin
Whitestone, William	565	stationer, 29 Capel st, Dublin
Whitfield, James	201	mcht, Ld
Whitten, W.	650	master coach mkr, Dominic st, Dln
Whittingham, J.	445	Letterkenny
Williams, Alexander	1078	attorney, Tullymore, co Donegal
Williams, Ambrose	311	Moyagh
Williams, James	650	master coach mkr, Mary st, Dln
Williams, James	661	bookseller, Skinner row, Dln
Williams, James	946	21 Skinner row, Dublin
Williams, John	1120	nr Carrigans, co Donegal
Williams, John	127	Buncranagh area
Williams, R.	151	Coleraine
Williams, Richardson	294	Bellaghy
Williams, W.	650	master coach mkr, Britain st, Dln
Williams, William	311	Ballynagallyglaugh
Williams, William	311	Tully
Willington, John	519	publican, (in or nr) Ld
Willson, Henry	341	Presbyterian, pr Ballykelly
Willson, James	341	Presbyterian, pr Ballykelly
Willson, John	341	Presbyterian, pr Ballykelly
Willson, Tho.	1098	Bogside, Ld
Willson, Will.	341	Presbyterian, pr Ballykelly
Wilson, Alexander	43	grocer, Ferryquay st, Ld
Wilson, David	471	ipo p/o Knockfair, Manor of Stranorlar
Wilson, Elizabeth	68	milliner, Ld
Wilson, Hugh	23	ipo p/o Ballow, co Down

Name	Issue	Location
Wilson, Hugh	74	employee of the Ld Poor House
Wilson, James	136	farm in Ga_key
Wilson, John	227	watchmaker, Ferryquay st., Ld
Wilson, John	586	Rosemary lane, Ld
Wilson, Joseph	766	ipo p/o Carrick
Wilson, Oliver	78	Ballybofey
Wilson, Robert	136	farm in Ga_key
Wilson, Robert	375	Raphoe
Wilson, Thomas	613	watch mkr, Pump st, Ld
Wilson, Thomas	871	ipo land nr Cloghglass, Liberties of Ld
Wilson, William	25	nr Cumber, co Down
Wilson, William	273	hse nr Rapho
Wilson, William	290	Tumnock in Burt, co Donegal
Wilson, William	593	fmr res Cross lane, Ld
Wiseheart, John	53	corp of Weavers, Dublin
Woods, David	190	pr Arbo, bar Loughinisholin, co Ld
Worthington, William	60	linen house, Watergate, Dublin
Wray, Alexander	42	Ballybofey
Wray, Hugh	285	Shellfield nr Letterkenny
Wray, William	307	Ards
Wright, Joseph	182	par Finvoy, bar Kilconway, co Antrim
Wynne, Folliott	775	Sligo
Yates, John	989	tailor, fmly London, Bishop st, Ld
Yeats, James	53	corp of Sheermen & Dyers, Dublin
Young, George	439	Culdaff
Young, James	116	ipo hse in Carrigans
Young, James	189	Cloonarell nr Castlefin
Young, Robert	1082	p/o Limnaherry, Mnr Cashel, co Antrim
Young, William	600	Castlefin